Praise for Joshua Hammer's
A Season in Bethlehem

"Hammer takes readers inside Bethlehem and its surrounding villages, stripping away the cliché image of Hallmark nativity scenes and bringing to life a place full of despair and trying to cling to hope under both the Israeli occupation and the corrupt leadership of Yasser Arafat's Palestinian Authority."

—*The Boston Globe*

"The author has a knack for getting the rich comment or detail, and he avoids the temptation to make snap judgments, carefully walking the line between sympathy and objectivity."

—*Publishers Weekly*

"*A Season in Bethlehem* examines this fascinating, historic city in microcosm, and uses it to explain why the situation in the Middle East is so explosive. Hammer's detailed portraits of all the actors and his incredible ability to create atmosphere bring the whole place to life. His moment-by-moment narration of the siege of the Church of the Nativity is riveting. You can't believe Hammer was so near all this, observing firsthand the terrible tension, the dangerous standoff. A brave book."

—Amy Wilentz, author of *Martyr's Crossing*

"Notable for the author's empathy with a tortured, misguided people, and the revelation of fanaticism's deadly causes and effects."

—*Kirkus Reviews*

"Joshua Hammer has achieved something truly remarkable here: by focusing on a single seminal event in modern Arab-Israeli history—the 2002 siege of the Church of the Nativity in Bethlehem—and letting its participants tell their stories, he has cast a piercing light on the passions and furies that plague the Holy Land. Rather than another polemic on the Middle East troubles, *A Season in Bethlehem* reads like a thriller—a particularly thoughtful and humane one."

—Scott Anderson, author of *The Man Who Tried to Save the World*

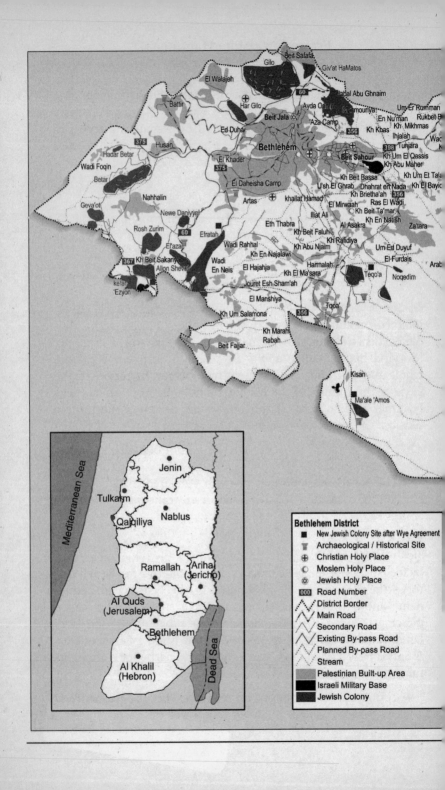

Bethlehem District

■	New Jewish Colony Site after Wye Agreement
⊼	Archaeological / Historical Site
⊕	Christian Holy Place
☾	Moslem Holy Place
✡	Jewish Holy Place
000	Road Number
⌇	District Border
⌇	Main Road
⌇	Secondary Road
⌇	Existing By-pass Road
⌇	Planned By-pass Road
⌇	Stream
	Palestinian Built-up Area
	Israeli Military Base
	Jewish Colony

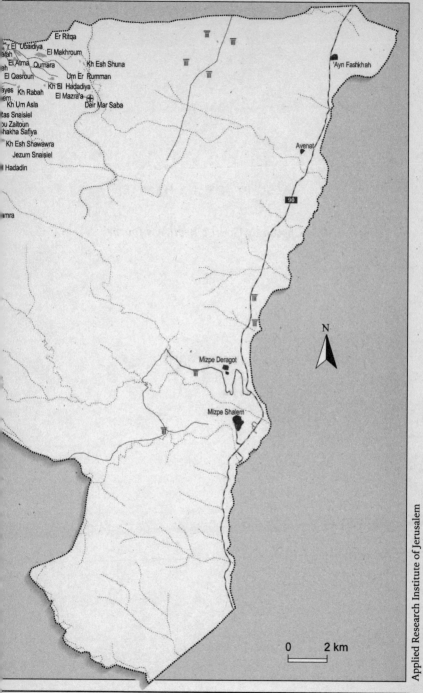

Er Ritqa
El Makhroum
Kh Esh Shuna
Um Er Rumman
'Ayn Fashkhah
z El 'Ubaidiya
alah
El Atma Qumara
El Qasroun
ayes Kh Rabah
em.
Kh Um Asla
itas Snaisiel
ou Zaitoun
shakha Safiya
Kh Esh Shawawra
Jezum Snaisiel
l Hadadin
amra
Kh El Hadadiya
El Mazra'a
Deir Mar Saba
Avenat
90
Mizpe Deragot
Mizpe Shalem

N

0   2 km

Applied Research Institute of Jerusalem

ALSO BY JOSHUA HAMMER

Chosen by God: A Brother's Journey

A Season in Bethlehem

Unholy War in a Sacred Place

◊

Joshua Hammer

FREE PRESS

NEW YORK · LONDON · TORONTO · SYDNEY

FREE PRESS
A Division of Simon & Schuster, Inc.
1230 Avenue of the Americas
New York, NY 10020

First Free Press trade paperback edition 2004

FREE PRESS and colophon are trademarks of Simon & Schuster, Inc.

For information about special discounts for bulk purchases,
please contact Simon & Schuster Special Sales:
1-800-456-6798 or business@simonandschuster.com.

Manufactured in the United States of America

1   3   5   7   9   10   8   6   4   2

The Library of Congress has catalogued the hardcover edition as follows:
Hammer, Joshua, 1957–
A season in Bethlehem: unholy war in a sacred place /
Joshua Hammer.
p. cm.
Includes index.
1. Al-Aqsa Intifada, 2000—Personal narratives, Palestinian Arab.
2. Al-Aqsa Intifada, 2000—Personal narratives, Israeli. 3. Bethlehem.
4. Military occupation. 5. Israel—Military policy.
6. Palestinian Arabs—West Bank—Bethlehem—Interviews. I. Title.

DS119.765.H354 2003
956.9405'4—dc21
2003049092

ISBN 0-7432-4413-3   0-7432-5604-2 (Pbk)

FOR NADJA AND MAX

CONTENTS

❧

CAST OF
PRINCIPAL CHARACTERS

ↄ‎ↄ

ATEF ABAYAT: Distant cousin of Hussein Abayat; commander of al-Aqsa Martyrs Brigades in Bethlehem, 2000–2001

HUSSEIN ABAYAT: Member of Fatah and commander of Abayat-clan militia in Bethlehem, October–November 2000

IBRAHIM ABAYAT: First cousin of Atef Abayat and his successor as al-Aqsa Martyrs Brigades commander in Bethlehem

AYAT AL-AKHRAS: Eighteen-year-old female student from Deheishe refugee camp; suicide bomber killed March 29, 2002

MIKE AVIAD: Israeli Defense Forces reservist: leader of platoon in battle of Bethlehem

CHRIS BANDAK: Christian from Bethlehem's Old City; member of al-Aqsa Martyrs Brigades

ABDULLAH DAOUD: Chief of Palestinian General Intelligence Apparatus, *mukhabarat,* in Bethlehem, 2001–2002

OMAR HABIB: Seventeen-year-old Bethlehem student trapped in Church of the Nativity

HANADI HAMMASH: Wife of Ahmed Mughrabi

KAMEL HMEID: Secretary-general of Fatah in Bethlehem; member of *mukhabarat*

ALA HOSNI: Chief of Police, Bethlehem, December 2001–present

JIHAD JA'ARA: Member of al-Aqsa Martyrs Brigades; one of the murderers of Avi Boaz, American Israeli slain in Beit Sahour in January 2002

LEOR LITTAN: Israeli Special Forces commander; chief negotiator for Israeli side during siege

MOHAMMED AL-MADANI: Governor of Bethlehem, October 2001–present

AHMED MUGHRABI: Commander of al-Aqsa Martyrs Brigades in Deheishe refugee camp and organizer of cell that dispatched suicide bombers to Israel

ALI MUGHRABI: Youngest brother of Ahmed and Mahmoud; member of Ahmed's suicide cell

MAHMOUD MUGHRABI: Younger brother of Ahmed; leader of protests at Rachel's Tomb

YUSUF MUGHRABI: Father of Ahmed, Mahmoud, and Ali Mughrabi

FATHER PARTHENIUS: Greek Orthodox priest; resident of monastery inside Church of the Nativity

SALAH TAMARI: Former Fatah commander in southern Lebanon; member of Palestinian Legislative Council; chief negotiator for Palestinians during siege

SAMIR ZEDAN: Christian businessman and journalist in village of Beit Jala

KEY EVENTS IN THE
ISRAELI-PALESTINIAN CONFLICT
1993–2003

JANUARY 1993 Secret talks between Israel and the Palestinian Liberation Organization (PLO) begin in Oslo

SEPTEMBER 13, 1993 Yasser Arafat and Israeli Prime Minister Yitzhak Rabin sign a Declaration of Principles in Washington, which becomes known as the Oslo Accords. Israel recognizes the PLO and gives Palestinians limited autonomy in return for peace and an end to Palestinian claims on Israeli territory

MAY 4, 1994 Cairo Agreement marks first step toward implementing the Oslo Accords. Israel agrees to withdraw from 60 percent of Gaza Strip, not including settlements, and from West Bank town of Jericho. A five-year period begins that is to lead to permanent resolution of disputes over Jerusalem, settlements, Palestinian refugees, and sovereignty over the Haram al-Sharif, or the Temple Mount

JULY 1, 1994 Arafat returns in triumph to Gaza to take up new position as head of Palestinian National Authority (also known as the Palestinian Authority [PA]), after twelve years of running PLO from Tunis

SEPTEMBER 28, 1995 Arafat and Rabin sign "Oslo II" in Washington to expand Palestinian self-rule in West Bank and Gaza and permit first Palestinian elections in January 1996

NOVEMBER 4, 1995 Yitzhak Rabin is assassinated by an orthodox Jewish student opposed to the Oslo Accords. Shimon Peres becomes Israel's new prime minister

DECEMBER 22, 1995 Israeli Defense Forces withdraw from Bethlehem; Palestinian Authority assumes control

MAY 29, 1996 Following a series of Hamas bus bombings that leave dozens of Israelis dead, Peres is defeated by Binyamin Netanyahu in Israeli elections for prime minister. The Likud leader opposed the Rabin-Peres peace program, campaigning under the motto "Peace with Security"

AUGUST 12, 1996 Israel lifts four-year freeze on settlement building in West Bank and Gaza

JANUARY 17, 1997 Israel hands over 80 percent of Hebron to Palestinian Authority, but retains control of Jewish settlements in the heart of the city

OCTOBER 23, 1998 Under intense U.S. pressure, Netanyahu ends eighteen months of stagnation in the peace process by signing Wye River Memorandum outlining further Israeli withdrawals from the West Bank

MAY 18, 1999 Ehud Barak defeats Netanyahu to become Israel's prime minister

JULY 25, 2000 Peace summit at Camp David ends without agreement after two weeks of negotiations. The main sticking points are the division of Jerusalem, sovereignty over the Haram al-Sharif, and the fate of Palestinian refugees

SEPTEMBER 28, 2000 Ariel Sharon, right-wing Likud leader, visits the Haram al-Sharif, sparking riots across the West Bank and Gaza and marking the start of the al-Aqsa intifada

SEPTEMBER 30, 2000 Caught in crossfire between Israeli and Palestinian gunmen, a twelve-year-old boy is shot dead in his father's arms. The killing, captured by TV cameramen, becomes a rallying cry for the intifada

DECEMBER 10, 2000 Barak resigns and calls for new elections in the face of continuing violence that has claimed three hundred lives, mostly Palestinian

FEBRUARY 6, 2001 Ariel Sharon defeats Barak in a landslide, calls for government of national unity with Labor Party to bring peace to the Middle East

SEPTEMBER 26, 2001 After a summer of suicide bombings, Arafat and Israeli Foreign Minister Peres agree to a truce, but cease-fire soon collapses

JANUARY 15, 2002 Ra'ed Qarmi, a leader of the al-Aqsa Martyrs Brigades, is killed in a bomb explosion, sparking calls for revenge and ending month-long period of calm

JANUARY 28, 2002 Wafa Idriss blows herself up in central Jerusalem, killing an Israeli and becoming first female suicide bomber of the intifada

MARCH 8, 2002 Thirty-nine Palestinians die in Gaza Strip, on the single bloodiest day thus far in the eighteen-month-long uprising

MARCH 27, 2002 A Hamas suicide bomber walks unimpeded into a ballroom at Netanya's Park Hotel and kills twenty-nine Israelis who had gathered there for Passover seder

MARCH 29, 2002 Sharon launches Operation Defensive Shield; Israeli forces roll into Ramallah and besiege Arafat in his headquarters

APRIL 2, 2002 Israeli troops/tanks invade Bethlehem; Church of the Nativity siege begins

MAY 10, 2002 Church of the Nativity siege ends

SEPTEMBER 20, 2002 Israeli forces enter the *muqata* (Arafat's headquarters) and destroy every building in the Ramallah compound except for Arafat's offices

NOVEMBER 5, 2002 Sharon calls for new elections following the collapse of his unity government

DECEMBER 22, 2002 Palestinian Authority postpones elections, which had been scheduled for January 2003, until Israel withdraws from all Palestinian cities and territories

JANUARY 28, 2003 Likud is big victor in Israeli elections; Prime Minister Sharon hails Likud triumph as "historic" and says he'll seek to create another broad-based government

PROLOGUE

❧❧

AT THE MILITARY CHECKPOINT ON THE HEBRON Road, the Israeli troops were in a relaxed, even jovial mood. It was Christmas Eve in Bethlehem, 2002, and the Israelis had lifted the curfew and pulled back the tanks and armored personnel carriers that had paralyzed the city for weeks. The troops were smoking and joking, waving a trickle of cars past cement barricades and a watchtower. "Merry Christmas," a Russian-born reservist told me, handing me back my press card with barely a glance.

As I approached Manger Square at the edge of Bethlehem's Old City, I began to encounter signs of celebration. The annual Christmas Eve procession led by the Latin patriarch of Jerusalem, Michel Sabbah, was expected to arrive at the Church of the Nativity momentarily, and a few men in civilian clothes directed the traffic that surged toward the plaza; the uniformed cops of the Palestinian Authority had disappeared six weeks earlier when the tanks and troops rolled in. Members of Bethlehem's Christian community walked through a chilly drizzle toward the square, mingling with Carmelite nuns, Franciscan friars, seminarians, and the occasional visitor from out of town. In front of the Door of Humility, the tiny main entrance to the fourth-century Basilica, the head of the Franciscan Order in the Holy Land chatted in Italian to a handful of reporters who'd come down to cover the event. This was the first Christmas at the Church of the Nativity since the thirty-nine-day siege in the spring of 2002, and the visit of the Latin patriarch was evidence,

1

the monsignor said, that "everything in the church has returned to normal."

Outside the church, the atmosphere was anything but. To protest the Israeli occupation, the mayor had ordered that no Christmas lights or ornaments be hung in Bethlehem this year. The patriarch's Christmas Eve procession to the purported birthplace of Jesus had drawn as many as fifty thousand spectators in years past, but this time around barely two thousand people had gathered in rain-slicked Manger Square. A large number of them had come to demonstrate, not to celebrate. European and American protesters joined a few dozen Israelis who had defied their government's ban on travel to the West Bank. Along with some of the locals, they waved placards proclaiming "End the Occupation" and "Curfew = Detention Camps." Here and there one encountered posters of Yasser Arafat. The Israeli government had denied him permission to visit Bethlehem on Christmas for the second consecutive year—a humiliation that had boosted, however temporarily, Arafat's sinking popularity among his people.

THE DISMAL CHRISTMAS celebrations seemed an appropriate way to end what had been, for most residents of the city, Bethlehem's *annus horribilis*. Four times in the past year the Israeli Defense Forces had occupied the city and held it for as long as three months. After invading Bethlehem in April and remaining for much of the spring and summer, the Israelis pulled out in late August under a plan to hand back control of certain West Bank towns to the Palestinian Authority once it had demonstrated a willingness and ability to halt terrorist attacks. Bethlehem enjoyed three months of calm. Then, on November 22, 2002, a Hamas suicide bomber from the village of al-Khader, in Palestinian-controlled territory next to Bethlehem, killed himself and eleven other people, including many children, on a bus in the southwest Jerusalem neighborhood of Kiryat Menachem. Hours later the Israeli army reoccupied Bethlehem and its environs—just in time to spoil Christmas. This time there was no talk about withdrawing, and the city resumed its downward slide. Festering piles of garbage accumulated on sidewalks. At the entrances to the Deheishe refugee camp, teenagers and boys burned tires and heaps of refuse and taunted the Israeli-made Merkava tanks that rolled by on a regular basis.

As a journalist covering the intifada, I found myself whip-sawed back and forth in my reactions to these repeated occupations. Talking to Israeli soldiers and civilians, I could fully understand their anger and frustration. It was hard not to sympathize with the argument that Israel needed to do everything in its power to protect its people from the scourge of suicide bombers. No doubt, since Israeli troops and tanks had rolled back into the Palestinian territories, the number of such attacks had dropped dramatically. But whenever I traveled to Bethlehem or other cities in the West Bank and felt the sullen rage and despondency of people shut indoors for days on end, or talked to family members of innocent civilians who had been shot dead for violating curfews, I was yanked back in the other direction. Then I felt again that the Israeli reoccupation was a dead end, a failed policy that could never stamp out suicide attacks completely, and that in the long run it fed the hatred and the hopelessness that had spawned such acts of "martyrdom" in the first place.

FOR MUCH OF THE past year I had been a witness to this grim cycle of occupation and withdrawal, traveling from my home in Jerusalem several times a week to chart the course of the al-Aqsa intifada as it raged through one West Bank town. I had gotten to know many of the people who lived there—Christians, Muslims, priests at the Church of the Nativity, civic leaders, Fatah commanders, and the families of suicide bombers—and become intimately familiar with the city's labyrinthine streets and diverse neighborhoods. I had talked at length with people who had partic-

ipated enthusiastically in armed attacks against Israelis, and I had
spent just as much time with those who vigorously opposed them.
I had roamed the packed warrens of Deheishe and Aida refugee
camps, sipped tea in Bedouin tents in the barren hills in the
Judean Wilderness just east of Bethlehem, attended weddings and
baptisms in the Christian villages of Beit Jala and Beit Sahour.
Gradually I had attained a degree of comfort and knowledge that I
had rarely achieved in any other city and had come to grasp the
complex personal histories, relationships, tensions, and rivalries
that lay hidden beneath Bethlehem's surface.

Why write a book on Bethlehem? I hadn't planned on such a
project when I arrived in Israel in the fall of 2000, a few weeks after
Ariel Sharon's incendiary trip to the Temple Mount or, as the Palestinians call it, Haram al-Sharif, Noble Sanctuary. For most of my
first year as *Newsweek*'s Jerusalem bureau chief, I was absorbed in
the daily coverage of the al-Aqsa intifada, the endless procession of
terrorist attacks, targeted killings of Palestinian militants, funerals,
and Israeli incursions into Palestinian territory that had come to
define the rhythm of life here. But after a time I wanted to go
deeper, to move beyond breaking news and convey the full texture
of life during the worst period of Israeli-Palestinian conflict in
recent history. I imagined not a book that would attempt to be an
all-encompassing examination of the intifada, but one that would
hold one piece of the mosaic under the light. It would be, for want
of a better term, a biography of a place.

A combination of events and circumstances led me to the city
in which, Christians believe, Jesus was born. About a year into
the uprising I hired as a "fixer" and translator a Palestinian Christian from Beit Jala named Samir Zedan. Until that point I had
barely been aware of the Christian presence in the Holy Land,
but as I began spending time in this hillside village just west of
Bethlehem, I found myself fascinated by the dynamics within the
dwindling community and its precarious position in Palestinian
society. Bethlehem's proximity to my home in Jerusalem also
drew me toward it as a subject. In the space of twenty minutes I

could walk out my front door, get into my car and drive through the Hebron Road checkpoint—or, when it was closed, climb over a pile of dirt and stones that the Israeli army had bulldozed across a road on the western edge of Palestinian-controlled territory—and find myself in Manger Square. The intifada raged in other towns in the West Bank, such as Qalqilya, Jenin, and Tulkarm, with perhaps even more intensity. But Bethlehem offered the advantage of proximity, the power of its name, and a problematic Muslim-Christian relationship that imbued it with a different level of tension and complexity.

I had pretty well settled on Bethlehem as a book subject when Israel invaded the town on April 2, 2002, and besieged the Church of the Nativity. The epic standoff at Jesus's birthplace—the army of the Jewish state surrounding dozens of Muslim militants who had forced their way into the second-holiest site in Christianity—added a whole new dimension of color and drama to the story. The siege seemed to capture the essence of the Mideast struggle: a seemingly intractable conflict fought between two stubborn and deeply distrustful enemies. Many of the people whom I had met over the past months, including Bethlehem's governor, the commander of the Fatah militia, a Greek Orthodox priest from Canada, and my next-door neighbor, an Israeli army reservist, found themselves by an eerie coincidence caught up in the standoff. A narrative arc took shape: I would follow the lives of a dozen characters whose destinies all converged at the church.

Finding a way to tell the story was one of the principal challenges of this book. Parts of the drama I witnessed personally: I watched the Israeli Defense Forces roll into Beit Jala in August 2001 to root out Palestinian gunmen who were shooting from the Christian village upon the neighboring Jewish neighborhood of Gilo. I was pinned down inside a hotel during the April 2, 2002, battle of Bethlehem; and spent hours at the barricades during the Church of the Nativity siege. But I did the bulk of the reporting during the summer and fall of 2002, traveling to Bethlehem several days a week to conduct interviews and fill in the details. To keep a sense of immediacy, I've injected many of these journeys into the book, weaving together the past and the present.

AT THREE O'CLOCK in the afternoon on December 24, 2002, the wail of a siren reverberated through Manger Square, and two police motorcycles emerged from the alleys of Bethlehem's Old City with their blue lights flashing. The motorbikes signaled the arrival of Michel Sabbah's entourage. I was standing behind a police barricade just in front of the Door of Humility when the sixty-nine-year-old Latin patriarch from Nazareth began his traditional walk across Manger Square. Two Greek Orthodox priests stood vigilantly on either side of the door: they were there to ensure that Sabbah obeyed the 1757 agreement, known as the Status Quo, that turned custody of the Basilica to the Greek Orthodox Church in perpetuity and granted the Latins only the right to pray in the Nativity Grotto and follow a strictly circumscribed path through the columns of the great hall. Resplendently garbed in a purple robe and pom-pomed miter, followed by a retinue of bishops and Palestinian Authority officials, the silver-haired prelate pushed through the adoring throng. Approaching the Basilica, he ducked beneath the three-foot-high portal and disappeared into the murky interior.

In Manger Square the crowds had already started to disperse. The demonstrators packed up their placards and began the journey back across the Israeli military checkpoint to Jerusalem. Many of the local Palestinians headed for Bethlehem's Municipal Market, taking advantage of the brief break in curfew to stock up on food for the coming week. Within a few minutes of the patriarch's arrival, the plaza before the church was deserted. The only sound was the rain landing in puddles on the paving stones.

THE CAMP

❦

HE HADN'T SET OUT TO BE A MARTYR THAT DAY, his best friend Sa'ed Ahmad assured me. We were walking through the warrens of Aida refugee camp on a scorching after-noon in July 2002, and I had asked Sa'ed to re-create for me the day that Israeli troops had killed Moayyad al-Jawarish, thirteen, during a clash at Rachel's Tomb, a heavily guarded Jewish holy site located at the northern entrance to Bethlehem. I was investigating the life of a man named Ahmed Mughrabi, one of the most chilling figures in Bethlehem, the leader of a suicide cell that had sent a half dozen teenagers to kill and be killed in Israel. I had traced the story here, to these early days of the al-Aqsa intifada, when Moayyad's death had set in motion a terrible chain reaction of murder and revenge.

Sa'ed was a jug-eared boy of sixteen who lived with his parents in one of those indistinguishable alleys found in refugee camps all over the West Bank and Gaza—a cramped quarter of ugly cinderblock buildings and kids playing with improvised toys such as unspooled reels of cassette tape that they find lying in the dirt. School was out for the summer when Sa'ed agreed to get into my car and head down the Hebron Road to Rachel's Tomb, a half mile away, to tell me about his friend's final hours.

With everything that's happened in the region since, it is not easy to remember the atmosphere back in those early days of the al-Aqsa intifada—Moayyad was killed on October 16, 2000—when madness, excitement, and the lure of martyrdom swept up the children of the refugee camps. Nearly every day violent clashes erupted at Israeli military checkpoints thrown up at the border between Palestinian- and Israeli-controlled territory: the New City Inn and Qalandia junction in Ramallah, Netzarim junction in Gaza, the entrance to the Abraham Avinu Jewish settlement inside Hebron. Boys as young as five hurled stones and even firebombs at Israeli soldiers. Palestinian security forces and Fatah activists often stationed themselves at the periphery of the crowds of stone-throwing youths, according to many witnesses, firing their Kalashnikovs in the air in an effort to provoke the Israelis to shoot back into the crowds. At the same time, the beleaguered government of Prime Minister Ehud Barak resolved to squelch the new uprising quickly with an overwhelming use of force. The result was carnage: in the eighteen days between Likud Party leader Ariel Sharon's visit to the Haram al-Sharif—what Jews call the Temple Mount—on September 28 and Moayyad's final morning, ninety-one Palestinians were killed, a third of them children.

The hours and days leading up to Moayyad's encounter at Rachel's Tomb were especially bloody. Israeli Apache helicopters leveled the Palestinian Authority police headquarters in Ramallah in retaliation for the October 12 lynching of two Israeli soldiers who had made a wrong turn and wandered into the seething city by mistake. Israeli troops injured scores in clashes across the West Bank and Gaza that had erupted in protest over Israel's closure of the territories. Israel sealed off Haram al-Sharif, the third-holiest site in Islam, to Palestinians under the age of forty-five, determined to avoid a repeat of the rioting that had followed Sharon's provocative visit.

As Sa'ed remembered it, teenaged street leaders of Yasser Arafat's Fatah movement, which was then trying to assume command of the uprising, had called for a "scholastic demonstration" at ten thirty in the morning on October 16 at Rachel's Tomb. Sa'ed had been there three times before, once with Moayyad. The fighting had been fierce, he told me: Molotov cocktails and stones met with tear gas, a hail of rubber bullets, and occasional rounds of live ammunition. Moayyad's father, an unemployed pipe fitter, and his mother had begged him not to go down to the tomb anymore, but many of the boys in his school were going, and Moayyad didn't want them to think he was afraid.

It began as a typical morning. Sa'ed met his best friend at seven fifteen in front of Moayyad's house. Moayyad's grandparents were refugees from the southern Jerusalem neighborhood of Malcha who had fled their home in 1948 and had rented the place on the outskirts of Aida camp from a Christian family, thus avoiding the crowded warrens of the camp itself, which is home to about thirty-eight hundred Palestinian refugees. Moayyad appeared at the front door wearing black jeans and a blue tee shirt, the standard school uniform of the boys in Aida, as well as the prized Reebok soccer shoes he'd received from his parents for his thirteenth birthday. He was the goalie of the soccer team of the Beit Jala Basic School for Boys, the United Nations–administered school he attended on Aida's outskirts, and was considered an enthusiastic player. On his back he wore a black-and-gray vinyl knapsack stuffed with a half dozen text- and composition books adorned with cheerfully colored sports-themed covers. Sa'ed remembers that they had both an algebra and an Islamic studies test that day and that they talked about the possible questions on the examinations as they walked to their seven thirty class.

The boys passed through the blue metal gate of the Beit Jala Basic School for Boys, a two-story stone edifice set behind a high green fence. Knots of students gathered in the courtyard, kicking soccer balls back and forth and talking enthusiastically about the demonstration. Moayyad and Sa'ed spotted Ali Mughrabi, a tough fourteen-year-old from Deheishe camp and the leader of the Young Tanzim, the Fatah youth organization, at the school. Moayyad braced himself as Mughrabi approached him. "Are you coming today?" asked Mughrabi. Moayyad hesitated for only a moment. "Of course," he replied.

*   *   *

It is a stark and forbidding no-man's-land. Situated at the northern limits of Bethlehem, off the main road that runs from Jerusalem to Hebron, Rachel's Tomb is an emotionally charged flashpoint imbued with contradictory and irreconcilable meanings for each side. To Jews it is one of the most sacred sites in their mythology, supposedly marking the place where "Mother Rachel," wife of Jacob, lay down and died while giving birth to her second son, Benjamin, during her southward journey from Beit El to Jerusalem. Her spirit, the faithful believe, blessed and comforted Jewish captives as they passed by her burial place on the way to slavery in Babylon in 586 B.C. To Palestinians the tomb is a constant source of outrage, a reminder of their powerlessness, and a symbol of the broken promises of the 1993 Oslo Accords, which created the framework for a permanent peace agreement and a Palestinian state. The deal signed by Yitzhak Rabin and Yasser Arafat in 1993 left unresolved the final status of the Jewish holy sites inside Palestinian cities, including Rachel's Tomb in Bethlehem, Joseph's Tomb in Nablus, and the Tomb of the Patriarchs in Hebron, although the Palestinian Authority did offer guarantees in perpetuity of access, prayer, and security for Jewish worshipers. Despite Palestinian assurances, the Israeli government moved to fortify all of the sites in the years immediately after Oslo. The Israelis argued that the Palestinians could not be trusted to safeguard this vulnerable part of the Jewish heritage; in the case of Rachel's Tomb, they cited such ominous developments as the published claim of Palestinian Authority officials in the mid-1990s that the tomb marked the burial site of an Islamic slave, not the revered Jewish matriarch. The Israeli army built a high wall around the modest, fifteenth-century domed structure that supposedly contains Rachel's remains. They added two forty-foot-tall watchtowers, narrowed the stretch of the Hebron Road that runs past the site, and stationed additional soldiers there to protect Jewish worshipers. Searches and identity checks of Palestinians who passed by the site increased, and as a result the commercial activity in the area sharply declined. In a part of the world where every square foot of land is invested with deep meaning, the Israeli Defense Forces also refused to withdraw from a few adjacent streets that the Oslo Accords had designated as "Area A"— under the control of the Palestinian Authority. The abrogated withdrawal from the area meant that four thousand Bethlehemites would remain against their will under Israeli military occupation.

Rachel's Tomb became a magnet for Palestinian protests. The demonstrators expressed their anger over both the fortification of the tomb and other perceived breaches of the Oslo Accords by the Israeli government. In 1997 Israeli troops fired tear gas at five hundred students from Bethlehem University during a march to protest the groundbreaking on the new West Bank settlement at Jabal Abu Ghneim—known to Israelis as Har Homa—that sprawled across a barren hill between Jerusalem and Bethlehem. (Har Homa perfectly illustrates the complexities of the Israeli-Palestinian conflict: although Israel forcibly expropriated land from some Palestinians to build the settlement, many other Palestinians sold their property willingly; in addition, several top Palestinian Authority officials obtained lucrative contracts from Israel to supply cement and other materials and services for the settlement's construction.) Two years after the Har Homa protests, a Palestinian was shot dead at the tomb after attempting to stab an Israeli soldier, a killing that precipitated three days of rioting. With the start of the al-Aqsa intifada, the clashes now occurred on a near-daily basis.

In Aida camp on that fateful morning two hundred boys, nearly one-third of the student body, poured out the gate of Beit Jala Basic School for Boys at ten o'clock. Moayyad walked arm in arm with Sa'ed at the front of the procession. Knapsacks on their backs, singing Palestinian national songs and thrusting their fists in the air, the boys were in high spirits. As they left the camp and entered the Hebron Road, they encountered busloads of boys and young men from the nearby Deheishe camp also heading for the demonstration. Ali Mughrabi waved to his brother, Mahmoud

Mughrabi, who stood in the front of the lead bus, a plastic jerri-
can filled with gasoline at his feet. He had stuffed the rear pockets of his blue jeans with shoelaces, which he would use to
fashion makeshift slingshots to hurl firebombs at Israeli troops.
The cries of *"Allahu akbar!"*—God is the greatest—resonated from
the buses as the Beit Jala Basic boys followed on foot toward the
tall stone watchtower that rose over Rachel's Tomb.

"THIS IS WHERE WE STOOD," Sa'ed told me, tensing visibly as we drew closer to the tomb. We were standing in the middle of the Hebron Road in the blistering heat, staring at the
forbidding column. The clashes at the tomb were history now,
but just the sight of it stirred up bad memories for him. I was
nervous myself. The scene reminded me of those sniper alleys I
had encountered in other war zones: burned-out, eerily deserted
places where the sense of danger and nearness of death make the
hair on your neck stand on end. Nothing much had changed
since Moayyad and Sa'ed made their final trip here. The Israelis
had sealed the street in front of Rachel's Tomb with cement
blocks. A shot-up Kando gas station loomed on my right; a weed-
choked, litter-strewn traffic median bisected the road. On the
left, on our side of the street, two unfinished and abandoned
apartment buildings rose beside neglected fields. Heaps of
garbage and concrete rubble lay strewn across the road; the remains of a corrugated-metal blacksmith shop and a garage stood
just a few feet from the watchtower. Everything was deserted,
shut down. No one could drive past the tomb anymore in either
direction, and anyone who tried risked being hit by a bullet fired
by one of those Israeli snipers sitting there, faceless, behind bulletproof glass.

We moved back two hundred yards from the tomb and stood
in front of the Hotel Intercontinental, a former Ottoman mer-
chant's villa once known as the Jasir Palace. When the hotel
opened in the spring of 2000, its Palestinian owners hoped that

the five-star establishment—with $200-a-night rooms and a graceful interior plaza in which fountains burbled beneath ancient shade trees—would attract flocks of well-heeled Western and Arab tourists. Six months later the intifada began, and the area directly in front of the hotel became a war zone. Now the Intercontinental's ornate pink-sandstone facade was scarred by a bullet hole or two; its doors were locked, its interior dark.

The turnout for the demonstration had been big—the biggest of the four that Sa'ed had been to, he told me. Four hundred boys from Bethlehem's refugee camps converged on the scene at ten thirty, and the violence began almost immediately. "There was a Ford Transit parked beside that big concrete block," he said, pointing down the Hebron Road at one of several ugly slabs that sealed the way. Two Palestinian police at a guard post behind the Hotel Intercontinental watched us with curiosity as we strolled around the former combat zone; this wasn't exactly a major pedestrian thoroughfare these days. "Just as Moayyad and I arrived," Sa'ed told me, "some *shebab* [teenagers or young men] from Deheishe camp raced up to the Ford, smashed the windows with stones, doused the interior with gasoline, and dropped in matches." As the flames shot in the air, the boys erupted in cheers.

The next two hours were chaotic. Two dozen helmeted Israeli soldiers took up positions in the center of the Hebron Road after the Ford was torched. Moayyad and Sa'ed hid behind a low cement wall seventy yards away from them, rising to hurl stones and chunks of concrete at the troops. A jeep roared up to the gas station and a half dozen soldiers leapt out, firing tear gas; the boys tossed the canisters back and hurled a barrage of stones, forcing the soldiers to take cover behind the jeep.

Mahmoud Mughrabi from Deheishe camp was, as usual, at the center of the fighting. A goateed and muscular man, he was clad that day in jeans and a white tee shirt, with a checkered *kefiyeh* (headscarf) around his neck. At twenty-five he was the most fearless of the demonstrators at Rachel's Tomb, the shebab acknowledged, and the most adept among them at making and hurling firebombs. Several times a week Mahmoud organized trips to the tomb, made sure participation was high, herded the youths onto public buses, and usually managed to persuade the bus drivers to waive the one-shekel fare because, he argued, the shebab were going to do "national work." Most of the boys preferred to remain in groups, but Mahmoud Mughrabi worked solo in the clash zone, creeping as close as possible to the Israeli soldiers, darting from tree to garbage dumpster to concrete wall, often scoring direct hits with his missiles. Today he carried his usual weapon, a soda bottle that he had picked off the street, filled with gasoline, and plugged with a crude fuse fashioned from a rag. Moayyad and Sa'ed observed him with nervousness and admiration as he hid behind a wall, out of sight of the Israeli soldiers, extracted a shoelace from his pocket, and twirled it around the bottle. He lit the fuse. Then he darted from behind the wall, swung the weapon over his head, and hurled it toward the Israeli position. The cocktail slammed against the pillbox and burst into flames, infuriating the soldiers inside.

The troops were everywhere now, perched on the Kando gas station roof, standing in the middle of the Hebron Road, creeping through the Islamic cemetery that lies behind a grove of pine trees at the rear of Rachel's Tomb. The shebab were conversing on their mobile phones, keeping track of the soldiers' movements, warning one another when and in which direction to run. At one thirty Sa'ed received a call from another Aida boy telling him that twenty soldiers were advancing quickly through the cemetery toward the field where he and Moayyad were lying low. He told Moayyad, "Time to go home." The two boys stood up simultaneously and ran in the opposite direction from Rachel's Tomb. At that moment a live bullet slammed into the back of Moayyad's head. Moayyad gave a little grunt, walked two steps, then fell down dead.

Sa'ed just stared. Moayyad lay face down in the grass, the blood from his fatal head wound trickling down his neck and back and staining the black-and-gray knapsack stuffed with his books. Sa'ed looked on disbelievingly. The boy started to weep, stroking his best friend's shattered skull. Mahmoud Mughrabi ran from his cover to Moayyad's corpse. His younger brother Ali joined him. Gingerly Mahmoud took Moayyad in both arms and carried him to a Palestinian Authority jeep waiting past the Bethlehem Hotel Intercontinental. Sa'ed ran home and, sobbing, told his parents about Moayyad's death. "After Moayyad died, I never went back to the clashes," he told me. "I couldn't bring myself to do it. He was like a brother to me." Mahmoud rode with the body to the government-run al-Hussein Hospital in Beit Jala, his tee shirt soaked with Moayyad's blood.

THE CITY OF BETHLEHEM sprawls across limestone hills rising twenty-five hundred feet at the edge of the Judean Wilderness, five miles south of Jerusalem, and lacks any natural landmarks such as rivers or lakes to form easy points of orientation. As you drive south out of Jerusalem on the Hebron Road, Route 60, you leave the carefully cultivated greenery of that city behind and begin to taste the breathtaking aridity of this part of the Middle East. The land is bleached out, windswept, and treeless except for a few swaying cypresses and gnarled olives. Past the thousand-year-old Mar Elias Greek Orthodox monastery situated on a hilltop to the left, past the fluttering Israeli flag, the gunmetal-gray watchtower, and the soldiers at the Hebron Road checkpoint, past the Palestinian taxis waiting on the other side, you arrive abruptly in front of Rachel's Tomb at an ugly concrete wall that blocks further movement south along the Hebron Road. Detouring left around the holy site, you pass an Israeli military encampment, surrounded by a low wall and barbed wire, that effectively cuts this part of Bethlehem off from the rest of the city. Beyond the camp lies Manger Street, curving through a newer part of the city, lined with shawarma restaurants, landmark hotels such as the Paradise and the Bethlehem, and many shuttered souvenir shops that, in better times, did a brisk business selling olive-wood religious scenes to some of the hundreds of thousands of tourists who visited annually.

You skirt the edge of a deep canyon, or wadi, to your left, that extends north toward the hulking apartment blocks and cranes of the unfinished hilltop settlement, Har Homa. Then you bear to the left and see, directly in front of you, the Old City clinging to the slopes of the second-tallest hill in Bethlehem. It is a hive of twisting alleyways, thousand-year-old stone houses, archways, tunnels, souks, steep staircases, and churches of a half dozen denominations—Syrian Orthodox, Lutheran, Roman Catholic, Greek Catholic, Greek Orthodox, Ethiopian Orthodox. On a second hill just east of the Old City, separated from it by Manger Square and the smaller Nativity Square, stands the Church of the Nativity, the fortresslike complex built above the Nativity Grotto where Jesus is said to have been born and the center of Bethlehem's life for the past 1,650 years. The church perches on a promontory at Bethlehem's eastern edge; far below, in a wide valley, the largely Christian village of Beit Sahour extends east toward the emptiness of the Judean Wilderness. If you turn your back to the Church of the Nativity and the Old City and face west, you will see another long line of densely populated hills directly in front of you. This is the Christian village of Beit Jala and, just to the north, the annexed Jerusalem neighborhood of Gilo, built on land captured in 1967, separated from its Palestinian neighbor by another steep canyon.

Over the last half century the city has expanded across the surrounding hills and valleys. Except for the main Hebron Road, recently renamed for Yasser Arafat, there is almost no flat ground, and each turn opens up a new vista of dusty wadis—pale brown eight months of the year, covered with a thin layer of grass during the winter rain. The wadis are peppered with flat-roofed homes built of blocks of Jerusalem stone, along with ubiquitous terraced fields of olives, one of the few crops that will thrive naturally in this semiarid climate. Besides the sense of sprawling verticality, the other powerful impression one obtains while driving around Bethlehem is the unfinished nature of the place. Half-built office complexes, hotels, and private residences seem to rise on every hilltop and at every turn in the road: exposed girders and steel supports emerge from the top floors of these window-less stone hulks, construction having stopped dead at the begin-ning of the al-Aqsa intifada. And of course there are the refugee camps.

MAHMOUD MUGHRABI'S FAMILY lives inside Deheishe, the largest refugee camp in the Bethlehem area. Created in 1950, Deheishe is one of nineteen camps established by the United Na-tions in the West Bank and Gaza to take in thousands of Palestin-ian refugees who fled their villages and towns after the first Arab-Israeli war. Originally a sea of tents pitched on 160 acres donated by the Jordanian government, which ruled the West Bank at the time, the camp took on an air of permanence in the 1950s, when the United Nations constructed cinderblock huts to replace the tents. UN administrators introduced electricity and running water and hooked up sewer lines to the Bethlehem mu-nicipality. More and more huts arose, and refugees added second and third stories, gradually accepting that they would not be re-turning to their original homes in the near future.

Deheishe has been a hive of political activism since its cre-ation. Every family inside the camp has at least one living mem-ber who vividly remembers the terrifying flight into exile, the loss of land, the chaos and sorrow of 1948; the *Nakba*—catastro-phe—has fueled an uncompromising hatred of Israel and a dream, however unrealistic, of return. In many conversations with residents of Deheishe, I have heard that the land of Pales-tine extends "from [the Mediterranean] Sea to [the Dead] Sea" and that only the Jews who arrived before the 1948 war have a le-gitimate right to live there; the Poles, the Russians, the Ethiopi-ans, the Americans who have immigrated in the years since then are illegitimate occupiers. During the first intifada the Israeli

army surrounded the entire camp with a fence to prevent
teenagers from throwing stones at passing cars; the only way in
or out was through a guarded turnstile. The fence came down
when the Palestinian Authority took control of Bethlehem in December 1995, but the anger hasn't dissipated. The twelve thousand refugees of Deheishe remain among the most politically
active in the West Bank. The two most popular movements in
Deheishe, Fatah and the Popular Front for the Liberation of
Palestine, stood at the forefront of the first intifada and took an
active role in organizing demonstrations at Rachel's Tomb during
the second uprising. Later, only later, would come the guns and
the bombs.

The camp sits on a hill that slopes sharply up from the Hebron Road. On a September day in 2002 my translator and I
drove into the camp through the main entrance, marked by a
huge mural depicting Ghassan Kanafani, the Akko-born Palestinian poet, playwright, and Popular Front for the Liberation of
Palestine activist who was assassinated by a car bomb, allegedly
planted by Israel's Mossad agency, in Beirut in 1972. We zig-
zagged through a maze of rutted alleyways, most of them barely
wide enough for a single car to pass, each lined with two- and
three- and even four-story cinderblock homes. The sky was visible only in slivers, cut up by a tangle of power lines. Minarets
peeked above the shabby warrens, and political graffiti and paint-
ings in a multiplicity of colors seemed to cover every inch of wall
space: Palestinian flags, Israeli soldiers, Fatah fighters, Kalashnikovs, along with occasional English slogans such as "Occupation is a crime" and "Resistance ≠ terrorism." Old men wearing
the traditional Arab kefiyehs gossiped in doorways. An army of
schoolboys in starched white shirts and black pants headed to
class; their paths crossed those of schoolgirls, clad in white-and-
green uniforms and white headscarves, known as *hejab*, walking
in the other direction.

Yusuf Mughrabi, Mahmoud's father, met me at the gate of his
borrowed rooms in the center of Deheishe. He was a personable

bear of a man with a broad, melancholy face, a prominent Roman nose, and a salt-and-pepper beard. He thumped around on a pros- thetic right leg. He had lost his limb during the Six-Day War, he told me, when he went to look for the remains of a downed Israeli fighter jet near the Mar Elias Greek Monastery and stepped on a land mine in a field. Mughrabi now spent his days crafting wooden furniture in the courtyard of his quarters and brooding about the tragic course his family's life had taken since the start of the intifada.

The toll was nearly unfathomable. When I met him, one son, Mahmoud, was dead, two were in Israeli jails, and the remainder of his family—two other sons, a daughter, his wife, and the wife of his son Ahmed—were homeless. After his eldest son, Ahmed, became the organizer of the Deheishe suicide cell, believed re- sponsible for the deaths of eighteen Israelis, Israeli troops de- stroyed his own place, which he had purchased and remodeled with ornamental gates and mosaic floors and a small landscaped garden in 1997. As he led the way across the courtyard to his rooms, Mughrabi told me that the United Nations had promised to give him eighteen thousand dollars to rebuild his house, but he guessed that it would require more than four times that amount to do the job right. So for now he was stuck where he was. The only personal touches on the otherwise bare walls were two framed photographs of Ahmed on his wedding day in De- cember 2001—Ahmed was already assembling bombs in a work- shop inside the refugee camp by the time of his marriage—and an almost life-sized poster of Mahmoud, caught in the act of hurling a firebomb in front of Rachel's Tomb.

We sat on cushions on the floor in Yusuf's living room. He took off his prosthetic leg and stood it in the corner, and he rubbed the stump periodically as we talked. Yusuf's wife, a strik- ingly beautiful, dark-skinned woman in her fifties, with a blue- henna dye mark on her forehead that indicated her Bedouin origins, brought in coffee and a tray of fruit and then, at my invi- tation, joined us. Deheishe residents had told me that the mother of the Mughrabi boys had shown up at Mahmoud's funeral in December 2000—female appearances at funerals are a rare occurrence in Palestinian Muslim society—and fired a Kalashnikov assault rifle in the air. "It was a pistol," she corrected me, as she fingered her rosary beads. "I fired seven shots." Mahmoud's parents had initially turned down a ten-thousand-dollar check proffered to them by representatives of the Iraqi dictator Saddam Hussein as compensation for the loss of their son; Yusuf Mughrabi told me nobody should expect a financial reward for such a sacrifice. But neighbors had prevailed upon them to accept the money, and they had used it to build a second-floor apartment for Ahmed in the family home in Deheishe. "Then the Israelis came and blew it up," Yusuf said.

Omar, the Mughrabis' six-foot-six-inch, seventeen-year-old son, also came in briefly. Like many other siblings in Deheishe camp, the Mughrabi sons had been deeply divided about the uprising when it began in September 2000. Mohammed, now twenty-one, and Omar had decided after a couple of trips to Rachel's Tomb that the stone-throwing and firebombing would lead them nowhere except perhaps to the cemetery. The other three boys—Ahmed, Mahmoud, and Ali—went to confront the Israelis as often as they could. Omar told me that fierce arguments would break out among them over dinner at the Mughrabi home. "Ali believed that we had to fight 'by any means necessary,'" Omar told me. "I thought he was making a mistake and I told him so." Ali was only fourteen at the time; within a year he would be building bombs with his brother Ahmed in a Deheishe explosives factory. The lives of Omar and Mohammed had followed a different course: Omar now studied heavy equipment maintenance at a vocational school in Bethlehem, and Mohammed worked for his uncle, Yusuf Mughrabi's half brother, at a supermarket the man owned on the Hebron Road.

I wondered whether Yusuf Mughrabi felt he bore responsibility for the disaster that had befallen his family. Palestinian acquaintances told me that even before the al-Aqsa intifada Yusuf

Mughrabi had earned a reputation in Deheishe as an angry man, a revolutionary, filled with uncompromising hatred toward Israel. They also told me that he had driven his children to Rachel's Tomb and had wished them good luck as they headed off to throw firebombs and rocks at Israeli troops. Yusuf denied it. "I could not prevent them and I could not support them," he told me. "It was their decision." In several visits to Yusuf Mughrabi over the next months, I found him to be a compassionate man, extraordinarily warm and welcoming, professing measured political views; at one point he told me that "Israel needs another man like Yitzhak Rabin."

But it was hard to discount that awful family history. His half brother, the supermarket owner, offered a harsher view of Yusuf when I met him later at his thriving establishment on the Hebron Road. He told me that when Yusuf came back to the Palestinian territories in 1996 after twenty-nine years abroad, he was still mouthing the slogans of his youth, still talking of war while everyone else was concerned with making money. "Yusuf didn't understand the game," the half brother, also named Mahmoud Mughrabi, told me. "I told him it's a different time now from 1967; it's no time for revolution." Yusuf Mughrabi, the uncle told me, seemed to encourage his sons' most nihilistic impulses. "He was careless towards his kids. He couldn't control them," he said. I suggested that the loss of his leg as a teenager may partly explain the passions that drove him, but his brother assured me that it was the aftermath, the horrific journey that followed, that shaped his character—and those of his sons—more than the accident.

YUSUF MUGHRABI, the grandson of a Tunisian immigrant to Palestine and his Palestinian wife, was born a refugee in Hebron in 1950 and moved to Deheishe with his family ten years later. Soon after the mine blast that tore off his leg, he traveled to Amman, Jordan, to be fitted with an artificial limb. There he resolved not to return to the Israeli-occupied West Bank, and he subsequently joined the Palestinian Red Crescent Society, part of Arafat's Fatah movement, which the Palestinian leader had set up with other exiles in Kuwait in 1958 to wage a military struggle against Israel. Over the next decade and a half, the Fatah leadership dispatched Mughrabi to do clerical work in medical clinics in Jordan, Syria, and Lebanon. In 1973 he and his wife moved from the Sabra and Shatila refugee camp on the outskirts of the Lebanese capital, Beirut, to the Ayn al-Hilweh refugee camp in the port of Sidon. Ahmed was born there the next year, and Mahmoud arrived in 1975. Then came Mohammed in 1979 and their only daughter, Dareen, in 1980.

Disaster soon followed. Ayn al-Hilweh was one of a number of refugee camps in southern Lebanon considered by Israel to be guerrilla strongholds of the Palestinian Liberation Organization, the umbrella group of armed factions chaired by Yasser Arafat, whose Fatah movement constituted the largest number of fighters. After a series of deadly mortar and rocket attacks launched against the civilian population of northern Israel from southern Lebanese bases, a massive Israeli force swept across the border on June 6, 1982. The stated aim of the invasion was to drive twenty thousand Palestinian militants out of southern Lebanon, but Defense Minister Ariel Sharon would ultimately order his troops and tanks to advance all the way to Beirut. Gunboats shelled the refugee camps from the sea; warplanes strafed everything that moved on the roads—passenger cars, pickup trucks, donkey carts—and bombed the camps indiscriminately, according to reporters and United Nations officials at the scene. More than twenty thousand people, most of them civilians, are believed to have died. The battle inside Ayn al-Hilweh went on for two weeks. Israeli troops arrested Yusuf Mughrabi along with the entire staff of the health clinic; they blew up his house and forced his family to seek refuge from the bombing in basement shelters filled with hundreds of terrified refugees. "We lived in total darkness, without even a flashlight and only water and stale bread to eat," remembered *Imm* Ahmed (mother of Ahmed), as Yusuf's wife is known respectfully after the name of her eldest son. "Everybody was shouting for ten days continuously. A decomposing body of a woman lay on the floor." The family emerged to find the camp flattened and corpses flung about the ruins. Yusuf Mughrabi had vanished. For his family the effect was profound. "The kids started feeling the pain and bitterness of occupation early in their lives," their mother told me. "They saw their house, school, clinic, and camp destroyed, all destroyed. These memories were kept inside their heads, and nothing could ease it for them."

Released from Israeli custody after a week, Yusuf Mughrabi located his family in the ruins of Ayn al-Hilweh and slipped his wife some money. Then he fled to Beirut and jumped on a rickety boat with six hundred Palestinian guerrillas bound for Port Sudan. Yusuf's vessel was the first ship to leave Lebanon as part of the Palestinian Liberation Organization's withdrawal from the country negotiated by the United Nations; Mughrabi had no passport, no papers, and no idea of what the future held for him. "My morale was very down," he told me. Sudanese authorities reunited Yusuf with his family in a dusty refugee camp about ninety miles outside Khartoum, but it was just a way station. Under the terms of the negotiated withdrawal from Lebanon, Arab governments agreed to take in the exiled fighters and activists from the Palestinian Liberation Organization. But fearful that the exiles would be a destabilizing force, the Arab governments dispersed the Palestinians and their families to "military camps," often in remote and undeveloped corners of the country where they would not pose a threat.

The Mughrabi family's first home was a grass-roofed mud hut in Sinkat, a market town of ten thousand people in a drought-stricken corner of northeastern Sudan. The local tribes wore nothing but loincloths, carried spears and knives, and still practiced ritual scarification with razor blades. The town had no electricity and no running water, and Mughrabi, his wife, and their children lived alongside fifty Fatah fighters who were supposed to spend their days in military training but in reality ended up idling away their lives. To supplement his one-hundred-dollar monthly Fatah salary, Yusuf Mughrabi built a crude wooden boat and fished for his family in the nearby Red Sea; his children attended government schools alongside Sudanese children, picking up tribal languages along with their Arabic. After seven years there a dispute developed between the PLO and the Sudanese government; the PLO leadership ordered Mughrabi and his family to uproot themselves again, this time to the Libyan oasis of Kufrah in the middle of the Sahara. Just outside of Kufrah lay the desert, four hundred miles of nothingness in every direction. Periodic sandstorms would howl across the oasis. The sense of remoteness, the boredom, was overwhelming. Ahmed Mughrabi applied to study chemical engineering at a university in the port city of Benghazi, but, according to his father, the college administrators rejected him and told him that if he wanted to attend college, he should wait until he went home to Palestine. It was a crushing disappointment. "The housing in Libya was better than in the Sudan, and we had water and electricity," Yusuf Mughrabi told me, "but psychologically it was much more difficult."

The family endured seven more years in Kufrah. Ahmed and Mahmoud grew into adults there, having experienced no other life since their childhood than the harsh regimen of military camps in desolate surroundings. At the end of December 1995 the PLO leadership informed Yusuf Mughrabi that he and his family could return to the Palestinian territories under the terms of Oslo. "I felt like I could be a human being again," he said. Shortly afterward he traveled with his eldest son, Ahmed, by bus one thousand miles to Rafah, on the border between Egypt and the Gaza Strip, to lay the groundwork for the family's homecoming. But their ordeal was not yet over. The Israelis denied Ahmed Mughrabi entry, and he lived in a refrigerator carton in the no-man's-land between Egypt and Gaza for two months while his father sorted out the paperwork. Another eight months passed before Israel granted entry permits to the rest of the family. Then the Libyans refused to allow Yusuf Mughrabi's five other children to cross into Egypt without their father, forcing him to make the two-thousand-mile round trip across the Sahara to retrieve them and his wife. Reunited in the Rafah refugee camp in October 1996, Yusuf embraced his family and told them that their decades in the wilderness had ended at last. "This is your homeland," he said. "Nobody can kick you out of here. You can even cut down your almond trees and nobody can tell you that you're not allowed to do this. This place belongs to you."

AHMED MUGHRABI'S WIFE, Hanadi, came into the room. She was a round-faced, softly pretty woman with doe eyes and three prominent beauty marks on her cheeks. She exuded an air of vulnerability and sweetness, but as we talked, I could detect a steely self-confidence and sharp intelligence. She had graduated the spring before the outbreak of the intifada with a degree in Arabic studies from Bethlehem University, and she spoke some English; the mere fact that she approached me to talk about her husband without being asked was a sign that she had been more influenced by Western culture than most Muslim women in the West Bank. I asked her if she had been able to speak to Ahmed Mughrabi since he had been arrested and charged with being the leader of Deheishe's suicide cell, and she told me that she had recently been to see him at a hearing at the Israeli military court in the settlement of Beit El, near Ramallah. During a lunch break she had forced her way through the crowd and approached an Israeli soldier standing guard in front of the room where Ahmed was being held. In passable English she had introduced herself as Ahmed's wife and demanded that he let her see her husband. "Aren't you a human being?" she asked him. The guard relented. "He was inside a cage, with two meters between us, and my mother and three other soldiers present in the room. We told each other we loved each other, we talked about our families, and he told me, 'I'm going to be here in prison for not more than two years. They have to let me out, because this is our land, and they are intruders.'" When I told her that the Israeli authorities had rejected my requests to visit Ahmed Mughrabi in Nafha prison in the Negev Desert, she replied that she wasn't surprised. "The Israelis are worried, because they know that anyone who meets Ahmed comes to love him," she said. Ahmed Mughrabi had stunned those in attendance at his Beit El hearing by launching into a defiant speech that was reported in *al-Quds* and other Arabic papers. Pronouncing the Israeli court "void," Mughrabi had told the judges, "You should be sentencing the ones who killed my brother Mahmoud, demolished my home, and scattered my family." Then the tall, bearded militant declared, "You have shut down hope for the future. If you were in my place, you too would have fought against the state of Israel."

After the Mughrabi family returned to the Palestinian territories in 1996, the National Security Force hired Yusuf Mughrabi as a border guard in Rafah. His son Ahmed went to work for the same force in Ramallah. Mohammed, still a teenager, found a job driving a tractor on a farm in Jericho, and Yusuf's half brother hired Mahmoud to pack bread at his bakery in Deheishe camp. (He would later expand his business to include the supermarket as well.) In 1997 Yusuf secured a transfer to Bethlehem with the rank of major in the National Security Force. The family pooled their resources and purchased a house on a ridge at the summit of Deheishe, with sweeping views of the Judean Wilderness. Thirty years after he had left the West Bank, Yusuf Mughrabi was back where he had started.

Yet the Mughrabis struggled to find a place in the community. Mohammed Laham, a longtime Fatah leader in Deheishe who spent fourteen years in Israeli jails, welcomed the family when they arrived and tried to help them integrate into the tightly woven fabric of Deheishe society. "The Mughrabis were isolated. They had no tribe, no real family, no money, and no friends," said Laham, a wiry, tough-looking man in his late forties who has served as a godfather to two generations of Fatah activists in the camp. "They were complete outsiders, and they were desperate to find acceptance," Laham told me. Yusuf Mughrabi's half brother Mahmoud, who had not seen Yusuf or his family in three decades and had spoken to them only rarely, also did his best to make the Mughrabis feel at home. "[Yusuf Mughrabi] was full of resentment; he had an inferiority complex," Mahmoud said. "He wanted to distinguish himself from his other brothers, who had been successful in business. So he became a *haj* [made the pilgrimage to Mecca] and stuck with this idea of revolution."

Yusuf Mughrabi vehemently rejected his brother's optimism about the peace process. He was disheartened by the unchecked growth of Israeli settlements, the harassment at checkpoints, the curtailing of Israeli entry permits issued to Palestinian workers, and, above all, the bloody clashes of September 1996, which started when Israel opened an archaeological tunnel near Jerusalem's Dome of the Rock and the al-Aqsa Mosque. Seventy-five people, most of them Palestinian, were killed in three days of rage across the West Bank and Gaza. Convinced that the Oslo Accords were meaningless, Yusuf Mughrabi said that there would never be a Palestinian state and spoke often about the inevitability of war. His brother chastised him. "Stop playing this old game," he said. "It's time to move on."

Yusuf Mughrabi's sons also had a hard time adjusting to their new community. Mahmoud Mughrabi lasted three months at his uncle's bakery, quarreling constantly, demanding pay raises, even threatening his uncle. "He resented the fact that we were doing well and his family was not doing well," his uncle told me. "He wanted to have everything at once—a house, money, and standing in the community. I told him it had taken me years to build what I had." Like his father, Mahmoud seemed insecure, yearning for recognition. Mahmoud Mughrabi lifted weights obsessively; he also turned to Islam, an unusual path in secular Deheishe camp, where the Islamic fundamentalist groups Islamic Jihad and Hamas have never gained a foothold. Mahmoud's older brother, Ahmed, became even more devout, swearing off cigarettes and liquor and praying dutifully five times a day; friends suspected that he was considering joining Islamic Jihad. The National Security Force sent him to Jericho to become a trainer, considered a prestigious position, but he quarreled with his colleagues and angered the powerful head of the National Security Force, General Haj Ismail, who had spent years in Jordan and Lebanon with Ahmed's father. Banished to a lowly job in Hebron, Ahmed quit the force.

Ahmed and Mahmoud tried to put their lives on track. Although the unemployment rate in the Palestinian territories was near 50 percent in the late 1990s, both brothers found steady jobs connected to the tourism industry. Ahmed built and maintained cable cars for the new Téléphérique and Sultan Tourist Center, a gondola system linking the ancient city of Jericho with the Mount of Temptation, the site of a Greek Orthodox monastery. The work was dangerous, requiring Ahmed to hang several hundred feet off the ground, but it paid the equivalent of four hundred dollars a week—a considerable income in the West Bank. Ahmed's religious commitment weakened, his uncle says. "Ahmed started making money; he got a taste of this life; he started growing his hair longer; he was becoming a modern boy." Mahmoud found a job cutting stone and laying tiles for a Bethlehem construction company that had European Community and UNESCO contracts to rehabilitate the Old City as part of the $300 million Bethlehem 2000 Project. Later he looked for a job at the Bethlehem Hotel Intercontinental near Rachel's Tomb. The manager promised Mahmoud an entry-level position if he graduated from a hotel management course. Mahmoud would finish cutting stones and commute five times a week to class at the prestigious Talitha Kumi Academy in Beit Jala. He told his friends at Deheishe that he loved the new hotel and that he was excited about the prospect of working there. At the same time, his uncle told me, Yusuf Mughrabi's uncompromising views exerted a powerful influence on his son. "Mahmoud was a good worker but he was confused," says his uncle. "He was always pulled in the other direction."

That other direction led straight to Rachel's Tomb. "Mahmoud was very nationalistic, he got very carried away," said Basel Afandi, twenty-four years old, a Popular Front for the Liberation of Palestine activist in Deheishe camp. "He'd yell to the kids 'Let's go! Let's go,' on the way to Rachel's Tomb. He was always recruiting kids in Deheishe to go to the checkpoint and always the first to carry away the wounded." The biggest clashes took place on Fridays, when teenagers would congregate around Mahmoud in front of the al-Kabir Mosque at the Deheishe camp entrance after midday prayers and pack onto buses for the mile commute to Rachel's Tomb. Mahmoud's bravado—and hatred of the Israelis—seemed to grow after Moayyad al-Jawarish's death. At a Friday clash two weeks later, Samer Afandi, Basel's seventeen-year-old brother, watched in amazement as Mahmoud launched a firebomb at an Israeli pillbox sheathed in camouflage netting, then took off down the Hebron Road pursued by four dozen angry soldiers. Mahmoud clambered to the roof of a nearby abandoned building and rained down bricks, chunks of concrete, and even an empty water tank on the soldiers, smashing the hood of an Israeli jeep. "Mahmoud was fearless," Samer told me. "He always went further than anybody else."

THE DAY BEFORE Mahmoud Mughrabi's first, and last, guerrilla attack against Israel, Moataz Taylach, fifteen years old, became the third young protester to be shot dead by an Israeli soldier at Rachel's Tomb. A stocky ninth grader who liked horseback riding and breeding pigeons on the roof of his house in Deheishe camp, Moataz was struck in the head with a rubber-coated steel bullet during a Friday demonstration on December 8. Mahmoud carried the fatally injured boy to an ambulance, berating the driver for not bringing the vehicle to the scene fast enough. He was angry and depressed at dinner that night, telling his father that "they're trapping each one of us."

On Saturday morning Taylach's funeral procession left the al-Hussein Hospital in Beit Jala and proceeded to the al-Kabir

Mosque, a domed octagonal structure made of pink and white blocks of Jerusalem stone and sandwiched into a small square just inside the camp's main entrance. The *imam* said a prayer for the dead. Then six of Taylach's classmates from the Iskander Khouri United Nations School in Beit Jala and two of his brothers bore his Palestinian flag–wrapped body on a stretcher to a new martyrs' cemetery that had been consecrated at the beginning of the intifada in the village of Irtas, just south of Bethlehem. A cold rain began to fall, and thick droplets of water splattered on the waxen face of the dead boy, running down his eyelashes and moistening his colorless lips, which were curled into a faint smile. Hospital workers had tightly wrapped the top of his head with white cloth, hiding the gaping wound in the back of his skull. Mahmoud Mughrabi led five thousand mourners along a winding road at the top of Deheishe camp heading south above a deep chasm filled with a dense gray mist that parted occasionally to reveal an old Roman Catholic monastery far below. "*Shaheed* [martyr]," Mahmoud shouted, addressing the dead boy, "we will continue the struggle. Martyrs, we will continue to Jerusalem!" Soaked and freezing, the procession clambered up the steep path that led to the martyrs' cemetery, a bare patch of ground surrounded by a few scraggly olive trees.

Taylach's plot had been dug the night before, next to the grave of another Deheishe camp martyr, Abdul Kadr Abu Laban, who had been shot dead on December 5. The gravedigger removed the stone slabs that had covered the earthen pit, and the rain quickly turned the bottom into mud. Mohammed Laham and Mahmoud Mughrabi stretched a tarpaulin over an adjacent olive tree, partially shielding the grave. They gently lowered Taylach's corpse inside, replaced the slabs, and slathered cement from a plastic bucket over the stones. The crowd watched intently, the only sound the scraping of the trowel and the roar of heavy rain. "Even the skies are crying for you, Moataz," Laham said. Then he, Mahmoud, and the gravedigger shoveled wet earth on top of the cement and smoothed it evenly across the surface.

At that point, Laham remembers, Mahmoud Mughrabi praised the gravedigger for fitting his grave so precisely to the size of Moataz's body.

"Make mine longer, please," he told him. "I want to be able to rest."

Laham looked at him in surprise. "How can you talk like that?" he said.

Mahmoud just smiled.

That night the Mughrabi family gathered around the dining table for *iftar*—the big evening meal that breaks the dawn-to-dusk Ramadan fast—and over lamb, rice, and yogurt discussed the worsening violence in the West Bank. At ten o'clock on that cold and rainy night, Mahmoud and Ahmed Mughrabi left the house together, as they often did. This time they met another Deheishe resident named Jad Salem Attala, a bespectacled recent graduate of Bethlehem University, who had also been a frequent participant in the clashes at Rachel's Tomb. Mahmoud Mughrabi had a Kalashnikov rifle; Jad Attala carried a homemade bomb in a backpack. The three planned to lay the explosive on a road just outside Beit Jala, in Israeli-controlled territory. Israeli jeeps and armored vehicles passed along this road frequently on their way to a hilltop military base.

After midnight the three men drove to the top of Beit Jala and climbed over an earthen barricade that blocked the exit leading into the Israeli-occupied West Bank. At the start of the intifada Israeli military bulldozers had blocked many such roads to seal Palestinian-controlled towns and prevent militants from driving out. As the men laid the device in the road, an Israeli patrol opened fire, hitting Mahmoud Mughrabi in the legs. "Mahmoud started crawling back painfully through the rocks," Yusuf Mughrabi told me, basing his account on what Ahmed had reported to him. "Ahmed reached him, and he took the Kalashnikov from his brother. Immediately he wanted to start shooting at the soldiers, but then he had a vision of his mother standing in front of him, and he felt it would be too painful for her to see both of her sons killed at the same time." With Mahmoud unable to walk and the Israelis fast approaching, Ahmed and Jad Attala retreated across the earthen barricade and into the safety of Beit Jala, leaving Mahmoud to his fate.

At dawn the next morning the Israeli army turned over the body of Mahmoud Mughrabi to the District Coordination Office, an agency on the Beit Jala border that functions as a liaison between the Israeli military and the Palestinian National Security Force. He had bullet wounds in his head as well as his legs: Dr. Peter Qumri, director and chief surgeon of Beit Jala's al-Hussein Hospital, who examined Mahmoud's body later that day, told me that the evidence pointed to an execution. "There was lots of earth on his legs that shows he was dragged," Qumri says. "He was shot in his head from a very short distance." (The Israeli Defense Forces ignored several requests I made for their version of events.) Yusuf Mughrabi smiled as he stood over his son's corpse in the morgue, a Palestinian journalist who witnessed the scene told me. He touched his fingers softly to his lips and pressed them against Mahmoud's lips, as if sending him a good-bye kiss. Moments later, when his fourteen-year-old son Ali began to cry, Yusuf slapped him across his face. "Cut it out," he told his youngest son. "Your brother is a shaheed and you are crying?" Ahmed Mughrabi also came to say good-bye to his younger brother, betraying as little sentiment as his father. "Congratulations," he had told his mother upon learning of Mahmoud's death. "Your son has become a martyr." Few people will ever know whether Ahmed felt guilty about leaving his brother to face execution, but those acquainted with him said a change came over him that day. As he gazed intently at Mahmoud's corpse, he was perhaps already plotting the course of revenge that would transform him into one of Israel's deadliest enemies. "Bastard," the Palestinian reporter heard Ahmed Mughrabi say in front of his brother's body. "He made it before I did."

THE TRIBE

ञ९ऽ

ON A MOONLIT NIGHT IN OCTOBER 2000, A KNOT of young men stood at the top of Wad al-Sawahra Street in the heart of Bethlehem, gazing at the glittering lights of Beit Sahour spread across the valley below. From their vantage point high above the predominantly Christian village, described in the Bible as the site where an angel told shepherds of the birth of Jesus, they could see the illuminated steeple of the Greek Orthodox church soaring above the low-slung skyline. Just to the left of the church rose the five-hundred-year-old Omar Ibn al-Khatab Mosque, with its distinctive green-tipped minaret. To the right, a circle of bright yellow lights delineated the perimeter of an Israeli military camp, known as the Crow's Nest, that Israel had established on the site of an old Jordanian army base after the Six-Day War. Its main function was to guard a road that led from Jerusalem to the isolated Jewish settlements of Teqoa and Noqedim in the Judean Wilderness.

The Palestinian uprising was less than a month old, but many members of the group were already experienced hands in carrying out armed attacks against Israeli targets. As they drove under the three-quarter moon down Doctor Geminer Street, the main thoroughfare through Beit Sahour, named after the founder of a well-respected orphanage, they chain-smoked and clutched their guns in anticipation. Parking their cars in front of the large campus of the YMCA, they crept down a dirt alley past some darkened white houses, recently abandoned by their terrified owners.

Israeli bullets and tank shells had damaged many of the buildings during the gun battles of the previous weeks. When they reached a clearing, they found themselves on a ridge looking out across a treeless gulch. The army camp stood five hundred yards away on a flattened hilltop in the gulch—a cinderblock house, a fluttering Israeli flag, and a lone cypress tree surrounded by barbed wire and illuminated by fluorescent lights. The camp, which the Israelis had promised to dismantle under the terms of the Oslo Accords, made an easy target. Chris Bandak, a Palestinian Christian from Bethlehem's Old City, inserted one of his two clips filled with .45-caliber bullets into his borrowed Kalashnikov assault rifle. It made a loud snapping sound that startled him. This was his first "operation" against the Israelis, and he was petrified.

ALMOST ALL THE FIGHTERS involved in shooting at the Crow's Nest, which the Israelis called Shdema camp, came from a Palestinian clan known as the Abayats, a group of interlocking families who lived in the dusty hills on the eastern edge of Bethlehem. The Abayats belonged to a tribe of former Bedouins called the Ta'amra, traditionally fighters and weapons smugglers who inhabited the Judean Wilderness. It was here that the biblical King David grazed his flocks of sheep and goats as a boy and where Greek Orthodox monks still dwelled, as they had for fifteen hundred years, in cliffside monasteries in total isolation. The Abayats had begun moving into Bethlehem in the 1940s, and now several thousand of them lived within the city limits. Until the beginning of the uprising Bethlehem's citizens—and their own Ta'amra brethren—had largely disparaged them as outlaws and troublemakers. But now the Abayats stood on the front lines of the Palestinian "national struggle," and their role had transformed them.

I had first become aware of the Ta'amra in the fall of 2000, the early days of the al-Aqsa intifada, when the sounds of gun battles between militiamen based in Beit Jala and Israeli troops in the annexed Jerusalem neighborhood of Gilo were a standard feature of nightlife in the city. The late-night whirring of helicopter blades over my head and the thud of nearby Israeli tank fire would jolt me awake in my home in the German Colony quarter in the southern end of town. I quickly learned that a cell of masked gunmen was infiltrating the mostly Christian village of Beit Jala at night and sometimes during daylight hours, firing M-16s and heavy machine guns wildly across the gorge dividing the two hilltop communities. If they were lucky, they would score a direct hit against a building—or a person. The Israeli Defense Forces would retaliate by firing back large-caliber bullets and tank shells, turning houses into rubble and occasionally killing civilians.

Sniper shootings accompanied the random firing at Gilo by the Palestinian militia. In the first weeks of the uprising, the gunmen killed seven Israeli soldiers and settlers in the Bethlehem region. Abayat fighters shot dead a petroleum-truck driver who had been delivering fuel to the Israeli army camp at the edge of Beit Sahour. They ambushed and murdered a settler near Teqoa, killed a Gilo resident in a ravine near Beit Jala, and shot dead two Israeli soldiers at a checkpoint in the village of al-Khader just south of Bethlehem. On November 10 an Israeli sentry guarding Rachel's Tomb was killed with a single shot in the neck. The leader of the group was a burly figure named Hussein Abayat, a thirty-seven-year-old baker, gun dealer, and car thief who liked to threaten people with his Browning M2 .50-caliber machine gun. Hussein Abayat had a son named Saddam, loved the Rambo character played by Sylvester Stallone, and often sold arms and ammunition to people off the back of his bakery truck. One of Abayat's top lieutenants was Ibrahim Abayat, then twenty-seven, Hussein's distant relative, who had become notorious in Bethlehem two years earlier for carrying out the first "honor killing" in the region in at least two decades: he had shot to death his first cousin, a mother of six, on the suspicion that she had been carrying on an extramarital affair. Now the peculiar dynamics of the al-Aqsa intifada had thrust these violent figures from the margins of their community to the front lines of the conflict.

The Abayat phenomenon had exposed deep fault lines running through Bethlehem's society. Many members of the city's Muslim population, not just the Ta'amra, viewed the Abayat militiamen as national heroes. To the Christians of Bethlehem and the outlying villages of Beit Sahour and Beit Jala, they were mercenaries and criminals who were creating havoc in their communities. The government in Bethlehem was similarly divided. As the intifada gathered force in Bethlehem, some officials tried to curb the power of the Abayats. Others supported them with arms and money. This schism reflected a larger struggle within the Palestinian Authority in the West Bank and Gaza over the direction of the uprising. The struggle would ultimately bring disaster upon the entire Palestinian territories—and the Abayat clan itself.

For the moment, however, the Abayats were on a roll. Their exploits were already being celebrated in songs, poems, and video montages, whose artful blend of martial music and gory imagery had become a staple of Palestinian television and a powerful propaganda tool. In a matter of months the Abayat guerrillas would transform themselves from a small cell into a mass movement that numbered as many as four hundred fighters. They were among the most powerful of the new armed groups that were springing up all over the West Bank and Gaza, and they continued to draw sustenance from their Bedouin identity.

LATE ONE AFTERNOON during the second summer of the intifada, in July 2002, I drove from Bethlehem deep into the Judean Wilderness to visit Abu Mohammed Sabeh, one of the oldest living members of the Ta'amra. I was seeking to learn about the mentality of the men who had sowed chaos in and around Bethlehem. Sabeh lives in the village of Za'atara in the heart of Ta'amra country, a narrow belt that extends from Hebron to Bethlehem and is bordered on the east by the Dead Sea and on the west by Israel. My Palestinian translator Samir Zedan and I passed through the village of Beit Sahour and drove through an

abandoned checkpoint marking the end of Palestinian-controlled
territory. We found ourselves on a ribbon of tarmac that wound
through a sweeping expanse of barren hills dotted with cinderblock and stone houses and scraggly olive trees, their silvery
branches wilting in the heat. Here and there Bedouins grazed
modest herds of sheep and goats. The summer sun had baked the
thin layer of scrub grass to a monochromatic beige, and our car
kicked up dust as we switchbacked up and down the precipitous
slopes.

Three miles to the east across the barren vista rose the distinctive conical form of Herodion, a seven-story hilltop palace constructed by King Herod the Great as a birthday present for his wife
in 37 B.C. The Judean desert lay beyond this semiarid zone, a
nearly rainless sliver of jagged limestone mesas and yellow dunes
cast half in light, half in shadow by the late afternoon sun. Abraham and Lot camped here as they journeyed to Egypt; Lot's wife
cast her backward glance at the burning cities of Sodom and
Gomorrah from these desert wastes, and the future King David
fled to these inhospitable climes to escape King Saul's fits of jealous rage. Beyond the desert the escarpment dropped straight to
the Dead Sea, a continuation of Africa's Rift Valley. The valley and
the Jordanian mountains beyond were clearly visible during the
winter months, but now a summer haze obscured them.

Fifteen minutes past Beit Sahour we arrived in Za'atara, the
main village of the Ta'amra. Two mosques and several hundred
houses all constructed from rough-hewn blocks of Jerusalem
stone—the newer ones white, the older ones weathered to
ocher—spread over rocky slopes at the very edge of the desert.
Little clusters of men stopped their conversations and watched
us, exuding neither warmth nor hostility. Ta'amra society is
tight-knit and suspicious of outsiders, I had been told, and the
"TV" signs plastered over my Isuzu Trooper, meant to ward off
attacks from roadside West Bank snipers, served to underscore
that we were strangers in town.

Sabeh dwelled in a family compound at the top of the village.

The old man ushered us inside his sitting room, filled with Oriental carpets, plush pink sofas and chairs, and engraved marble pages of the Quran on the walls, and served us a large platter of fresh fruit and cups of pungent Arabic coffee tinged with cardamom. Sabeh was a rail-thin man with a well-trimmed silvery beard and a copper complexion, and he wore the traditional white *dishdasha* (robe) and a white kefiyeh with a black headband. Alert and energetic, he seemed two decades younger than his ninety-two years. When I asked him what his first memory was he described being a boy of seven watching barefoot, bedraggled Turkish soldiers trudge past his Bedouin tent in Za'atara on their way to surrender to the British conquerors of Palestine in Jerusalem in 1917. "They begged us for water," the old man remembered, as he nibbled on a ripe fig. "We threw stones at them instead." Later the British swept into Za'atara on horseback, a hundred men in desert khaki uniforms led by a mustachioed commander, who announced to the Ta'amra that their land had been liberated. The British ordered the nomads to turn in their guns and ammunition and warned that they would execute on the spot anyone who didn't. "We dug deep holes in the earth and buried our weapons there," the old man said. "The Ta'amra cannot be without their guns."

The harsh desert existence, the lawless tribal culture in which they lived, had bred in the Ta'amra a fierce attraction to weaponry. Sabeh received his first gun from his father when he was fourteen years old, he remembered: a .22-caliber bolt action German-made Ruger hunting rifle with a fish carved on its walnut stock. The Bedouins gauged their manhood according to their skill with weaponry. At wedding feasts and other celebrations, Sabeh and the other Ta'amra men and boys would place the head of a sheep on a post and try to shoot it from 300 yards away, a contest that still takes place at many Ta'amra weddings today. "We were all excellent shots," he said. During the Arab Revolt that began in 1936 he joined one hundred Ta'amra guerrillas who attacked Jewish villagers and British army and police in a campaign to force the British to end Jewish immigration to Palestine. His band had sought sanctuary from the British legions in the caves near Mar Saba, a fifteen-hundred-year-old Greek monastery built into desert cliffs five miles from the Dead Sea. They had been strafed, shelled, and bombed from the air until only thirty members of the band were left. "When I was growing up, the British were kings of the world, and the United States was nothing," he said with a slight smile. "Now God rules in the skies, and America rules the earth."

The Ta'amra nomads eventually succumbed to the lure of the sedentary lifestyle—and of peaceful coexistence with their occupiers. In the 1930s, after years of drought, Sabeh and his family settled down along with most of their tribesmen. They planted olives, lentils, and barley, sold their camels and livestock, and sent their children to schools set up by the British rulers and later the Jordanians, who succeeded the British in 1948. "Life became easier for us then," said Sabeh, who never learned to read or write but lived to see his own grandchildren and great-grandchildren attend universities in Europe and America. Still, the Ta'amra's transition to the modern world came relatively late. Weeks after my visit to Sabeh I talked to Edward Khamis, a Palestinian politician from Beit Jala, who as a young district officer based in Bethlehem traveled through the Judean Wilderness in 1950 to register Ta'amra men over age eighteen for the Jordanian civil guard. "I was shocked. We could not find any houses. They had only tents," recalled Khamis. "We measured the height of the Ta'amra men using the tall wooden post that held up their tents. But their lives began to change."

The main instrument of change was Sabeh's close friend, Sheik Mohammed Salem Dueb, the son of a camel trader from Za'atara, who became one of the most influential men in all of Palestine as well as the Ta'amra tribe's bridge to the modern world. The Ta'amra gunmen regarded Dueb as their tribe's greatest leader—an inspiration and a symbol of "Ta'amra power." Indeed Hussein Abayat once told an Israeli reporter that "we

[fighters] are all Mohammed Dueb's successors now." Abu Mohammed urged me to meet Dueb's family, still prominent figures
among the Ta'amra.

At sunset, I left Sabeh and drove across Za'atara to visit the
home that the late sheik had built for himself in 1952, while a
member of the Jordanian Parliament, out of the fortune he'd
earned from the contraband trade. A three-story pink sandstone
villa with a colonnaded portico, it perched on a knoll that offered
breathtaking views of the desert. Swirls of rose tinged the sky, and
the dunes seemed to glow with luminescent energy. Just beyond
the house the property fell away into a gorge that Dueb had
planted with pine trees and that his family kept watered with a
now-computerized sprinkler system (almost nothing green grows
naturally in this barren part of the world). We sat down in the
madafeh—an outdoor pavilion where Dueb had presided over tribal
court sessions. "My father designed this house himself," said
Salem Dueb, Mohammed's fifty-year-old son. "He needed a home
that would suit his stature. They called him the sheik of sheiks."

Dueb's fortune derived from two commodities that future
generations of Ta'amra would also turn to with great success:
hashish and guns. In partnership with a Jordanian general named
Sharif Nasser bin Jamal Ali (a relative of King Hussein) and a
Bedouin leader from the Israeli town of Be'er Sheva in the Negev
Desert, I was told, Dueb organized shipments of cannabis from
Lebanon's Bekaa Valley to the Jordanian port of Aqaba and also
brought in rifles and ammunition from Britain, Italy, and Germany. Camel caravans then transported the drugs and guns across
the ancient Bedouin routes: north from Aqaba through the Negev
Desert, Be'er Sheva, Hebron, and the Dead Sea region, or west
across the Sinai Peninsula. Dueb lavished much of his fortune on
building houses, schools, and mosques for the Ta'amra—he died
of a heart attack in 1979 at the age of sixty, leaving fifty thousand
dollars in debts—and supposedly struck deals with the Israeli
occupiers to keep the smuggling routes open in exchange for tips
about anti-Israeli activity in Ta'amra country. (The relationship

collapsed in 1968 when Fatah guerrillas fired Katyusha rockets at Jerusalem from Ta'amra territory and Defense Minister Moshe Dayan had Dueb deported to Jordan for four years in retaliation.)

As we sat in the gathering darkness in the madafeh, Salem Dueb opened a small box that contained old photographs of his father, a round-faced, broad-shouldered man with a thick gray mustache. In one he pays a condolence call on King Hussein after the death of Queen Alia; in another he's posed before a statue of a caliph during a visit to Cairo. "It was the only time he ever wore a Western suit," his son told me. "He hated it." Dueb's influence as sheik extended far beyond Ta'amra country: from the same box Dueb extracted a braid of black hair, a gift from a young woman in Ramallah who had been attacked with an axe and injured, her hair chopped off, by a spurned suitor. After local authorities refused to become involved, the sheik traveled from Za'atara to Ramallah, persuaded the police to jail the man, and received a hefty compensation for the young woman from her attacker's family. Then, according to his son, he told the assailant, "If you get close to her again, I will declare war on you with the whole Ta'amra people."

We took a walk around the grounds in the early evening. The aroma of fresh bread wafted from a traditional clay oven known as a *taboun* in an attached bakery in back. A white stallion pranced in a rocky field beside the stables. Salem Dueb's nineteen-year-old son Mohammed came out to greet us. He was an engineering student at Hebron University and an English speaker, part of the new generation of Ta'amra who had left the world of their grandparents behind. Mohammed Dueb told me that he and other Ta'amra teenagers once a year hiked deep into the desert, climbing down the escarpment to the Dead Sea. "Our ancestors lived there for years, but for us one day is enough," he said. Now some Ta'amra had come full circle. At the outset of the intifada young Dueb had found himself torn between pursuing his education and joining the Ta'amra fighters led by the Abayats. "They are heroes," he told me. Abayat friends had taught him to

shoot an M-16 semiautomatic weapon in a field outside Bethlehem, he told me, and had encouraged him to join the gunmen.
He had finally rejected their entreaties, instead braving road-
blocks and checkpoints each day to travel from Za'atara to Hebron University. Still, he said, he felt the lure of the battle. "We
are always being pulled back to our Bedouin roots," he told me.

ONE OF THE NEW gunmen who fit that description was
Ibrahim Moussa Salem Abayat, perhaps the most notorious
member of the Ta'amra tribe. Ibrahim Abayat's so-called honor
killing of his first cousin and her supposed lover, and its violent
aftermath, had shaken up the town like no other event in recent
memory. It divided Bethlehem society between traditionalists
who believed such killings were justifiable and modernists who
considered them backward and barbaric; it pitted the Bedouin
code of honor against the nascent secular justice system of the
Palestinian Authority, which had come to power only three years
earlier; and it identified the Abayats as a rising and potentially
dangerous new force in the city. Moreover it foreshadowed the
struggle that would soon erupt between the Palestinian Authority and the tribe during the intifada—and would bring Bethlehem
to the point of utter chaos. In the summer of 2002 I visited the
family of Ibrahim Abayat to hear more about the murders and the
men who committed them.

Wadi Shaheen, the Valley of the Condor, is a hillside neighborhood in eastern Bethlehem now populated almost entirely by
members of the Abayat clan. The area has a rural feel to it, with
blocky, flat-roofed houses scattered among cactuses and terraced
olive groves. But the sense of being in a heterogeneous urban environment is always present: the Crusader- and Byzantine-era
buildings of the Old City hug the slopes directly across the valley
from the Abayat home, and the bells from the Greek Orthodox
tower of the Church of the Nativity were pealing as I drove up to
the Abayat compound. Unlike their brethren living in the Judean

Wilderness, the Abayats rub shoulders frequently with Palestinian Christians. The first generation of Abayats to arrive in Bethlehem, before the 1948 Arab-Israeli War, lived in the Fawagreh neighborhood of the Old City, at a time when Bethlehem was a village clustered on two hillsides and dominated by one Muslim and seven Christian tribes. (These tribes take their names from the professions of their ancient forebears in Bethlehem, including the Najajareh, or carpenters; the Kawawseh, who walked in front of the Greek Orthodox patriarch during religious processions; the Kanawati, guardians of the wells of Bethlehem; and the Tarajime, who translated for the pilgrims at the time of the Crusaders. The Fawagreh, who had lived in Bethlehem for more than a thousand years, were the only Muslim tribe among the original eight.) Salah Tamari, a former Fatah guerrilla chieftain from the Ta'amra tribe who is now a popular member of the Palestinian Legislative Council, told me that he and many of his Ta'amra friends were baptized as teenagers in the Basilica of the Church of the Nativity as a symbol of friendship with the Christian community. Tamari and others also attended Christian schools such as the Franciscan-run Terra Sancta High School, brought offerings to Bethlehem's churches at Easter and Christmas, and still abided by an old pact that united the Christians and Ta'amra of Bethlehem in property disputes and other kinds of conflicts against the Muslims of the southern West Bank town of Hebron.

Our car raised clouds of dust as we wound up the hill leading to a four-house compound. The rusting carcasses of dozens of abandoned cars and trucks lay in the sun at the base of the hill; Wadi Shaheen was one of many automobile graveyards scattered across Bethlehem, a reflection of the chronic shortage of municipal services that dated to the Israeli occupation. A dozen children surrounded us excitedly, and Ibrahim's widowed mother, Fatima Abayat, emerged from the main house and welcomed us inside. She wore the traditional white hejab and the finely embroidered black gown of the Ta'amra women, known as a *thob*. She had a timeless look about her, stocky, matronly, with a strong nose and a broad forehead and a weirdly high-pitched voice that didn't correspond with her physical heft. Imm Khaled, as she is known respectfully after the name of her eldest son, told me that the Church of the Nativity had been a constant presence in her family's life since 1967, when the Abayats took refuge there during the Six-Day War. "When we first heard the planes, we thought it was the air force of King Hussein, not Golda Meir," she told me. "We said *hamdilullah*—thank God. But it was the Israelis bombing Jordanian positions in the city." She, her husband—a retired Jordanian army officer and plastics company accountant who died in 1994—and the three sons they had by then climbed up the hill and stayed inside the Basilica for two days. When they emerged, they encountered their new Israeli occupiers passing out bread and sweets to people in Manger Square—which before the Six-Day War the Jordanian government had cleared of densely packed houses and shops and turned into a tourist-bus parking lot.

Imm Khaled seemed marked by the stoicism and quiet fortitude that I had often encountered among Palestinian women of her generation, women who had suffered from war and occupation for so long that these conditions had become a given in their lives. Born in Beit Fajar, a poor village near Hebron, the daughter of a stonecutter, she had entered into an arranged marriage with Moussa Salem Issa Abu Jalghif when she was fifteen years old. (The Abu Jalghifs are one of eight families within the Abayat clan; many members of the tribe use their family name or Abayat interchangeably.) The Ta'amra soldier, originally from the Fawagreh neighborhood of old Bethlehem, took her to live in the house that his family had built in 1948 in Wadi Shaheen. A traditional Muslim housewife and mother, she eventually was forced into the role of family breadwinner. After the Six-Day War her husband journeyed to Kuwait to try to rescue stranded relatives and became stuck there himself after Israel sealed the border with Jordan. When he returned to Bethlehem five years later, his health was failing, and Imm Khaled supported the family as a maid for a well-to-do Christian family—a job she still has. She had held the family together during the trauma and humiliation of the Israeli occupation: her oldest son, Khaled, and second son, Issa, built a profitable construction business in Israel, while her third son, Suleiman, achieved degrees in both chemistry and Islamic studies at the prestigious Birzeit University in Ramallah.

But the honor killing, the al-Aqsa intifada, and the tragedy that engulfed the family overshadowed all of those accomplishments. Ibrahim Abayat, her youngest son, had become a member of Hussein Abayat's militia and had risen to commander. Two first cousins who lived in the compound had also joined the gunmen: Nidal Abayat, Ibrahim's partner in the honor killing, and Atef Abayat, Nidal's younger brother, who had also become commander of the al-Aqsa Martyrs Brigades in Bethlehem and one of the most feared killers and powerful warlords in the West Bank. Now one was in exile overseas, one was in an Israeli prison, and one was dead. The boys had been inseparable growing up, had thrown stones together in the first intifada; in the second uprising they had played for higher and deadlier stakes—and lost.

Ibrahim always seemed the one most destined for trouble, his family told me. "Ibrahim was spoiled, conceited, and he caused a lot of problems at school," said his brother Suleiman, a black-bearded Islamic scholar with penetrating dark eyes. "He always had a lot of fights. Our father wanted to beat him, but he could never bring himself to punish him." When the first intifada broke out in 1987, Ibrahim's brother Khaled and a group of friends in their twenties led a Fatah cell, and Ibrahim and Atef begged the older men to let them join. Though Ibrahim was only fourteen at the time and Atef thirteen, Khaled gave in. "There were about ten of us, all cousins and brothers, and we were well organized," Khaled, forty-three, told me.

In retrospect the first intifada seems quaint: the money Khaled received from his underground Fatah leaders went to buy jogging suits, running shoes, Palestinian flags, and paint to splash political graffiti on walls. The boys would frequently skip classes and spend their mornings and afternoons tossing rocks at

Israeli troops guarding the Caserna—the police station built catty-corner to the Church of the Nativity during the British Mandate—or engaging in running cat-and-mouse games through the alleys of the Old City. But then the games turned ugly. In 1989 an Israeli soldier beat Khaled and shot him in the calf during a skirmish near the souk; the troops seized his identification papers, then dropped him at al-Hussein Hospital in Beit Jala and released him with a warning to stay off the streets. The same year, the Israeli army conducted sweeps through Wadi Shaheen, first arresting Nidal, then Atef, and finally Ibrahim. Ibrahim and Nidal, both sixteen, received thirty-month sentences at Megiddo prison in northern Israel. Atef, fifteen at the time of his arrest, was incarcerated for the same period in Dahariyeh prison near Hebron. The interrogations were brutal—solitary confinement, days without sleep, a variation of Chinese water torture—but perhaps the most insidious consequence of their jail time was that it deprived all three boys of a chance at a decent education. Ibrahim, Atef, and Nidal Abayat all emerged from prison in 1992 barely literate.

"It was raining the day that Ibrahim came back," his mother says. "I was making sweets in the kitchen and my daughter said, 'Mother, Ibrahim has returned!' He was walking up the road, just with the clothes on his back." Ibrahim began working in his cousin Atef's bakery and later as a bulldozer driver for a family construction company, clearing land for development in Israeli towns such as Beit Shemesh, midway between Jerusalem and Tel Aviv. Political change was in the air, the Oslo process had begun, and hope swept the Occupied Territories. "Ibrahim simply hoped to keep working, improving himself, get married, and raise a family," Suleiman said. "He didn't talk about his prison experience. He wanted to put it behind him."

Imm Khaled showed me a snapshot of Atef and Ibrahim taken during the first intifada: Ibrahim with a thin adolescent mustache and a deadly serious expression, Atef clean shaven, with a sensuous mouth curled into a charismatic smile, a lick of hair tumbling down the center of his forehead. Then a second portrait taken during this intifada: the boys now in their khaki fatigues, carrying guns, involved in a bigger and deadlier game this time, with no sense of where it was all going to lead, except no place good. As I studied the two photographs taken twelve years apart, I couldn't help thinking that to some extent the Israelis had brought the current turmoil upon themselves. The uprising was being fueled by young men like Nidal and Ibrahim and Atef Abayat—ripped out of schools as teenagers, beaten and made to languish in Israeli jails for years, then tossed back onto the streets to brood and wait for the opportunity to get even.

IN 1995, THE YEAR after his father's death of a heart attack, the newly established Palestinian General Intelligence Apparatus hired Ibrahim along with hundreds of other members of the Abayats. The agency, known as the *mukhabarat*, was one of a dozen security forces established by Yasser Arafat according to the terms of the Oslo Accords. (The Palestinian Authority overall security apparatus has come under sharp criticism from international human rights groups, who say that its pattern of corruption and contempt for the rule of law has been exacerbated by its bloated size. In Switzerland, for example, there is one police officer for every three thousand Swiss; under the Palestinian Authority, by contrast, there is one officer for every sixty Palestinians.) As the Palestinian Authority prepared to assume power in Bethlehem, the mukhabarat was in desperate need of reliable local muscle to make arrests and serve as security guards. The Abayats, who had earned a reputation as Bethlehem's toughs, were the obvious choice. Ibrahim performed such tasks as guarding a circus in Beit Sahour; shadowing activists from the Popular Front for the Liberation of Palestine, Hamas, and Islamic Jihad, all of whom had opposed the Oslo Accords; and protecting the intelligence agency's West Bank chief, Tawfik Tarawi, whenever he came from intelligence headquarters in Ramallah to Bethlehem.

But Ibrahim Abayat chafed at following orders and grumbled that he considered the work undignified; months after he was hired, when a colleague made a disparaging remark about the Ta'amra, calling them bandits and camel herders, Abayat struck the man and quit the agency in disgust. "He was hot-tempered, and he was always ready to fight for the honor of the tribe," said his brother Suleiman.

He would have his chance two years later. In the winter of 1998, Ibrahim and his brothers began hearing clan gossip that their first cousin Sara Abayat, a married mother of six, was having an affair. Her husband was in Cairo most of the year working as a ticket agent for the startup company Palestinian Airways, and Sara Abayat admitted that she wasn't happy in the marriage, that her husband cared little for her or the children. Sara Abayat, whose sister was married to Ibrahim's brother Suleiman, her own first cousin, insisted that the rumors of an extramarital liaison were false. On a visit to Wadi Shaheen, she told the Abayat brothers that her husband's older relative, a man named Mahmoud Judeh Ibrahim Ayish, had come to her house when her husband was away, begging her to have sex, but she swore that she had always refused him.

Skeptical of her story, Ibrahim and his next-door neighbor Nidal Abayat, also a first cousin, shadowed the man, lurking outside his home in the nearby village of Irtas, even planting a cassette recorder under his bed that caught sounds, they claimed, of the couple having sexual relations. That tape sealed their death sentence. Soon after they made the recording, Ibrahim and Nidal took their nine-millimeter Browning pistols registered to the Palestinian Authority intelligence agency and set out for Irtas.

I followed the route that the two men took that fateful morning in February 1998, a cold and dreary day. Nidal was at the wheel of a borrowed 1994 purple Mazda; Ibrahim sat beside him. Atef had begged his brother Nidal to let him take his place— Nidal was married with several young children, while Atef had only one infant daughter at the time—but Nidal had rejected the offer. "This is Ibrahim's and my business," he had told him. "We'll take care of it." At ten thirty in the morning the two cousins wound through Wadi Shaheen, then followed the road to Irtas, ten minutes away, out past Solomon's Pools, three ancient stone reservoirs built during the time of King Herod, and out along a pine-forested ridge. They waited in front of Ayish's house and trailed him to the local barber shop. Brandishing his gun, Ibrahim forced Ayish into the front seat and tied a rope tightly around his wrists and mouth. They continued to Sara's home, made her sit in the back, then drove to the Omar Ibn al-Khatab Mosque in the Abayat neighborhood of Bethlehem, where Suleiman Abayat occasionally serves as the imam. (This mosque is one of several in the Bethlehem area named after the Arabian caliph who conquered Jerusalem in 638 A.D. bearing the new faith of Islam, and renamed the city al-Quds.)

It was eleven thirty in the morning. About twenty members of the Abayat clan were gossiping in the plaza of the modern green-domed mosque when the Mazda stopped in front of the building. Ibrahim and Nidal had planned it this way, later telling Ibrahim's brother Suleiman that they had wanted to commit the act in public. I could picture the scene: Mahmoud Ayish was making little sounds of protest through the gag tied tightly around his mouth, Sara Abayat whimpered in the backseat. Nidal opened the front passenger door and kicked Ayish to the ground. As he lay there, hands still tied behind him, Ibrahim and Nidal fired a total of nine bullets into his back. Then they both stepped out of the car and each shot once more into his brain at point-blank range.

They drove back to the Abayat family compound. Wordlessly they parked the car beside Ibrahim's house and marched Sara up a steep hill to an olive grove behind the highest house. I imagine that Sara must have been pale and terrified, crying and begging them to consider her six young children. Suleiman was home at the time. "I heard shots and I ran up the hill, and I found her ly-ing there, with four bullet holes in her back," said Suleiman. "I tried to revive her, but she was dead." Ibrahim and Nidal returned to the house and calmly ate a meal of rice and vegetables. Then they got back in the car and fled east to the Ta'amra village of Za'atara, still under the control of the Israeli government, where they knew they could find refuge.

The Palestinian police and intelligence agents swarmed over Wadi Shaheen, searching for the fugitives and interrogating the family. Tawfik Tarawi spoke to Ibrahim on his cell phone and demanded that he turn himself in. After two days in hiding, Ibrahim and Nidal surrendered to Tarawi's representatives in Bethlehem and were imprisoned in the *muqata,* the local security headquarters, to await trial.

The honor killing was the talk of Ta'amra country and beyond. While the act appalled some in Bethlehem, Nidal and Ibrahim Abayat's decision to "clean" the family's stigmatized reputation made them a cause célèbre in their community. Friends and relatives visited their prison cell to express support. The Palestinian prison guards, who did nothing to hide their own sympathy for their captives, permitted the Abayat cousins to leave on frequent weekend furloughs back to Wadi Shaheen, where their clansmen celebrated them as heroes. Nearly everyone within the Ta'amra and many non-Ta'amra Palestinians as well believed that the men's actions had constituted justifiable homicide. "Our pride and dignity are more important than life itself, and our pride is concentrated in our women," Suleiman Abayat told me. "I wish the murders had not taken place, but things got out of hand. They were compelled to do it." Even the victim's father, Ali Abayat, came from his home in Amman to file an affidavit in which he absolved Nidal and Ibrahim Abayat of blame for the killing of his daughter. Ibrahim expressed no remorse, only anger at the Palestinian Authority for keeping him and Nidal in jail. The more I learned about him, the more he seemed to be a classic paradox: the urbanized Ta'amra, trying to build a modern life, yet dragged back to his Bedouin origins.

I visited the Bethlehem Municipal Courthouse, a modern one-story building on a hilltop near Deheishe camp, where the judges finally rendered the verdict on February 6, 2000. It came after a year and a half of on-again, off-again hearings, forensics presentations and eyewitness testimony, and the protests of many members of the defendants' tribe, who believed they should never have been tried in the first place. One hundred Ta'amra men, most of them from the Abayats of Bethlehem, poured into a small whitewashed courtroom to hear the judgment; several hundred more waited outside. "The courtroom was packed," said Judge Fadhi Musleh, a distinguished-looking man with silvery hair and a thin gray mustache, "and you could feel the tension in the air." The three judges gazed solemnly at the defendants. They pronounced Ibrahim and Nidal Abayat guilty of two counts of premeditated murder and sentenced each to life imprisonment with hard labor—immediately reduced to fifteen years because of "the age of the defendants" and the fact that they had committed the crime "to defend the family's reputation."

The Ta'amra reacted with ferocity. "There was a huge shout, and the crowd began breaking the seats," one of the judges, Fatih Abu Srour, told me. "People were yelling, 'This is an injustice! This will encourage adultery! We are defending our pride, our dignity!'" As police hustled the convicted killers out of the courtroom, several hundred Ta'amra attacked the building with bricks and stones. A large rock smashed through the window of Judge Fadhi Musleh's chambers and nearly struck him; he showed me how he'd been sitting at his desk, trying his best to ignore the crowd shouting for his blood, when the projectile sailed past his head and gouged a chunk out of his wall. "I thought at that point it would be wise to stop working and find a way of leaving," he said. The crowd spilled into the streets of Bethlehem. Protesters discharged their guns in the air, set cars alight, and torched a grocery store belonging to residents of Irtas, the home village of the two victims. In Irtas women and children sealed themselves indoors and men gathered on streets preparing for a Ta'amra attack. "I have never seen people so frightened," one Israeli journalist who visited the village told me. "They were expecting a massacre." (The Abayats' fury dissipated after their rampage through the city, and they never invaded Irtas.)

The riot deeply unsettled Palestinian Authority officials. For hours the Abayats had raged through the streets of Bethlehem unimpeded—even supported by Abayats who served in the PA's security forces. Tribal power had trumped the new government, and the Authority's own men had revealed to whom their loyalty belonged. The following day Yasser Arafat rushed to Bethlehem to meet with tribal elders and government officials and try to end the crisis. And the Palestinian Authority worked alongside Ta'amra leaders to speed Ibrahim and Nidal Abayat's release from jail almost as soon as the verdict was delivered. Many emotional meetings took place between the families of the murder victims and the families of their killers; Fatah leaders in Irtas and Bethlehem and tribal sheiks served as mediators. In the fall the Palestinian Authority gave financial compensation to the bereaved children of Sara Abayat and those of Mahmoud Ayish, in return for a letter from the victims' families offering their forgiveness to Ibrahim and Nidal Abayat "for the national interest." In October 2000, eight months after they were sentenced and two weeks after the al-Aqsa intifada began, Ibrahim and Nidal Abayat were granted a full pardon and exited the Bethlehem police jail as free men. "People came to the house in Wadi Shaheen to welcome them back," Chris Bandak told me. "But the situation in Bethlehem was chaotic, and there wasn't any time for a real celebration."

MUCH HAD CHANGED in the two and a half years since Ibrahim and Nidal had been arrested and jailed. A distant cousin of Ibrahim's named Hussein Abayat had been amassing power and money—and guns—in Bethlehem. By some estimates Bethlehem residents, including many Abayats, now had forty thousand unregistered weapons, thanks in large part to a deal that Hussein had struck with high Palestinian officials. This relationship, founded on mutual self-interest, would prove essential in transforming the Abayats from an unruly mob into the well-organized shock troops of the al-Aqsa intifada. Yet little in Hussein's background suggested that this figure would be the primary agent of the Abayat clan's metamorphosis.

Born in 1963 on Bethlehem's eastern outskirts, down the road from Wadi Shaheen, Hussein Abayat dropped out of school at the age of fifteen because of family financial problems. Like tens of thousands of other Palestinian teenagers living under Israeli occupation, he joined Yasser Arafat's then-illegal Fatah movement. In 1982 the Israelis arrested him, charged him with Fatah membership, and sentenced him to five years in the British-built Ramallah Prison, now used as Arafat's headquarters. "He was one of the cattle," says one fellow inmate, a member of the Popular Front for the Liberation of Palestine, a hard-line resistance movement and a rival of Fatah. "He was a weak guy, an insecure guy, who tried to act macho all the time as if he had something to prove." Released from prison during the first intifada, Hussein returned to Bethlehem, where he was lightly injured while throwing rocks at Israeli soldiers. But he never rose above the level of a street stone thrower. "He was a withdrawn, inconsequential person in those days, and he wasn't worth a penny," says one Fatah activist from Deheishe camp who spent eight years in Israeli jails.

Hussein seemed determined to make an impression on people. He buffed up his body with a brutal weightlifting regimen at a local gymnasium. When his eldest son was born during the Gulf War, he named him Saddam in honor of the Iraqi dictator. Establishing contacts with members of the Israeli underworld, he and other Abayats ran a car theft ring, stealing vehicles in Israel and selling them in the West Bank. Hussein moved easily between the two societies. He spoke Hebrew, mastered during his five years in Israeli jails, owned part interest in a bakery in the Bakah neighborhood of West Jerusalem, and had a permit to cross the checkpoints that divided the West Bank and Israel.

When Hussein's Israeli cronies came to Bethlehem, he would slaughter a lamb and prepare a Bedouin feast in their honor. Although a biographical pamphlet about him insisted that he "hated Zionism," in fact, acquaintances say, he believed a permanent peace deal with Israel would be excellent for business.

The Palestinian Authority took control of Bethlehem on December 22, 1995 in a joyous ceremony held in Manger Square and attended by Yasser Arafat. By then Hussein had achieved the kind of notoriety that drew the attention of powerful officials. Recruited by mukhabarat chief Ismail Faraj into the intelligence division, Hussein Abayat spent eight weeks in a training camp in Jericho, where instructors put recruits through a course of body building, weapons assembly, and marksmanship. He graduated from the course in early 1996 and was inducted into the Executive Force of the mukhabarat. Dozens of other members of the Abayat clan, including Ibrahim, entered the ranks as well, but few profited from the arrangement as much as Hussein. He was on the agency's full-time payroll, but he had minimal responsibilities, allowing him to pursue the vocation that had now risen to the top of his agenda: weapons dealing. According to Abayat family members, top mukhabarat officials guaranteed Hussein protection against arrest by other Palestinian security agencies and even helped find him customers. In return they received Hussein's loyalty—as well as a percentage of his profits.

Hussein Abayat's weapons business flourished. He purchased guns and ammunition from Bedouins in Be'er Sheva, Jordanian dealers, and Israeli middlemen who received their supply from Israeli soldiers. He transported the guns into Bethlehem hidden in the trunk of a Mercedes taxi and often sold them off his bakery truck as he made the rounds. "He could get you anything," says Mazzin Hussein, a former member of the Palestinian police who often bought small-caliber bullets from him. "Hussein would ask, 'You want to buy a weapon?' Then he would open the trunk of his car and say, 'This is an M-16, this is a Kalashnikov, this is a Galil. Take your pick.'" Once the police arrested Hussein Abayat's bakery partner after a street fight broke out between him and his neighbors. Minutes later "Hussein showed up at the police station with an arsenal, intending to make trouble," Mazzin Hussein recalled. "The police called me and said, 'Please come, your friend is carrying many huge guns.' I showed up and calmed him down."

When the intifada began in late September, Hussein Abayat and a small group of men began appearing armed and masked at demonstrations at Rachel's Tomb and Bethlehem University, shouting anti-Israeli slogans and declaring that they were ready for war. "We are a new generation," he told an Israeli reporter at the time. "We are not like our fathers. We know you Israelis and we know how to fight you." The men carried out their first attack on October 6, according to a member of the original group, firing on the Crow's Nest in Beit Sahour. It is still not clear just what Hussein Abayat's motives were. Some Palestinians believe that he was simply a hired gun of the Palestinian intelligence chief, Ismail Faraj, who was seeking to bolster the agency's position as the main sponsor of the uprising. Others told me that the collapse of the Camp David talks, Ariel Sharon's visit to the Temple Mount, and the dozens of Palestinian deaths in the first week of the uprising filled him with genuine rage. The most likely scenario is that officials of the mukhabarat in Bethlehem wanted to use Hussein Abayat but viewed him as a loose cannon and gave him wide latitude. "Hussein Abayat was both under the control of and not under the control of the Palestinian intelligence division," I was told by Najih Faraj, a Palestinian journalist in Bethlehem and the younger brother of Ismail Faraj.

IN MID-OCTOBER 2000 Chris Bandak crouched behind a wall on the ridge overlooking the Crow's Nest, surrounded by Abayat gunmen. As his finger rested on the trigger of his borrowed Kalashnikov assault rifle, he experienced a frisson of excitement. If the Palestinian intelligence chief in Bethlehem was paying Hussein Abayat and other members of his tribe to shoot at Israelis, Bandak didn't know about it and wouldn't have cared. All he knew was that he had watched repeatedly the televised killing of Mohammed Durra, the twelve-year-old boy shot dead in cross-fire between Palestinian and Israeli troops in late September at Netzarim junction in the Gaza Strip, and the scene had filled him with anger. "I wanted revenge against the Israelis," he told me much later. "We all did." Two hours earlier he had run into his old friend Ibrahim Abayat at the Mundo Pizzeria on Manger Street in central Bethlehem. Ibrahim Abayat, just released from prison, had joined forces with Hussein and Atef Abayat's militia. He had invited Bandak to accompany them, and Bandak had accepted.

Shifting his feet nervously, with the harsh lights of the Israeli camp in his eyes, Bandak glanced at the other fighters. They had covered their faces with black woolen ski masks, but he could easily recognize the burly form of Hussein Abayat. Hussein carried a huge .50-caliber machine gun, and bandoliers of bullets swathed his black shirt. The dozen other guerrillas possessed an astonishing selection of weaponry, mostly consisting of new M-16 semiautomatic rifles, which sold in Bethlehem for as much as twelve thousand dollars apiece. The leader set up a tripod and gave the signal. Then the men opened fire.

The shooting was intense, Bandak recalled. The Abayats fired their guns wildly, darting out from the cover of the abandoned Christian homes to spray entire clips of bullets at the Crow's Nest, then dashing back behind the walls to reload. A few shouted *"Allahu akbar!"* as they fired. The Israelis extinguished the lights the moment the shooting began and returned fire with heavy machine guns. Red tracer bullets lit a fiery arc through the night sky; the bullets smashed through windows and sent chunks of masonry and stone flying. Bandak expended his two clips—a total of sixty bullets—in fifteen minutes, but the Abayats seemed equipped with an unlimited supply of ammunition, and the firefight went on for two hours. Exhilarated, exhausted by what he had witnessed, Bandak told his friend Ibrahim Abayat that once wasn't enough. "Any time you're going out again," he said, "make sure to bring me along."

SIX WEEKS AFTER the uprising began, on the morning of November 9, 2000, Hussein Abayat and Ibrahim Abayat set out from Wadi Shaheen in two cars to inspect houses near the Crow's Nest that had been damaged by Israeli shelling the previous night. They had no idea that a twenty-eight-year-old car mechanic from the Ta'amra tribe named Mohammed Deifallah was watching them. According to a confession that Deifallah would later give to Palestinian intelligence—his family insists he was tortured into confessing—Deifallah had been shadowing Hussein Abayat for several weeks and providing information to an Israeli military intelligence agent in clandestine meetings just across the Hebron Road checkpoint in Jerusalem. Deifallah told Palestinian intelligence that he had begun working for the Israelis inside Ramallah Prison a decade earlier and had informed on militant groups sporadically since then. Starting in early October 2000, he said, he was paid one thousand shekels—then worth $250—for each weekly report he supplied about the activities of the gun-dealing militiaman. At nine thirty on the morning of November 9, Deifallah confessed, he had called his handler, who went by the code name Captain Mudi, and told him that Hussein Abayat had left Wadi Shaheen in his green Mitsubishi Magnum 4X4, followed by a Fiat Uno. "It looks like they're going to shoot in Beit Sahour," he said that he told Captain Mudi.

Ibrahim Abayat heard the whine of helicopters and looked up to see three Apache warships sweeping through the sky above the Judean Wilderness. He thought the helicopters were on a routine surveillance mission, until they circled as if zeroing in on a target and then drew lower and lower to the ground. Two one-hundred-pound Hellfire missiles launched by one of the Apaches struck Hussein's car and exploded, killing him instantly. Flying shards also cut down two women, fifty-two-year-old Aziza Shaibat and fifty-five-year-old Rahma Shahin, as they stood in front of a nearby house waiting for a taxi. A third missile hit Ibrahim's car but didn't explode. Deafened in one ear and grazed by shrapnel, Ibrahim staggered out of the Fiat Uno and collapsed to the ground beside the smoldering remains of Hussein's Mitsubishi.

This "targeted killing," Israel's first assassination of a Palestinian militant during the al-Aqsa intifada, galvanized the Abayat clan. Family members carried Hussein Abayat's battered body to Beit Jala's al-Hussein Hospital, where the biggest crowd of Abayats since the honor-killing trial gathered to gaze at the remains. The explosion had torn out Hussein's brain and ripped away most of his right arm. Twenty thousand people assembled at his funeral the next day; they chanted, "Oh, beloved Saddam, bomb Tel Aviv," as they bore his flag-wrapped corpse on a two-mile journey from the hospital to the Omar Ibn al-Khatab Mosque in the Abayat neighborhood and then to a new cemetery for martyrs of the Abayat clan donated by the Waqf, an Islamic organization based in Jordan. Hours after the funeral ended, Abayat's gunmen opened fire on Israeli soldiers guarding Rachel's Tomb, killing twenty-year-old Shahar Vekret with a bullet in the neck. During the next few days posters showing the beefy militiaman brandishing his trademark .50-caliber machine gun were pasted on walls and shop windows across the city. Hundreds of members of his clan with other surnames adopted the nom de guerre Abayat in his memory. A paperback hagiography called *Spirit of the Intifada: The Epic of Hussein Abayat* appeared in Bethlehem shops. It contained an ode to the fallen gunman written by a local physician that ended with the lament "Oh father, my daughter cries, they have killed the most noble among men."

Almost two years after the killing, in August 2002, I drove down a winding road on the eastern edge of Bethlehem, above a dusty wadi where many members of the Abayat clan live, to visit the Abayat family cemetery. I was joined on the journey by Suleiman Abayat, Ibrahim's brother, who had recited a prayer at Hussein Abayat's funeral and had helped carry his body through

Bethlehem to his grave. Suleiman wore his customary white dishdasha, a symbol of both his conservative Islamic faith and his Bedouin roots. He shifted uneasily in the front passenger seat. During the summer of 2002 the Israelis had occupied Bethlehem for the second time that year; Suleiman had already been stopped twice and interrogated by Israeli troops about his relationship to the notorious Ibrahim Abayat. They had confiscated his ID the second time, and the prospect of encountering another Israeli patrol terrified him.

"*Fi jaish?*" he asked a white-bearded Ta'amra standing outside the local mosque. Is there any army?

The old man shook his head. "*Fish jaish,*" he said, there is no army, and Suleiman sat back, relieved.

The Abayat family cemetery lay on a barren plateau overlooking a rocky valley. There wasn't a tree in sight. The land seemed as harsh and unforgiving as the conflict now being waged upon it. A hot wind blasted in our faces as we walked past roughly hewn slabs of marble and open pits that had been dug for the next Abayat martyrs. Hussein Abayat's polished white marble gravestone, the first to be laid, contained a carving of the al-Aqsa Mosque and the inscription "Martyr of the al-Aqsa Brigades and leader of the [Fatah] military wing of the south area." After circling the grave, we stepped back in the car and drove a few hundred yards down the road to the dead man's house, a two-story stone building with a satellite dish and three water tanks on the roof. His widow still lived there with her seven children, including the oldest boy, Saddam. In front of the house sat the mangled remains of the Mitsubishi Magnum 4X4 in which Hussein Abayat had been killed, towed there by his family as a kind of ghoulish memorial. I could see that the Israeli missile had scored a direct hit. The driver's seat was bent forward, the steering wheel crumpled, the body of the vehicle pocked with shrapnel holes, and pieces of melted metal curled upward like twisted fingers. I saw dark stains on what remained of the upholstery, and I could still detect the faint odor of blood.

THE CHRISTIANS

✺

ONE DAY IN THE MIDST OF THE INTIFADA I received a telephone call from Samir Zedan, a businessman turned journalist who lived in the beleaguered Christian community of Beit Jala. A fluent English speaker who had studied for several years in the United States, Zedan had heard through the grapevine that I was unhappy with my Palestinian translator; he was calling to offer me his services. His unsolicited call took me aback, but in fact he was right, so I arranged to meet him at his home on a Sunday afternoon.

The entrance to Bethlehem on the Hebron Road was closed, so I chose an alternate way into the village: the Route 60 "bypass road" built on expropriated Palestinian land by Israel's Labor government in the 1990s that detours around Bethlehem. The government had undertaken the project to allow Jewish settlers to avoid the potentially hostile Palestinian city on their drive between their settlements in the southern West Bank and Jerusalem, but since the beginning of the intifada the bypass road had become nearly as risky. After passing through a tunnel, I found myself on a long bridge that spanned the ravine between Gilo and Beit Jala; on the rocky slopes to my left stood the houses from behind which Ta'amra militants often fired at the Jewish neighborhood. The Israeli Defense Forces had erected twelve-foot-high concrete pillars to shield motorists from gunfire by Palestinian snipers on the hillside, but the often wide gaps between the pillars were unnerving. I hoped that if the Ta'amra gunmen were watching me, they would catch sight of my "TV" stickers before reaching for the trigger.

Zedan had called me twice that morning to make sure that I was coming down to meet him. I wondered what I was getting into. He had struck me on the phone as a self-promoter, and I began to doubt that he had any authentic journalistic credentials to back up his sales pitch. The Palestinian territories teemed with desperate people who had lost their jobs during the al-Aqsa intifada; I supposed that Zedan was one of them. I considered driving back to Jerusalem. But something kept me going—a dissatisfaction with my current situation, a curiosity about the village of Beit Jala. I could always not return the fellow's phone calls, I decided, if this initial encounter didn't work out.

An Israeli checkpoint just past a second tunnel marked the official exit from Jerusalem. I was now in the West Bank. Beyond the military post I turned left and climbed a steep hill that brought me, as Zedan had directed, to the "back entrance" of Beit Jala, which the Israeli army had sealed with a ten-foot-high mound of earth and stones. The view from the ridge looking west toward Israel was stunning: a Grand Canyon–like vista of pinkish slopes contoured with stone terraces of olive trees receding into the hazy blue hills of Beit Shemesh. The scene contrasted sharply with the ugly pile of rubble that greeted me across the road. Though the Christians of Beit Jala were mostly bystanders to the uprising sweeping the West Bank, they lived inside Palestinian-controlled territory, known as Area A, and so they were subject to the same hardships as everyone else. Palestinians stoically unloaded TV sets, sacks of flour, and other merchandise from trucks and cars and reloaded them into vehicles on the other side of the barricade, while a steady stream of people trooped over footpaths carved into the dirt pile. Zedan waited in a battered red Mazda Protegé four-door with Texas license plates. He had bought the car before graduating from the University of Texas at Austin in 1995, he explained, and had decided to bring his car home with him. Zedan was supposed to have registered the vehicle with the

Israeli government after shipping it to Haifa, but he had never bothered; now he made certain never to drive it in Israeli-controlled areas.

Zedan was an ebullient, stocky man in his late thirties whose dark eyes radiated a lively intelligence. With his thick black mustache, a Dallas Cowboys cap on his balding head, and a large gold crucifix dangling around his neck, he could have passed for a Latino as easily as a Palestinian. He chain-smoked Marlboro Lights and spewed smoke as he drove down Virgin Mary Street, Beit Jala's steep main drag, which skirted the stone-walled warrens of the small Old City and passed the Municipality Building and most of Beit Jala's half dozen churches. Despite the volatile situation, this main artery of Beit Jala life hummed with activity. Families poured out of religious services, greeting friends and relatives, and preparing to head home for the traditional Sunday feast. Beit Jala's women were as fashionably turned out as their counterparts in Vienna or Rome, and the men too had a distinctly Western look—handsomely attired, almost all of them beardless, many adorned as Zedan was with crucifix pendants.

In the plaza in front of the imposing Virgin Mary Orthodox Church, the city's oldest Greek Orthodox house of worship, teenaged boys waited to chat with teenaged girls emerging from the Sunday Divine Liturgy, engaging in the kind of easy public mixing of the sexes that is unheard of in the Muslim parts of the West Bank. The scene was the same just down the road at the even more impressive Saint Nikolas's Church, a silver-domed stone cathedral that had been built in 1925 over the ruins of a much older church, Beit Jala's first house of worship. Below those ruins was the grotto that once served as the home to Beit Jala's patron saint, Nikolas of Lykia, who made a pilgrimage here from Asia Minor in the fourth century.

The details of Beit Jala's founding have been lost over time, and no artifacts have been discovered to shed light on the distant past. What's known is that at the height of the Ottoman Empire in the sixteenth century Beit Jala was a thriving community of several hundred people from five Christian tribes, drawn to the hillside village because of its proximity to the Church of the Nativity in Bethlehem and the Church of Saint Nikolas. Zedan was descended from one of two brothers from the Deir tribe who had come to Beit Jala from Lebanon between six and eight hundred years ago, he told me. The overwhelming majority of the Christians of Beit Jala were Greek Orthodox—affiliated with the eastern wing of the Christian church, now headquartered in Istanbul, which had broken from Rome in the Great Schism of 1054—but the religious character of the town had shifted owing to the European missionaries who began coming to the region in the nineteenth century. The Roman Catholic, or Latin, Church had made inroads here, comprising 20 percent of the Christian population (Lutherans make up the rest). Zedan couldn't resist getting his digs in at the Greek Orthodox's principal rival as we drove past the Annunciation of the Virgin Roman Catholic church on Virgin Mary Street. "We look at [the Catholics] as poor bastards who converted to get money and food from the Franciscans," he told me with a laugh.

The prosperity of Beit Jala has also set it apart from other communities around Bethlehem. In 1907 the Ottoman rulers began forcing Palestinian Christians to serve as porters and servants for their army, and many Beit Jalans boarded boats for the Christian lands of Latin America to escape the draft. Samir Zedan's great-grandfather, one of the first of Beit Jala's *turcos*—as the locals called these Palestinian immigrants to Latin America— had caught a freighter to El Salvador in 1914. He had worked first as a street peddler and then prospered in the import-export business. (Zedan's grandmother separated from her husband and brought her infant son, Zedan's father, back to Beit Jala in 1931.) Nearly everyone in Beit Jala has relatives in El Salvador, Panama, Honduras, Peru, Ecuador, Colombia, and other countries in Central and South America; there's a community of thousands of Palestinians in Santiago, Chile, who trace their roots back to Beit Jala. Many people have spent a few years or decades in that part of the world, made money, and then returned to Beit Jala, imprinting the village with both signs of wealth and a Latino flavor. Zedan and I drove past the El Pollo chicken restaurant, known for its *salsa verde*, past the Amigo clothing boutique, the Cactus shoe store, and the Chile Girls School. The sounds of Spanish wafted through the air from motorists greeting each other from passing cars. *"Qué tal, amigo?" "Cómo estás?" "Adónde te vas?"* I had to remind myself that I was traveling through a West Bank village and not a hamlet in El Salvador.

SAMIR ZEDAN LIVED in a small rented apartment in Beit Jala with his wife, Denisa, the daughter of a local cardiologist and his Czech wife; and their son, Nikolas Andreus, born in Brno in the Czech Republic, baptized in the Church of Saint Nikolas in Beit Jala, and now a kindergarten student at an English-language school staffed mostly with American and Canadian teachers. This international breadth was typical of Beit Jala's residents; where else could you meet a Palestinian, as I did, who had named his twin sons Vladimir and Voltaire? But the case of Samir Zedan seemed so kaleidoscopic that it was often hard to remember his true origins. He traveled interchangeably on a Salvadoran or a Palestinian Authority passport, Denisa had both Czech and Palestinian passports, while Nikolas Andreus had the option of three—Salvadoran, Palestinian, and Czech. Zedan had lived half his life abroad, shuttling among four continents: most recently the family had resided on and off in Montreal between 1998 and 2000 while Zedan worked for the Canadian Pacific import-export firm. In spite of the increasing difficulties Palestinians faced trying to leave the country, Zedan and his family escaped on a regular basis. He and Denisa had recently returned from a wedding in Prague, and Zedan planned to take his family on a whirlwind tour of the United States, including a weekend at Disney World.

As a teenager growing up in the Occupied Territories, Zedan had experienced the humiliation of Israeli occupation and flirted briefly with anti-Israeli activity: often Israeli troops dragooned him and his friends to mop the floors and clean the toilets of occupation headquarters in Bethlehem. "They never realized the damage they were doing, the hatred they were sowing," he told me, as we sat in a popular grilled chicken joint across the street from the Beit Jala Municipality Building on Virgin Mary Street. (The grill had been a favorite of Ariel Sharon's, Zedan told me, in the pre-intifada days when Israelis were regular visitors to Beit Jala.) When Zedan was seventeen years old, he and a friend ignited a gasoline fire near Rachel's Tomb and were pursued to their homes by the Israeli police. "But they could tell we had been smoking marijuana, so they let us go with a warning," he said, laughing.

The experience made a deep impression on him—and helped to keep him out of further trouble. By 1983 the Popular Front for the Liberation of Palestine, one of the most uncompromising anti-Israeli factions, had become a strong force in the village. Many local youths admired George Habash, the Palestinian Christian physician and intellectual living in exile in Damascus who had founded the movement and who had spent part of his youth in Beit Jala. Another hometown hero was Ja'el Arjah, a Popular Front airplane hijacker who was killed by Israeli special forces during the raid on Entebbe Airport in Uganda in 1976; Arjah was the older brother of Jamal Arjah, the owner of Beit Jala's popular Everest Hotel. But while many of his friends were throwing rocks and Molotov cocktails at Israeli soldiers during what became known as the "mini-intifada" in Beit Jala in 1983, Zedan, then nineteen, followed the route of many Beit Jalans and escaped overseas.

He fled first to El Salvador, where his uncles lived. On the dusty streets of Sonsonate, the country's fourth largest town, he connected for the first time with the Latin side of his family—including the spirit of his late grandfather Salomon, whom Zedan describes as a notorious gambler and philanderer. "I met this beautiful woman at my great-uncle Emilio's photo shop," Zedan told me. "I asked her, 'Will you go out with me? Meet me on that

street corner at nine o'clock tonight.' Later Emilio said to me,
'Did you tell this girl to meet you over at that particular street
corner? That's exactly what your grandfather did with his
women. It's fucking genetic.'" After a year in El Salvador, he left
to study business administration at California State University in
Sacramento. Then he traveled the world as an importer-exporter
for a decade, living out of suitcases and flying rattletrap airlines
from Barranquilla to Managua to Tegucigalpa, branching out later
to such Asian capitals as Taipei, Bangkok, and Seoul. The business was a constant hustle—bringing in counterfeit Reeboks
from South Korea to Panama, selling New Zealand powdered
milk in El Salvador—but Zedan was a natural entrepreneur, and
he managed to make a small fortune. Zedan's best-selling items
in Latin America, he told me, were heat-sensitive stickers of
naked women that were glued to coffee mugs and became visible
only when boiling liquids were poured inside. Along the way he
learned fluent Spanish and English and drifted farther from his
Palestinian roots. "I got a D in Arabic studies at university," he
told me. "I've lived all over the world, and I'm not sure where I
belong. Some people say that I'm more Latin than Palestinian,
and that may be true."

Yet like many Beit Jalans who emigrate abroad, Zedan also
found himself drawn back to his homeland. Zedan was in San
Salvador in 1993 when he watched the historic handshake between Yasser Arafat and Yitzhak Rabin on the White House lawn.
"My girlfriend called me at that moment, and she said, 'Are you
crying?' I said, 'Of course.' I told myself, 'My God, this is amaz-
ing. When peace comes to this place, it's going to be the next
Singapore.'" The next year Zedan finished his business administration degree at the University of Texas at Austin, then returned
to Beit Jala and prepared for the new era. Shortly after he came
back, he received a sobering reminder of what might have been.
Zedan ran into his old best friend William Shaer, a classmate at
the Franciscan-run Terra Sancta High School, who had joined the
Popular Front for the Liberation of Palestine in 1983, the same

year Zedan traveled abroad. As Zedan prospered as an entrepreneur, Shaer languished in an Israeli jail for six years for throwing a firebomb at a busload of Jewish settlers. "We hugged each other," Zedan told me. "I was an international businessman, wearing Ralph Lauren clothes, smoking Vantage cigarettes imported from America. I asked, 'What are you doing?' and he said, 'I'm milking cows now.'"

In the mid-1990s Zedan poured his $200,000 life savings into three dunams of undeveloped land just up the street from his parents' home on the edge of Beit Jala's Old City and built a three-story building on a ridge overlooking his property. (One dunam, a unit of land that dates back to Ottoman times, equals one quarter of an acre.) In the new construction, which he called the Maya Building, after the pre-Columbian civilization in Mexico, he installed a printing press, a food import business called Blue Rose Lines (owned by Zedan's oldest brother, Majid), and the Maya Supermarket, which Zedan called "the first American-style grocery in the Bethlehem area." The Maya Building became a regular congregation spot for Zedan's family—he had one brother living in Argentina, but his parents, two other brothers, and a sister and their families all remained in Beit Jala—and one of the new centers of commercial activity in the village. Then Zedan put the finishing touches on his new life: Israel had stripped him of his Palestinian residency while he lived abroad, forcing him to travel on his Salvadoran passport and enter the country repeatedly on an Israeli tourist visa. After a decade-long fight with the Israeli Ministry of the Interior, which continues to control immigration even in autonomous Palestinian areas, he finally won back his Palestinian residency. In 1998 Zedan acquired a Palestinian Authority passport, just in time to watch Beit Jala begin its slide to disaster.

MY RELATIONSHIP WITH Zedan developed after that first meeting in the fall of 2001. Intrigued by both the volatile situation in Beit Jala and the Christian community there, I came back several times throughout the late fall of 2001 and the winter of 2002 for Sunday afternoon feasts with his wife, son, parents, siblings, nieces, and nephews and was overwhelmed by the family's hospitality in the middle of dangerous times. The television set in Zedan's parents' living room was usually airing an Egyptian soap opera, a refreshing change from the fiery intifada propaganda I had grown accustomed to seeing in other Palestinian homes. (The family got its news from al-Jazeera, considered the most neutral of the many Arabic-language stations available in the Palestinian territories.) The family, including Samir's wife, Denisa, and son, Andreus, would crowd around the dinner table for a traditional meal of lamb and rice, washed down with Fanta Orange soda or Coca-Cola, and often, in Zedan's case, bottles of Tayibe beer brewed in Ramallah. Most of the children in the Zedan family attended German or American private schools in Beit Jala partially staffed with foreign teachers who commuted from Jerusalem, and even four-year-old Andreus spoke a few words of English. Zedan joked that the Zedan kids were among the few Palestinian children who were able to stay home from school on the Jewish holiday of Yom Kippur—because with traffic banned from the streets in Jerusalem on the holiday, their teachers couldn't travel to the West Bank. All the members of the youngest generation of Zedans had received Western rather than Arabic names—Nikolas Andreus, Daniel, Anton, Angelina, Matthew, Luis, Maria Theresa.

Sometimes relatives or friends would visit from Latin America, and they would sprinkle their conversations with Spanish expressions and gossip about people in San Antonio del Monte, San Salvador, Santiago, or Mendoza. The family discussed upcoming baptisms, marriages, and the Greek Orthodox Church, which had come under fire because of secret land sales made by the patriarchate in Jerusalem to the Israeli government. The Greek Orthodox bishops of Jerusalem had recently elected a new patriarch, Irineos, who openly criticized Israel's policy toward the Palestinians and promised to undo the seamier transactions of his predecessors. But the Israeli government had refused to recognize him—confirmation, in the Zedan family's eyes, of how politics tainted everything in the region.

Inevitably the conversations would turn to the current crisis: Samir's oldest brother, Majid, might be on the telephone with his Israeli partners in the port of Ashkelon, explaining in his near-fluent English that his Israeli permit to leave the West Bank had been delayed another week. Samir might be talking about a scheme to approach the televangelist Pat Robertson to publicize the Christian plight in the West Bank. The venom toward Israel that I frequently heard in Palestinian Muslim homes was notice-ably absent here; this lack of malice reminded me that Palestine's Christians had not been driven from their land and forced to re-settle in refugee camps (though many Beit Jalans, including Samir's paternal grandmother, had lost valuable property in Jerusalem and elsewhere during the wars of 1948 and 1967). The Zedans felt nearly as removed as I did from the self-pity and dreams of revenge and return that soaked up the energies of so many Palestinian Muslims living in the camps.

Family members heaped scorn on the Ta'amra fighters who had made the lives of Beit Jalans hellish. The Zedans considered themselves Palestinian nationalists—Samir's younger brother, Johnny, remained a committed supporter of the Popular Front for the Liberation of Palestine—but the al-Aqsa intifada had tested their loyalties. The corruption of Arafat's inner circle disgusted them; they were furious at the leadership for instigating the up-rising. They were also angry at Israel for its brutal acts of retalia-tion that, they declared, served only to perpetuate the cycle of violence. But Israel was like an older brother who had lost his way, whereas the Palestinian Authority under Arafat, they be-lieved, could never be trusted. Like many others in Beit Jala, the family was torn between its Palestinian identity and its admira-tion of the secular, Western values embodied by Israel. "I want to be a citizen of Israel, and I want my children to serve in the Is-raeli Defense Forces," one guest at the dinner table told me dur-ing an unguarded moment, reflecting a common sentiment in

Beit Jala. "But any collaborator I see who betrays his people and cooperates with Israel, he should rot in hell."

I noticed other significant differences between the Zedans and the Muslim families I had met. Many Islamic men in the West Bank and Gaza consign their women to strictly defined roles as housewives and mothers and often restrict their interaction with strangers. The Zedan women held jobs, expressed opinions, and were garrulous participants in the discussions at the family dinner table. Zedan's wife, Denisa, was a feisty woman in her twenties who had put aside her aspirations to become a lawyer in order to be a full-time mother; she spoke Czech, Arabic, and English, clashed openly with her husband over the upbringing of Nikolas Andreus, and often mocked Zedan's struggle with his addiction to nicotine and junk food. "Samir has started a new diet," she told me during a family dinner once with a laugh. "I predict it will last three hours."

True, Beit Jala was still very much a man's world in comparison to the United States or Western Europe. Funerals, for example, were a male-only affair, according to Greek Orthodox tradition. Politics was also strictly the provenance of men: no woman had ever served on Beit Jala's city council, and the crisis meetings I attended to deal with issues such as the Ta'amra shootings were exclusively male events. But the Zedan circle seemed filled with women who had independent lives outside the home. Magda, Zedan's sister, managed the family's Zoom Printing Press and frequently bought printing molds and other materials in the ultrareligious Jerusalem neighborhood of Mea She'arim, where as a working woman she was treated with disdain by some of the Hasidic Jews she dealt with. When I met her, she had recently returned from a solo trip to El Salvador—unthinkable in a traditional Muslim household, where women are forbidden to travel anywhere outside the home without a male member of the family.

As time went on, I worked with Zedan not only in Beit Jala and Bethlehem but—when he could arrange the necessary permits to travel outside of his village—elsewhere in the West Bank. Zedan's main assets were an expansive personality, a sense of humor, and an ability to put at ease almost everybody he met, from Islamic Jihad militants to Deheishe camp refugees, from top officials of the Palestinian Authority to Israeli Defense Forces commanders who were responsible for handing out precious entry permits into the country. Zedan was an operator, befriending everybody, betraying as little of his own political views as possible. It was through Zedan that I began to look at the world through Palestinian Christian eyes. For them the game was about survival, about negotiating a path of least resistance between the Israelis on one side, Muslims on the other.

DURING THE PAST twelve months, however, the fragile shelter that Beit Jala's Christians had built for themselves had crumbled, and they found themselves menaced from both sides. Zedan took me down to al-Maskariyeh Street, the front line of the Ta'amra gunmen's campaign against Gilo, where the homes offered an unobstructed view of the Jewish neighborhood rising on the opposite ridge and the bypass road bridge over the gorge below it. House after house stood damaged, scorched, and abandoned, their residents having fled their homes to move in with relatives or stay in hotels in Bethlehem. We drove past the house of Harald Fisher, Beit Jala's first fatality, a German social worker and chiropractor who had moved to Beit Jala in 1981 and married a local Christian woman. On November 15, 2000, during heavy shelling of Beit Jala, Fisher heard screams of "Fire!" coming from his neighbor's house. He grabbed a fire extinguisher and ran down the street—and was struck and killed by an Israeli shell fired by a tank perched on the ridge a half mile away. "I got there three minutes later," Zedan told me. "It took off his legs. It was a direct hit." Israeli fire had killed two more Beit Jalans since then and injured a dozen.

Zedan believed that the gunmen had chosen Beit Jala partly

because it offered an excellent vantage point from which to shoot at the Jewish neighborhood, and partly because of their conviction that the Christians were not sufficiently committed to the al-Aqsa intifada and needed to be dragged into it. Most of the eleven thousand acres of olive fields and rock quarries expropriated by Israel in August 1970 to create the annexed Jerusalem neighborhood of Gilo had belonged to residents of Beit Jala, and yet, in the gunmen's view, the Christians were unwilling to fight for what was rightfully theirs. "The Muslims have always suspected the nationalist credentials of the Christians," Zedan told me. "They view us as Israel's spoiled children. This was an attempt to involve us in the struggle, to make us suffer too."

TENSIONS BETWEEN the Ta'amra and the town were nothing new, I soon discovered. Farah al-Araj, the former mayor of Beit Jala, told me that the crisis represented a stirring up of enmities and jealousies that had first surfaced during the Arab Revolt of 1936, at the time of the British Mandate, when Arab militias began attacking British troops and Jewish settlements across Palestine. Al-Araj, now eighty-eight years old, was a twenty-one-year-old olive farmer in Beit Jala when the British garrison abruptly pulled out of the then entirely Christian village, leaving its citizens defenseless. The Bedouin gangs from the nearby Judean Wilderness—the ancestors of the people shooting at Gilo—had long envied the Christians' prosperity and now saw them as easy pickings. "The Ta'amra started pressing the people of Beit Jala for protection money," he told me when Zedan and I visited him in his palatial, eighty-year-old home on Beit Jala's outskirts. "They came armed with Enfield rifles; they would knock on the door, and people would throw out their cash." In 1936 the Ta'amra kidnapped eighteen Christian leaders of Beit Jala and held them in caves in the Judean Wilderness for a week until their families agreed to pay a ransom. When the former hostages returned to their homes, ragged, filthy, and insect-infested, the residents of Beit Jala took action. Al-Araj and a dozen other young men from the village formed a civil guard, keeping watch from rooftops on the village outskirts. They had only a few aging rifles among them, but when a Ta'amra raiding party showed up one night, the guards opened fire, killing one and injuring another. The Ta'amra fled, al-Araj told me, and never came back—until the start of the second intifada.

After that al-Araj had fought repeatedly to preserve Beit Jala as a tranquil island in the face of both Muslim and Jewish incursions. He was the commander of Beit Jala's military guard when the Arab-Israeli war broke out in 1948. "Moshe Dayan and his gang tried to enter Beit Jala, and we shot three shells at them," he said. "We killed two mules carrying ammunition but no soldiers, and they retreated. In 1967 Dayan came back and he told me, 'You almost killed me.' I told him, 'We were only trying to protect the town.'" Later in 1948 al-Araj watched with consternation as Muslim refugees streamed into Beit Jala from towns that had been seized by the Israelis. Christian families took in some of the refugees temporarily, but al-Araj and other civic leaders sent them the message that they would not be welcome in the community. "We sprayed their heads with DDT because we were afraid of lice, and we told them to move on," he said. The refugees were herded down Virgin Mary Street and set up camp on neighboring hills, which were later to become the camps of Aida, Azza, and Deheishe.

The twenty years that Farah al-Araj spent as mayor of Beit Jala still evoke misty-eyed reminiscences from many Beit Jalans, including Samir Zedan. Although his tenure coincided with the years of Israeli occupation, al-Araj saw to it that his Christians wore the yoke lightly, establishing friendly relations with Israeli politicians, including Ariel Sharon. "We were used to being occupied—by the Turks, the British, Jordanians," he told me. "There was poverty and no work before 1967, but after the Israelis took over, there was a flow of labor to Jerusalem, and things improved for the people of Beit Jala. It was like one country." His view of

Beit Jala as an endangered Christian enclave surrounded by Muslim hordes struck a chord with many of the village's citizens, especially in the 1980s when a tide of Islamic fundamentalism swept across the West Bank and the Gaza Strip. In the early 1980s al-Araj—kept in power for two decades by Israel, which banned all elections in the West Bank and Gaza after 1976—redrew Beit Jala's boundaries to exclude a hillside neighborhood called Doha populated by Muslims who had moved there from the adjacent Deheishe camp. Overnight the mayor cut Doha's citizens off from Beit Jala's sewers, water, and electricity. Fatah and other nationalist factions fiercely attacked al-Araj as a Muslim-hater, but the mayor made no apologies. "I will not annex Muslims to my town," he declared.

But in his later years as mayor, al-Araj's hopes of keeping Beit Jala a purely Christian town were dashed. In the 1970s the Islamic Waqf, a religious council headquartered in Amman, Jordan, bought land in Beit Jala's Old City and constructed a mosque on the site. During the 1980s hundreds of Christian families immigrated to Latin America, Canada, and the United States, driven out by unrest and deteriorating economic conditions. Many sold their homes to Muslims, who today make up 30 percent of Beit Jala's population.

The coming of the Palestinian Authority to power in 1995 was, for many Christians, the turning point toward catastrophe. In 1996 doctors diagnosed Farah al-Araj with throat cancer and removed his larynx; two years later his family and colleagues nudged him into retirement, and the Palestinian Authority named Raji Zaidan, a Christian civil engineer—and cousin of Samir Zedan—as his replacement. Tensions rose to a fever pitch. Muslim members of Fatah from outside of Beit Jala began buying property at cheap prices and building houses in "green zones," public land set aside by the Beit Jala municipality for parks and other recreation areas. Although the Christian-dominated city council protested, the mayor refused to block the illegal land deals. On June 1, 1999, all nine Christian members of the twelve-member council, not including Mayor Zaidan, resigned in protest. Zaidan, they said in an open letter, was "the puppet of the Palestinian Authority." Days later a group of Beit Jala citizens, including some Zedans, wrote a letter to the United States Embassy in which they accused the Palestinian Authority of plotting to drive out the Christian population and replace them with Muslims. "In ten years," the letter declared, "we fear that there will be only a few Christians left in Beit Jala."

AFTER OUR VISIT to al-Araj, Zedan and I descended Virgin Mary Street in his aging Mazda Protegé on our way back to his parents' house for lunch. It was approaching afternoon prayer time, and the wail of the muezzin from Beit Jala's mosque carried through the winding streets, a jarring reminder of the growing Muslim influence in this village. Zedan grimaced at the sound. "The mosque calls have gotten louder since the beginning of the intifada," Zedan told me. "They turn up the speakers and read long verses of the Quran. It's like they're trying to draw attention." During unguarded moments Zedan manifested his discomfort with certain aspects of Muslim culture. He fretted about the increasing visibility of Islamic fundamentalists on the streets of Bethlehem. "These imams are complaining, 'Our Muslim girls are becoming like Christian girls,'" he told me. "What's that stuff supposed to mean, 'like Christian girls'?" Once during the summer I caught him staring with undisguised perplexity at two Muslim teenaged girls who were shopping at the Maya Supermarket. "How do they wear these things in this heat?" he muttered, pointing to the headscarves. "Try wrapping that around your head and see how you feel."

At certain moments, Zedan demonstrated a tribalism, I thought, that seemed out of place for a man of such education and experience in living in heterogeneous Western societies. Wasn't he guilty, I asked him, of the same small-mindedness that had condemned Israelis and Palestinians to a seemingly ceaseless cycle of violence, an unwillingness to accept the humanity of the other side? Zedan insisted I had pegged him wrong. He told me that he would never object to his son marrying a Roman Catholic or a Lutheran—there were plenty of such interfaith marriages in Beit Jala, he said—and could even accept his marriage to a Jew, though he knew that the social problems that such a relationship could cause were immense. But he drew a "red line" at the idea of his son marrying a Muslim. "I forbid it," he told me. The way he saw it, the Christians of Beit Jala were waging a desperate struggle to defend a dying way of life, and he wouldn't allow anything to happen that would speed them to extinction. "We are like the Jews in *Fiddler on the Roof;* we're living inside a ghetto," he told me.

THE TENSIONS IN Beit Jala rose during the fall of 2000. The shooting at Gilo was erupting almost every night, further poisoning relations between Christians and Muslims. A sizeable number of Christian militants from the Popular Front for the Liberation of Palestine still lived in Beit Jala, but their leader, a close friend of Zedan's named Khader Abu Abbara, had made a decision early in the intifada not to join the Abayats at the front lines. That decision too had fomented interreligious enmity. In November vandals entered the Greek Orthodox Cemetery on Virgin Mary Street and broke the crosses off dozens of marble tombs, including several belonging to the Zedan family. Most Beit Jalans were convinced that the Abayat militia was responsible, while others raised the possibility that Israeli intelligence had paid a Christian collaborator to drive a deeper wedge between the Christians and the Muslims. That was hardly necessary; relations were already strained to the breaking point.

One by one, symbols of Christian life in Beit Jala were coming under threat. The Arab Orthodox Club, once Samir Zedan's favorite hangout, a Christians-only social center where Beit Jalans had gone since 1907 to drink alcohol, talk politics, and play bingo and cards, was on the verge of shutting down for good. Before the intifada Fatah activists had launched a campaign to force the exclusive club to open its doors to Muslims, outraging the village's Christians, including Zedan. "It's not enough that they want to live in Beit Jala, now they want to control our social life," one Christian told me. Now the shooting on Gilo from nearby was making the Muslims' campaign moot. The club had taken Israeli rounds in the fall of 2000, and nobody wanted to go near a place that sat on the edge of the combat zone.

Inside the gloomy and deserted Arab Orthodox Club, Zedan introduced me to Khader Abu Abbara, the forty-five-year-old firebrand whose decision not to join the Abayats in the shooting at Gilo had placed even more stress on the fragile Christian-Muslim relationship. An intense man with a shaved head, brush mustache, and ever-present beige workman's cap, Abu Abbara was one of Beit Jala's most outspoken and controversial figures. For many years Abu Abbara had been a symbol of violent resistance among Palestinian Christians to Israeli occupation—the counterpoint to the town's former mayor, Farah al-Araj. Many of the town's brightest young men had followed him to the front lines in the 1980s, hurling Molotov cocktails and stones against Israeli troops and settlers; a half dozen had wound up languishing alongside Abu Abbara in Israeli prisons. His resolve to keep the Popular Front out of the second intifada had represented a stunning turnaround, a reflection of the fissures in Palestinian society that had widened since the start of the uprising.

The son of a housepainter, Abu Abbara had become attracted to the radical politics of George Habash's Popular Front for the Liberation of Palestine while at Bethlehem University in the late seventies and founded a small Popular Front cell in Beit Jala after his graduation. The group began as a social reform movement—he and his gang of a dozen friends slashed the tires of cars parked outside a Beit Jala gambling den and conducted burnings of hashish in public—but it graduated quickly to anti-Israeli protests. Abu Abbara accused Mayor al-Araj of collaborating with Israel and hurled firebombs at the Municipality Building on sev-

eral occasions. In 1983 Abu Abbara and five members of his Beit
Jala cell attacked a bus filled with Jews heading for a nearby settlement; Israeli occupation forces tracked down and arrested all
of them, and all were sentenced to six years in prison. (Among
those sentenced was Samir Zedan's friend and Terra Sancta classmate William Shaer, with whom Zedan had the poignant reunion
upon his return from the United States.) After his release from a
jail in Israeli-occupied Ramallah in 1989, Abu Abbara returned to
the streets, organizing more demonstrations during the first intifada.

Abu Abbara remained a hard-liner even after Arafat signed
the Oslo Accords in 1993. The Popular Front viewed the Accords
as an unacceptable compromise: the group maintained that the
Palestinians should keep up the struggle until Israel removed all
its settlements from the West Bank and Gaza and withdrew to its
pre-1967 borders. In 1995 a fellow Popular Front militant impli-
cated him in the murders of two Israeli hikers in the Wadi Qilt
valley near Jericho. Abu Abbara denied any involvement in the
killings, but he wound up high on Israel's most-wanted list: he
was among several alleged terrorists that Israeli Prime Minister
Binyamin Netanyahu demanded Arafat arrest when the two leaders met with President Bill Clinton at Wye River, Maryland, in
October 1998 to discuss the implementation of the Oslo Accords. While living in fear of Israeli assassination, he also experienced harassment at the hands of Arafat's security apparatus.
Throughout the 1990s Palestinian intelligence agents detained
Abu Abbara several times for his "rejectionist and hard-line" opposition to Arafat and Rabin's peace agreement. Locked up in
Bethlehem's jails, he says, he received a disturbing firsthand look
at the excesses of the Palestinian Authority—routine demands
for bribes to free prisoners, brutal interrogations—and it intensified his disillusionment with the new government. "The oppression by your relatives," he told me, "is far more painful and bitter
than the oppression by your enemies."

By the time bloody clashes erupted at the al-Aqsa Mosque and

Israeli military checkpoints in September 2000, Abu Abbara—
then working as a counselor in a Bethlehem orphanage—considered himself as much an enemy of the Palestinian Authority as of
the Israeli government. The start of the uprising elated him: in his
view, the outpouring of grassroots anger was an expression of
contempt for both the corruption of Arafat's circle and the brutal-
ity of Israeli occupation. "You can't strike out against your father,
so you bang your hand against the door instead," he explained.
Abu Abbara believed that the unrest spreading across the West
Bank and Gaza offered a chance to wipe the slate clean—both to
topple the Palestinian Authority and to force the Israelis to declare
a unilateral withdrawal from the territories. "We were excited
about the uprising, because we saw it as the end of the Oslo
Accords," he told me. But when Hussein Abayat and his gunmen
began shooting at Gilo from Beit Jala, Abu Abbara surprised many
by siding with his Christian community, and his former nemesis
Farah al-Araj, against the Muslim militiamen. He believed that by
militarizing the intifada, the Palestinian Authority was dragging
the Christians into an unwinnable armed conflict with Israel and
creating discord at a time when all of Palestinian society should be
working together to end the occupation. Abu Abbara had begged
his counterparts in Fatah to curb the shooting, to no avail. He
himself nearly became one of the victims of the Beit Jala–Gilo violence. In March 2001, a few months before our meeting, Israeli
helicopters fired two missiles at the Beit Jala home in which Abu
Abbara was temporarily residing, injuring the owner, William
Shaer, and narrowly missing the Popular Front leader. It wasn't
clear whether the Israelis had targeted Abu Abbara for assassination, as he believes, or whether he had been caught in the crossfire
of the battle between Israeli troops and the Abayat gunmen.

THE FIRST ANNIVERSARY of the al-Aqsa intifada found
Samir Zedan in a gloomy mood. Despite his expanding career opportunities, not all was well with the Zedan clan. The Palestinian

militants' incursions and Israeli reprisals were taking a toll on the health of his parents, both of whom were in their seventies. Linda Zedan, the family matriarch, was suffering from angina pains caused, her family believed, by the stresses of the intifada; the Zedans had decided to send her to a hospital in Amman for a catheterization for her ailing heart, but the family feared that the Israelis would close the Allenby Bridge to Palestinians and she'd be trapped in Jordan. The family's businesses were in a precarious state. Israel's tightening closure of the territories had put tens of thousands of people out of work. Maya Supermarket had barely any customers anymore. The food import business, Blue Rose Lines, was in deep trouble. Containers languished at Israeli ports because Zedan's brother Majid couldn't collect them; banks had cut off lines of credit; clients scaled back their orders. Majid, to whom Samir had given the business in 1997, was ten thousand dollars in debt, on the verge of bankruptcy, and Zedan spent some of the cash he was earning to keep Majid afloat.

Zedan despaired of any solution's being found to his village's predicament or to the wider Israeli-Palestinian conflict, as long as Sharon and Yasser Arafat remained in power. He feared that extremists were drowning out all other voices in both societies. "I take Route 60 to Jerusalem, I see these gun-carrying Jewish settlers in front of me," he told me. "Then I go to Bethlehem, and I see these bearded guys in dishdasha. I'm telling you, I'm under siege. It makes me just want to leave." He was beginning to think he had made the wrong choice by coming back to Beit Jala. At other times Zedan acknowledged that the only thing keeping him here was the opportunity to make a buck. "I'm not living in this place because I love this shitty country," he told me. *"Yo soy empresario."* Zedan was working on a freelance or contract basis for a half dozen Western news organizations now, including the *Los Angeles Times, Houston Chronicle, Christian Science Monitor,* the Spanish-language TV network Antenna 3, and *Newsweek.* He had begun spending the money he was making as a translator and fixer to turn the top floor of the Maya Building into a spacious new apartment for himself and his wife and son. Wags in the press corps had nicknamed the apartment-in-progress "Chez Intifada."

On a wintry day in late 2001, Zedan and I stopped in at the Maya Supermarket. His younger brother, Johnny, who ran the grocery, sat behind the cash register, smoking and playing solitaire. He looked depressed. "This place is dying, man," Zedan said. Christian iconography covered the walls inside the grocery: a Saint Nikolas calendar, pictures of the infant Jesus and of Saint George battling the dragon. But on the shop windows outside, I noticed, the Zedans had prominently displayed three martyr posters of Hussein Abayat, the Ta'amra gunman assassinated by Israel months earlier. Zedan explained that the posters had worked as a kind of insurance against the militants' predations. "We have to make these people think that we're on their side," he said. But the Zedans weren't sure how much longer such methods would remain effective. A neighbor of the Zedans, a prominent Christian doctor who happened to be shopping in the market when we walked in, had gotten a taste of the deepening hostility toward Beit Jala's Christians, he told us, when he had had a car accident with an Abayat gunman a few months earlier. Said the doctor: "The guy just glared at me and swore, 'I am going to make Beit Jala burn.'"

THE WARLORD

 ❧

IT WAS SAID THAT ATEF ABAYAT WAS CRAZY ABOUT his birds. He kept about five hundred of them in wire cages stacked on the roof of his house in the Wadi Shaheen neighborhood of Bethlehem, and he liked nothing better than to spend hours there in solitude, feeding them, cleaning their cages, stroking their clipped wings, even singing to them. The collection included doves, guinea fowl, finches, canaries, macaws, and most of all love birds of every description—Abyssinian, Madagascaran, black-cheeked, peach-faced, white-faced creaminos. Even in the summer and fall of 2001, when the al-Aqsa Martyrs Brigades commander was on the run from the Israelis and fearing for his life, he would still manage to sneak home for a few hours to take his four-year-old daughter, Ala, to the roof and linger with her in his aviary.

Atef Abayat never announced in advance his visits home. Once every two weeks or so he arrived by taxi from a hideout in Beit Sahour or Bethlehem, stepped out at the top of the hill above Wadi Shaheen, and then hiked down a few hundred yards through the terraced olive groves to the huge house with the six red-trimmed balconies he had constructed in stages for his family during the mid and late 1990s. The house, which dominated the hardscrabble landscape, was built on a hillside just above the more modest home where he, his siblings, and his cousins, including Ibrahim Abayat, had grown up. Silently Atef climbed the stairs to his third-floor apartment, always taking his wife and three young children by surprise. Ala was the oldest; then came his daughter, Asal, two years old, and then his infant son, Hussein, born in March 2001 during the Eid al-Adha Islamic feast, commemorating the end of the *haj,* or pilgrimage to Mecca. Atef had been at the hospital for Hussein's birth, but since then he had seen his son only a few times, and he savored each visit as if he might never see the boy again.

The sojourns with his wife and children were fleeting, but they seemed to invigorate the al-Aqsa Martyrs Brigades commander. Atef would sit with them in an ornately furnished parlor stuffed with velvet-covered Victorian-style sofas and bric-a-brac—carved olive-wood sparrows, white marble horses, framed gold-leaf Quranic quotations. He carried his son around the house, played with his two-year-old daughter on the floor of her room, then took Ala on the roof to inspect the bird collection, which Atef had begun accumulating when he was fifteen years old. They stayed up there for an hour sometimes, replacing the soiled newspapers, washing and disinfecting the cages, trimming flight feathers, and placing vegetables, pasta, beans, and fruit in the little plastic food trays. (By the end of the summer of 2001, Atef realized that many of his birds were dying during his lengthy absences. He instructed his younger brother Mazzin to sell as many of the creatures as he could. He was upset about it, but he realized it was better that way.) At the end of his visit he would slip quietly downstairs and greet his mother and father and his brother Nidal's wife—his own wife's older sister—and children. Then he walked downhill a few paces to surprise his aunt Fatima, his cousins Khaled, Issa, and Suleiman, and their large families. The children crowded around Atef excitedly, yelling, *"Abu Hussein! Abu Hussein!"*—father of Hussein, Atef's firstborn son. Atef quieted them down, not wanting to draw attention to his presence in the compound.

Atef's family didn't know much about what he did. Except for Mazzin Abayat, a former medical student in Kiev who had spent time in a Palestinian Authority jail in 2000 for being a member of

Hamas, Atef told them almost nothing, preferring to keep his life compartmentalized. He knew that the Israelis often considered the family members of militants to be as guilty as the militants themselves and would subject them to harsh interrogations if they were arrested. But they all knew that he was playing a highly dangerous game. Once he had brought home two freshly killed deer and prepared a venison feast for his family, explaining that he had been out "hunting Israeli soldiers" and had stumbled upon the game instead. The family knew about Israel's attempts to kill him, knew that shrapnel from an Israeli tank shell fired from Gilo had hit him in the groin and lightly wounded him. And they knew that Yasser Arafat himself had phoned Atef, begging him to drop out of sight before the Israelis located him. "Hide, Atef!" the president had urged him. During every visit his parents, sisters, and other members of the family made him promise to be careful and pressed him to go into hiding. He nodded, smiled, and said, "Yes, Father, yes, Mother." Then, after a stay that never lasted longer than four hours, he climbed back through the olive terraces and disappeared over the crest of the hill, his departure often accompanied by the drone of an Israeli military helicopter circling over Bethlehem.

IT HAD ALL BEGUN a decade earlier with a bakery. When the Israelis released Atef Abayat from Dahariyeh prison in 1992, after he had served a two-and-a-half-year sentence for throwing stones at Israeli soldiers, he was twenty years old, jobless, and semiliterate. Atef's employment prospects didn't appear promising. But he had done an apprenticeship as a baker's assistant in Bethlehem's Madbasseh neighborhood when he was twelve years old, so, based on that modest experience, he invited his older brother Nidal and their first cousin Ibrahim—also recently released from Israeli jails—to go into partnership with him. The threesome rented a small bakery in a section of the Old City known as Ras Iftes, or "head of the corpse"—so named because in biblical times it lay in the dangerous no-man's-land outside of the village gate, where bandits and murderers lurked. Atef, Nidal, and Ibrahim took turns manning the ovens and driving the delivery truck. The business thrived. In 1995 Atef and Nidal began building their own house in Wadi Shaheen, and the following year they installed a bakery with two electric ovens on the ground floor. Soon they were baking pita bread for the Abayat neighborhood; they steadily expanded their business to Bethlehem and surrounding villages.

Atef Abayat quickly diversified into the traditional pursuits of his clan. His distant cousin and longtime acquaintance Hussein Abayat introduced him to his Bedouin contacts in Israel, Mazzin told me, and Atef began smuggling pistols, English hunting rifles, and ammunition to Bethlehem. When the Palestinian Authority took power in Bethlehem in 1995, the opportunities multiplied. Atef's cherubic good looks served him well: he often filled the trunk of a Mercedes taxi in Israel with rifles and bullets, covered them with a blanket, put on a pair of black-frame glasses to enhance the harmlessness of his appearance, and sat innocently in the backseat thumbing through a newspaper as the car sped through Israeli and Palestinian checkpoints. In 1997 Atef handed the bakery over to Nidal and concentrated on his much more lucrative gun trade, protected, like Hussein Abayat, by the Palestinian intelligence division. (Like Hussein Abayat and Ibrahim Abayat, Atef was on the mukhabarat payroll and did occasional strong-arm work for the security force.) Suleiman Abayat, Ibrahim Abayat's older brother and Atef's first cousin, told me that Atef was the first gun dealer to introduce the M-16 assault rifle to Bethlehem. The price for a new weapon ranged between two thousand and ten thousand dollars, depending on availability, and Atef invested his profits in a third and fourth story for his house and a new Mitsubishi Magnum jeep, which one of his kinsmen had stolen from an Israeli. The only demand on Atef made by the mukhabarat, Suleiman Abayat told me, was that he refrain from selling weapons to the Palestinian Authority's rivals, Hamas and Islamic Jihad. "But Atef didn't listen to them," Suleiman told me. "He sold to anyone who could pay."

Snapshots taken of Atef Abayat during that period show a confident young man with full lips twisted into a slight smirk, an aquiline nose, and a shock of black hair that fell down the center of his forehead. There is a James Dean, rebel-without-a-cause quality about him. The charm and self-assurance that would draw into his orbit so many people, from teenaged foot soldiers to top Palestinian officials, come through in a variety of photographs: Atef on horseback in the fields of Wadi Shaheen; sunning himself on vacation at the Dead Sea; at his 1996 engagement to a young Ta'amra woman whose older sister had married his brother Nidal; cutting bread in his bakery; and posing in Jericho with a Kalashnikov in 1994, just after the turnover of the city to the Palestinian Authority. His friends told me that Atef's air of self-confidence and authority was noticeable from an early age. "Atef learned to bear responsibility since he was little," said Issa Mazook, a Ta'amra and an activist in Islamic Jihad in Bethlehem who knew the militia leader since childhood. "Abu Atef [his father] suffered a psychological disorder; he couldn't work, so Atef had to shoulder the burdens."

He was also an excellent marksman. Atef had learned to shoot as a teenager, but he perfected his skills during this time on hunting expeditions in the hills and wadis around Bethlehem. Before dawn on Friday, the Muslim holy day, Atef and a few close friends, most of them Abayats, would pile inside Atef's jeep with their Kalashnikovs and M-16s. Switchbacking over dirt tracks with their guns hanging out the windows, they descended into the uninhabited bush of Wadi Nar on the road to Ramallah or of Wadi Ahmad just north of Beit Jala, even crossing the border to hunt on the east side of the Jordan River. The arid land abounded with hyenas, wolves, foxes, ibexes, gazelles, hares, eagles, porcupines, even the rare leopard. Although unlicensed hunting is technically illegal in the region, the Jordanian and Palestinian police never bothered them. But the Israeli border police often chased them when they strayed into Israeli-controlled areas. Once, Mazzin told me, he discharged a volley of AK-47 shots into the air to divert a squad of Israeli patrolmen who were in pursuit of Atef Abayat's vehicle. Atef's favorite prey was the gazelle. He could hit one from a moving jeep from as far as three hundred yards away, Mazzin claimed, and he often returned to the compound in Wadi Shaheen with a buck tied to the roof. He then prepared feasts for his family as well as for powerful figures in the Palestinian Authority, including the mukhabarat chief Ismail Faraj, who became a regular guest in Atef's home.

After Ariel Sharon's visit to the Temple Mount on September 28, 2000, Atef Abayat's life underwent a dramatic change. When the current intifada began, Atef and his fellow hunters became the core of the clan-based militia that gathered around Hussein Abayat to shoot at Israeli prey. As in the case of Hussein Abayat, it is hard to know what motivated Atef Abayat to turn his guns against the Israelis; the answer is probably a mixture of genuine anger and opportunism. Atef worked side by side with Hussein, sharing his .50-caliber machine gun as they fired on Gilo and the Crow's Nest. Then, in November 2000, Hussein's killing in the Hellfire missile attack thrust Atef Abayat into the leadership position. "Atef was the only possible choice," said Chris Bandak, who by then had become Ibrahim Abayat's driver and a full-time member of the gang. Atef took command of a cell of between fifteen and twenty fighters; the group within months grew to more than a hundred. Many of the new guerrillas joined out of anger at the assassination of Hussein Abayat; the force of Atef Abayat's personality drew in others. "People came up to Atef on the streets of Bethlehem and said, 'I want to join,'" says Chris Bandak. "And Atef would say, 'Okay, but you'd better be ready.'"

Atef's ascension came at a critical moment in the narrative of the al-Aqsa intifada. The checkpoint clashes were losing momentum; the last shaheed at Rachel's Tomb in Bethlehem, for instance, was Moataz Taylach. As the rock and firebomb throwing died out, an emerging group of young gunmen known as the

Tanzim (organization) was beginning a campaign of shootings and roadside bombings across the Occupied Territories. The Tanzim were largely the creation of Marwan Barghouti, a charismatic physician and the secretary general of the Fatah Party, based in the West Bank capital, Ramallah. (The Israeli army would capture Barghouti in May 2002; he would be indicted for the murder of twenty-six Israelis.) West Bank intelligence chief Tawfik Tarawi was also allegedly a major backer of the guerrillas, and Yasser Arafat gave the green light to their campaign.

Arafat, many observers believe, had gambled that a guerrilla war against Israeli soldiers and settlers led by his Fatah cadres would keep the pressure on the Israeli government, raise his popularity on the Palestinian street, and steal the thunder of the resurgent Islamic fundamentalist movements Hamas and Islamic Jihad. Arafat's ultimate aim, many experts believe, was to draw an international military force into the Middle East—to "Kosovo-ize" the conflict. According to both Israeli and Palestinian sources, Arafat, Barghouti, and Tarawi underwrote, with weapons, money, and logistical support, a loose network of Tanzim across the West Bank and Gaza. The relationship between Arafat and Barghouti was never smooth: Arafat regarded the charismatic younger man as a rival for power, while Barghouti viewed Arafat as the leader of a system that reeked of favoritism and corruption. As time went on, Arafat found himself increasingly squeezed between pressure from the United States to curb the gunmen and pressure from Barghouti to continue a guerrilla campaign against soldiers and settlers in the Occupied Territories.

The Tanzim groups adopted the name the al-Aqsa Martyrs Brigades at the beginning of 2001. Many commanders had a long history of Fatah activism. The chief of the al-Aqsa Martyrs Brigades in Balata refugee camp near Nablus, for example, Nasser Awais, had been imprisoned in an Israeli jail for seven years for his Fatah activities, then sent into exile in Jordan after his release, a fate reserved only for the most influential Fatah leaders. (Upon his return to the West Bank he became a high-ranking officer in the National Security Force but quit to join the Tanzim.) Atef Abayat's résumé was different. He had been a low-level Fatah member during the first intifada and had had little to do with Fatah since his release from prison. Many regarded him as apolitical, concerned mostly with growing his weapons business, until the opening salvos of the intifada. But Atef Abayat, like his predecessor Hussein Abayat, had one important qualification for leadership: he had the power of his clan behind him.

ON A HOT SUMMER afternoon in 2002 Chris Bandak and I sat in a falafel shop on a cobblestone alley just off Manger Square in Bethlehem, drinking Coca-Cola and eating *foul*—fava beans and olive oil—and talking about the short, violent career of the militia chief he had lived side by side with for a year. At this point Bandak, a sturdily built twenty-three-year-old with a gentle demeanor, was one of the last members of the original Abayat gang who had not been arrested or killed. But he remained high on the Israeli wanted list, fingered by fellow Tanzim in prison for the murder of two Israeli settlers; Bandak told me only that he "might have hit them" when he sniped from the village of Irtas upon vehicles traveling down the Route 60 bypass road. During a recent incursion into Bethlehem the Israelis had blown up his family's house because, Bandak admitted, he had allowed an explosives engineer from Deheishe camp to assemble bombs in his bedroom. Talking about his activities in the Abayat gang with a tinge of remorse, Bandak made that episode in his life sound like an innocent lark that had gone badly awry.

Bandak had followed an unusual path to militancy. Born to middle-class Christian parents in Bethlehem's Old City in 1979, he was raised by an aunt and uncle following the death of his father in a mental institution. After graduating from the elite Talitha Kumi Academy in Beit Jala, he found a job in 1998 dealing cards at the newly opened Oasis Casino outside Jericho, which was considered one of the major success stories of the Palestinian economy. But the casino closed down at the start of the intifada, and Ibrahim Abayat persuaded his boyhood friend Bandak, who was idle and angry, to pick up a rifle. In November 2000 Atef put Bandak in charge of procuring weapons and ammunition for the nascent group of Tanzim, financing the deals with the profits Atef had accumulated as a gun dealer. "Atef had connections all over the West Bank and Be'er Sheva," Bandak said. Bandak smuggled armaments into Bethlehem through an ever-tightening Israeli cordon on five occasions, he said. On his first mission, he brought back ten thousand bullets from Hebron hidden in the trunk of a taxi beneath boxes of live chicks. On another occasion he secreted six M-16 rifles purchased from a Bedouin dealer in Be'er Sheva inside crates of plums. Atef had a constant need to replenish the supply, not only because the al-Aqsa Martyrs Brigades were growing, but also because members of the Palestinian Authority security forces were covertly joining Atef's group to fire on Gilo. At the end of every month these men, who came primarily from Arafat's elite bodyguard division known as Force 17 and from the National Security Force, were supposed to account for every round their commanders had issued them; Atef would have to replace their bullets. But transporting weapons and ammunition became an increasingly risky enterprise for the Tanzim: in early 2001, Israeli police arrested one of Atef's main suppliers in Be'er Sheva. Then the Israelis stopped Bandak at a checkpoint while he attempted to smuggle another load of bullets into Bethlehem. Bandak abandoned the ammunition along with his Palestinian identification card at the checkpoint and fled back to Bethlehem. Without this vital personal document, he risked arrest whenever he left Palestinian-controlled territory, so his weapons smuggling days were effectively over.

The loss of Bandak's services was a blow, but Atef Abayat soon received important help from other sources. His long-standing friendship with Ismail Faraj, the head of Palestinian intelligence in Bethlehem, led to an equally productive arrangement with Faraj's successor, Abdullah Daoud, a veteran Fatah activist originally from Nablus's highly politicized Balata refugee camp. "Atef would show up at the door of the intelligence head-quarters, carrying his M-16, and he would be greeted like a prince," Chris Bandak told me. The mukhabarat funneled weapons and ammunition to Atef and his fighters and also gave them information about Israeli troop positions on the edges of Bethlehem. Atef also enjoyed a close relationship with Abu Baker Thabet, the commander of the National Security Force, the Pales-tinian Authority's equivalent of an army. Bandak told me that Thabet approved the delivery of ammunition to Atef Abayat to shoot at Gilo and at the Crow's Nest in Beit Sahour. "Atef had a way with all the big people," Bandak told me.

Local leaders of the Fatah political party in Bethlehem also contributed to the maintenance of Atef Abayat's fighters. Begin-ning in December 2000, Fatah officials doled out monthly salaries to Atef's forces, eventually putting 150 fighters on the payroll. Bandak told me that he used to visit the Fatah office on Manger Street in central Bethlehem at the beginning of each month and receive an envelope stuffed with 450 shekels, or about $110, from "Dr. Nasser," a Fatah member who worked for the National Security Force's medical division. Atef, having de-cided who merited these payments, would hand a list of names to the local Fatah secretary general, Kamel Hmeid, who, Bandak says, became the Tanzim paymaster as well as their biggest pro-tector. The money went to support families and handle the fight-ers' operational expenses—including cellular phones, MIRS radio sets, gasoline, and auto repairs.

CURIOUS TO LEARN more about the links between Fatah's political wing and the al-Aqsa Martyrs Brigades, I visited Kamel Hmeid at his Fatah office off Manger Square in the summer of 2002. (By far the most popular political party in the Palestinian territories, Fatah consists of a central committee headquartered in Ramallah, as well as local committees in every municipality in the West Bank and Gaza. Yasser Arafat continues to serve as the chairman of Fatah, in addition to being the leader of the Palestinian Authority.) Hmeid, forty years old, is a slight man with hunched shoulders, a shock of prematurely white hair, a small black mustache, and an enigmatic smile. A member of the Ta'amra and a graduate of Bethlehem University, Hmeid spent a decade in Israeli prisons and then rose rapidly through the Fatah hierarchy. Several Tanzim told me that Hmeid became a key ally of Atef Abayat early in the uprising, though he always denied this and kept his distance from the gunmen in public. Besides bankrolling Atef and his men, I was told, he also played a critical role in neutralizing enemies of the militants. (Hmeid also serves as a colonel in the Palestinian intelligence division, the principal backer of the intifada among the security forces.) One reliable Palestinian Authority source told me that Atef Abayat and Kamel Hmeid conspired against a high-ranking Bethlehem police official. The official had been widely suspected of cheating on his wife. One night in early 2001, acting on a tip from Hmeid, Atef and another gunman burst into the man's house and caught him in flagrante with his mistress. From that point on, I was told, the police force never attempted to interfere with the activities of Atef and his Tanzim. Hmeid denied the story and swore that he never encouraged the fighters. "There's not a single gunman who can say that Kamel Hmeid gave an order to fire," he told me.

With charm and perhaps a measure of intimidation Atef Abayat established close ties to many other civic leaders. Judge Fatih Abu Srour of the Bethlehem court, who had sentenced Atef Abayat's brother Nidal Abayat and his first cousin Ibrahim Abayat to fifteen years in prison in February 2000 for the honor killing, developed an easygoing relationship with the guerrilla leader, Abu Srour told me. Atef strolled unannounced into the judge's chambers on several occasions, chatting up the judge's bodyguards about weaponry and then sharing Arabic coffee with Abu Srour as they discussed local politics and the intifada. When Abu Srour sentenced Mohammed Deifallah and two other collaborators to death by firing squad following a January 2001 show trial for helping Israel to kill Hussein Abayat, Atef paid him a courtesy call, thanking him for bringing his cousin's killers to justice. "Atef was honest, polite, full of charisma. You felt obliged to respect him," Abu Srour said.

Salah Tamari, the former Fatah commander from the Ta'amra tribe who became a respected member of the Palestinian Legislative Council, also built a close relationship with Atef Abayat. Tamari, whose real name is As'ad Suleiman Hassan, was born in the Old City in 1942, fled into exile in Egypt in 1963, joined Fatah at Cairo University, and became a member of the Fatah inner circle while still in his twenties. As Fatah's military commander in southern Lebanon, Tamari was captured by Israel during the battle of Sidon in 1982, jailed at the notorious Ansar prison, and released in 1983 in a prisoner exchange. He married Dina Abd al-Hamid, the first wife of Jordan's King Hussein, cultivated political contacts in the United States and Europe, and returned home in triumph in 1995. Tamari was now approaching sixty, but he still exuded raw physical power and charisma. As the paterfamilias to a generation of young fighters, Tamari regarded Atef as a wayward son who, like himself, had grown up under Israeli occupation and been drawn into violence because of a sense of hopelessness. "He was a young person deprived of a dream," the graying, imposing-looking councilman told me. "I identified with him, because I had become a *fedayee*—a freedom fighter—too."

Tamari often expressed his opposition to the shooting at Gilo. But he says he felt sympathy for Atef and tried to steer him away gently from the al-Aqsa Martyrs Brigades, encouraging him to find a job in the Palestinian security forces. "He would say, 'Yes, Uncle, all right, Uncle,' and then he would go out the door and fall under the same bad influences. . . . He and his friends needed compassion. They needed to have faith in the future," Tamari told me. "I liked him. I saw in him a great ability to evolve, to become a new breed of leader. The only difference between us is that I went to school and he was barely literate." Tamari lent Atef

Abayat and his fellow fighters more than just a sympathetic ear. "Atef would come to me all the time complaining about cash," Tamari said. "He was not getting enough of it, so I took out a twenty-thousand-dollar loan from the Arab Bank to keep the families going."

ATEF ABAYAT CULTIVATED an image of generosity and benevolence: a self-styled godfather, he often spent his own money to support the wives and children of gunmen killed or wounded in operations against Israel. At the same time Atef became a law unto himself in Bethlehem. He and his Tanzim openly displayed their M-16s and Kalashnikovs as they strutted around Manger Square, which became the central meetingplace for the fighters and the site of frequent memorial services and political rallies. They treated themselves to lavish meals in the city's restaurants and then walked out without paying, knowing that no restaurant owner would dare present them with a bill. The residents of Beit Jala and Beit Sahour were frequently awakened by gunfire to see jeeploads of masked fighters cruising the narrow streets. Often Atef was at the front of the convoy, L&M filter cigarette dangling from his lips, shock of thick hair blowing in the wind, one hand on the steering wheel of a stolen late-model Mitsubishi Pajero or Isuzu Trooper. Shopowners across Bethlehem made sure to display the images of fallen Tanzim prominently on their storefront windows, knowing that a refusal to do so could get them beaten up or worse. And many fell victim to an increasingly deadly extortion racket.

One day I went to see Charly Shamieh, a Christian real estate developer from Beit Jala who had received a visit from three members of the al-Aqsa Martyrs Brigades at his office near Rachel's Tomb in the spring of 2001. "They were polite, smooth," he told me. "They said, 'Help the shebab. Either donate money or purchase weapons for us.' They didn't name an exact figure." Shamieh, citing financial reversals, declined to help them. Two days later the men returned, still refusing to give a dollar figure. On the third visit, "They said they wanted me to purchase four M-16 rifles. The price was twenty-five thousand dollars. I told them, 'Sorry, I'm not paying.'" The next evening Shamieh was sitting on the porch of his home in Beit Jala when four men wearing black ski masks drove up in a red Daihatsu. Shamieh dropped to the floor just as the gunman in the front passenger seat opened fire with an M-16; the bullets chipped stone fragments off the wall of his house, which struck him in the head and injured him. Shamieh says the Bethlehem district attorney promised to investigate, and a half dozen police officers guarded his home for a week. Days after they withdrew, the Tanzim returned at eight thirty at night, breaking the windows of Shamieh's car and firing bullets into the air. Shamieh fled the house the next morning and never returned.

Shamieh wasn't the only Christian businessman who fell victim to Tanzim shakedowns. The Tanzim purportedly forced the Nasser family, wealthy owners of hotels, restaurants, and souvenir shops in Bethlehem, to hand over thousands of dollars as well as gold jewelry. (Even in the summer of 2002 they refused to talk to me about their experience, still fearing reprisals from remnants of the militia.) Refusing to pay could be fatal. A Christian real estate man named Faraq Botto was shot dead in front of his terrified twenty-three-year-old daughter, Sholine Botto, in Beit Jala in May 2001. And gunmen shot in the face and blinded a property owner from Bethlehem named Farid Azizi six months later.

Nobody has ever definitively linked Atef to these crimes; Chris Bandak, for one, insists that the extortion ring that preyed on Christians was organized by smaller satellite groups of Tanzim that had begun to form in the Bethlehem area at the end of 2000 and the start of 2001. (Bandak, a Christian who still admires Atef Abayat, is hardly a disinterested source.) Still, as the leader of the biggest pool of fighters, Atef Abayat wielded extraordinary influence and must have known about all such activi-

ties. Sholine Botto, the daughter of the murdered Beit Jala businessman Faraq Botto, received another glimpse of Atef Abayat's
power in July 2001. Tanzim gunmen from a rival group kidnapped her Arab-Israeli fiancé from in front of her home, accused
him of being a collaborator with Israel, and held him in an abandoned building in Deheishe camp. Botto managed through
friends to contact Atef Abayat, who agreed to intercede to save
the man's life. According to acquaintances, Botto still isn't sure
why Atef showed a compassionate side; he seemed to be one of
those people who could be homicidal one moment and sweetly
generous the next. Perhaps his fighters were responsible for her
father's murder and he felt that he owed her a favor. Whatever
the case, Atef came to her house, worked the phones, and quickly
secured the man's release.

Manuel Hassassian, the chief administrator of Bethlehem
University, had a similarly memorable encounter with Atef
Abayat. He looked up from his desk in August 2001 to confront
the Fatah commander, whom he had never met before, and four
armed bodyguards standing in his doorway. Days earlier Hassassian, a Christian of Armenian descent who lived in Beit Jala, had
refused to allow Atef's brother Mazzin Abayat to matriculate at
Bethlehem University, he told me, because his high school grade
point average fell below the college's minimum standard. "Atef
was wearing a white tee shirt and chinos and a pair of Ray-Bans.
He was a very cool character," said Hassassian. Atef was polite at
first; he wanted to know why Mazzin had been rejected, suggest-
ing that Hassassian must have made an error. Hassassian was
adamant, telling Atef that Mazzin might have better luck applying to the less selective Bethlehem Free University. Atef slammed
his fist down on the table, sending a glass coffee cup shattering
to the floor. "If Allah himself comes down to earth and tells me
no," Atef told Hassassian, "you will admit my brother into your
university." Hassassian, who had no idea that Atef Abayat was
the leader of the al-Aqsa Martyrs Brigades, leapt from his chair.
"Listen, are you threatening me, you son of a bitch?" he shouted.

"Get out of my office now." A few tense seconds passed, then Atef Abayat and his gang walked out. For a month Hassassian feared for his life. "People were coming up to me at work, saying, 'Do you know whom you shouted at?' But for some reason I never heard from him again." Atef moved on to other battles; Mazzin Abayat, never admitted to Bethlehem University, ended up joining the Tanzim and earning a place on Israel's wanted list.

In the spring of 2001 a delegation of Christian civic and political leaders from Beit Jala paid a desperate visit to Kamel Hmeid, the Fatah secretary general, begging him to intervene against Atef and his gang. The shooting at Gilo was occurring almost every night, often lasting until dawn, and Israeli retaliation was escalating. The extortion had touched nearly every Christian business in Bethlehem, deepening the economic woes all were experiencing as a result of the intifada. The group left disappointed. "Hmeid said he could not control [the Tanzim]," one member of the group told me. "He lied. Hmeid needed to stay on the shooters' side, because that's where the power was." The Beit Jala group next approached the National Security Force commander, Abu Baker Thabet. One participant remembered, "He told us, 'You can hit them. You can help me if you can hit them.' I said, 'What do you mean, hit them? We cannot take the law into our own hands. You have the guns, you have the power. You must stop them.' He just said, 'I cannot.'" The group also got nowhere with the ineffectual governor of Bethlehem, a former teacher named Rashid al-Jaabari, disparagingly nicknamed "the schoolmaster" by members of the security forces. Jaabari soon stopped coming to work altogether, preferring to remain at his home in the Jerusalem neighborhood of Beit Safafa rather than deal with growing anarchy in the streets.

ATEF ABAYAT AND his comrades lived a life of leisure, interrupted by moments of cavalier violence. The Tanzim commander would often awaken at one o'clock in the afternoon in one of the dozen safe houses he rented across the city. Then he might cruise the hills of Bethlehem, shoot targets in a rocky field where he trained with his men, search for new vehicles and weapons, dine out late in restaurants, and play cards or backgammon over strong Arabic coffee at his hideout. Atef's favorite sanctuary was the Russian Hotel, an eight-story pilgrims' hotel owned by the Russian Orthodox Church and located a few blocks east of the Church of the Nativity; Chris Bandak, who worked as a part-time security guard there, turned the usually empty establishment over to Atef and his Tanzim comrades. Then late at night Atef and his men would climb into their jeeps, drive to the border of Palestinian-controlled territory, and shoot at Rachel's Tomb, the Crow's Nest, Gilo, and a stretch of the settlers' bypass road that was an easy target from an overlook in the village of al-Khader. And they would make risky excursions outside of Palestinian-controlled Area A into the Judean Wilderness, to snipe at Jewish settlers traveling down deserted roads. (The Israeli Defense Forces captured Atef's brother Nidal at a roadblock just past Beit Sahour during one such trip on January 9, 2001; Nidal has been jailed in Nafha prison in the Negev Desert ever since.) Ibrahim Abayat was Atef's closest comrade in the al-Aqsa Brigades, although for security purposes they never traveled in the same vehicle and often went out on separate operations. Ibrahim called Atef "Abu Farwa," referring to an animal pelt, an allusion to Atef's passion for hunting, both animals and human beings.

The violence they committed involved little planning, and even a casual bet could spark it. One evening in April 2001, Atef and a half dozen comrades lounged about a safe house in Beit Sahour, playing a card game called fifty-one. The group typically played for a few Israeli shekels, but tonight one participant suggested that they play for bloodstakes: the loser would be obliged to kill an Israeli soldier. When Atef lost the game, he climbed to a rooftop in Aida refugee camp overlooking Rachel's Tomb and shot dead nineteen-year-old Danny Darai with two bullets to the chest as the private walked back to his compound following an evening of guard duty. "Atef was very happy afterward," Chris Bandak told me. "He believed that anytime you killed the enemy, you should celebrate."

Usually, however, Atef Abayat preferred to have others do the killing for him. During the first week of June 2001, for example, a resident of Azza refugee camp in Bethlehem named Hassan Abu Sha'aria began sending urgent messages to the al-Aqsa Martyrs Brigades commander in Bethlehem. "I must see Atef," he begged at one point. "I don't want him to be late, or else we'll both end up losers." Atef consented to a meeting, which took place in a house rented by the Tanzim just behind the Church of the Nativity. Abu Sha'aria—a skinny, pockmarked man in his late thirties—nervously entered the living room. Atef sat regally in a leather armchair, a pistol stuck in his belt. Abu Sha'aria embraced the al-Aqsa chief with a traditional kiss on both cheeks, then confessed, "I have been working for the Israelis for the past seven years." Abu Sha'aria told Atef that his handler was Captain Mudi, the same military intelligence agent who had met with Mohammed Deifallah and, according to Deifallah's confession, orchestrated the assassination of Hussein Abayat. "I have a flak jacket that was given to me by Captain Mudi," he told Atef. "The Israelis want to kill you with it." Abu Sha'aria said he had come to see Atef because he feared that the Palestinian intelligence division was aware of his activities and that if the mukhabarat arrested him, he would almost certainly be exposed as a collaborator and condemned to death. "I want to clean my reputation," he told Atef. "Tell me what I must do."

Abu Sha'aria trembled with fear. But, says Rami Kamel, a Tanzim gunman who was present at the meeting, "Atef was friendly toward him and made him feel secure." He asked Abu Sha'aria to bring him the flak jacket; when Abu Sha'aria returned with it the next day, Atef's bodyguards searched it, Kamel says, discovered a homing device, then blew it up in a field in Beit Sahour. Afterward Atef laid a fraternal hand on Abu Sha'aria's shoulder and made a proposal to him: "Go and kill Captain

Mudi," he said, "and I promise that you will become a hero." Atef handed Abu Sha'aria his personal handgun, a Belgian-made Browning nine-millimeter pistol, and ordered one of his men to teach him how to use it. Four days later Abu Sha'aria returned to the safe house for a final send-off. He had already arranged by telephone to meet Captain Mudi that morning, requesting that the intelligence officer come alone. Atef embraced him warmly and said, "After you kill him, bring me his personal bag. It must have a lot of files inside." Abu Sha'aria said, "If anything should happen to me, you will be held responsible for the welfare of my children." Atef agreed but assured Abu Sha'aria that he would come back unharmed.

Four Tanzim accompanied Abu Sha'aria on the short drive to Bir Una, a natural spring in the ravine underneath the bypass road bridge between Beit Jala and Gilo. Abu Sha'aria wedged Atef's nine-millimeter pistol in his belt, pulled out his shirttail to cover the gun, then climbed from the ravine to the highway. He had arranged to meet Captain Mudi, who was really Yehudah Edri, a lieutenant colonel in military intelligence, beside the entrance to the first tunnel on the bypass road just south of Gilo. Edri was waiting in his car at the appointed place—with two bodyguards. Abu Sha'aria approached, pulled out the Browning, and fired four shots through the open window, killing Edri instantly and wounding a bodyguard. The second guard chased Abu Sha'aria into the ravine and shot him dead.

Atef Abayat received word of the deaths of the forty-five-year-old Edri, the highest-ranking military officer killed during the al-Aqsa intifada, and Hassan Abu Sha'aria a few hours later. "He said, 'Allahu akbar,' and then went to congratulate the shaheed's family," Rami Kamel told me. Chris Bandak said that "Atef was delighted, because it was not so easy to kill such a big guy." The Israeli Defense Forces turned over Abu Sha'aria's body to the District Coordination Office; from there the National Security Force delivered it to the al-Hussein Hospital in Beit Jala. Atef Abayat arranged for a hero's burial at the Abayat cemetery, and

Abu Sha'aria was laid to rest in a pink marble sepulcher beside the tomb of Hussein Abayat. The burial service was an edgy affair, however, because the Tanzim suspected that the Israelis had booby-trapped Abu Sha'aria's corpse before handing it over. "Don't get too near the body," they whispered to one another as they gathered around the grave. Atef Abayat didn't make an appearance.

DESPITE THE KILLING of Captain Mudi, the summer of 2001 was a period of quiet in the life of Atef Abayat. Just before midnight on Friday, June 1, a twenty-year-old Hamas terrorist blew himself up while standing near the crowded entrance to a nightclub on the Tel Aviv beachfront, killing twenty-one young Israelis. The Dolphinarium bombing spurred an international diplomatic effort to quell the Middle East violence, and in early June U.S. Central Intelligence Agency director George Tenet negotiated a cease-fire between Israel and the Palestinians. Atef and his men agreed to respect the orders of Yasser Arafat and the Fatah leadership to stop the shooting, and the guns of the al-Aqsa Martyrs Brigades fell silent over Gilo for seven weeks. But on July 19 an Israeli Apache helicopter swooped over Wadi Shaheen and fired missiles at four Hamas militants tending their pigeons in an outdoor aviary. All four were killed; Atef Abayat and his men vowed revenge.

At the Hamas funeral the next day in Manger Square I caught my first and only glimpse of the chief of the al-Aqsa Martyrs Brigades in Bethlehem. It was a broilingly hot day, and I gulped down several bottles of mineral water as I stood in front of the Bethlehem Peace Center, a starkly modern two-story building erected on the site of the demolished Caserna. In better times the Peace Center was a busy meeting place that housed museum exhibits, photo galleries, a visitors' center, and the headquarters of the Tourist Police; now it was usually deserted. In the packed square I listened to fiery speeches from the leaders of all of Beth-

lehem's resistance movements—Hamas, Islamic Jihad, the Popular Front for the Liberation of Palestine, and the largest group,
the al-Aqsa Martyrs Brigades. The bodies of the four men lay on
stretchers in the square, draped in the green flags of Hamas and
buzzed by swarms of flies; hundreds of black-masked gunmen
flaunted a daunting display of weaponry. In the middle of one
speech, a Christian tour group made up of middle-aged and elderly Americans emerged from Star Street in the Old City, cameras
dangling around their necks, name tags appended to their tee
shirts, faces buried in Bethlehem tourist maps. At that precise
moment Manger Square exploded in gunfire, and shouts of *"Allahu akbar!"* rose up from the throats of the army of masked guerrillas. The Americans stared, astonished, and then retreated back
into the Old City.

Atef Abayat—as much a symbol of the new Bethlehem as the
Christian group was of the old Bethlehem—approached the mi-
crophone moments later. I didn't know who the clean-shaven,
bedimpled fighter was at the time; only much later, when I saw
videos of the event, did I realize that I had been watching Atef.
His speech was boilerplate intifada: "Israel doesn't scare us anymore," he proclaimed, as a procession of boys waving Hamas
flags marched before the podium. "Preserve the memory of the
martyrs by continuing the intifada. Their blood unifies all of the
factions. We will continue the struggle until liberation or death!"
The square erupted in another fusillade.

Atef Abayat returned to the front lines against Israel that
night. This time he was in a position to do far more damage.
Weeks earlier Atef had succeeded in acquiring two mortars and a
dozen 60-millimeter shells—all stolen from the Israeli army, according to Tanzim comrades. The evening after the funeral the al-
Aqsa Martyrs Brigades fired one of those shells at Gilo, and it
smashed into a house under construction—confirming the fears
of Jerusalem residents that the Palestinian militants were manag-
ing to obtain ever-heavier weaponry. Israel moved tanks, bulldozers, and additional troops to the entrances to Bethlehem and Beit

Jala. On August 14 Atef Abayat's men launched a predawn attack on Gilo that lasted for six hours. In response Jerusalem Mayor Ehud Olmert called for a "massive operation" against the al-Aqsa Martyrs Brigades in Beit Jala, and Prime Minister Ariel Sharon threatened to invade the village if the Tanzim fired "one more bullet" at Gilo. Then on Monday morning, August 27, a missile launched from an Israeli Apache gunship decapitated Mustafa Zibri (known by the nom de guerre Ali Mustafa) as the leader of the Popular Front for the Liberation of Palestine sat in his Ramallah office. In retaliation Atef and his gang immediately began shooting and lobbing shells again at Gilo. (Popular Front militants would assassinate Israel's former tourism minister Rehavam Ze'evi at the Jerusalem Hyatt Hotel in October 2001 in revenge for Ali Mustafa's killing.) None of these attacks caused more than minor injuries to Gilo's residents, and they damaged only a handful of houses. But the people of Gilo lived in a constant state of anxiety, and the government of Ariel Sharon considered the unchecked gunfire from the sanctuary of Palestinian-controlled territory a provocation that had to be answered. At one o'clock in the morning on Tuesday, August 28, Israeli tanks roared out of the darkness onto Beit Jala's Virgin Mary Street and Israeli troops established bases and sniper posts in buildings throughout the village. Atef Abayat's shooting spree had led directly to one of Israel's biggest operations in the West Bank to that point since the Six-Day War.

I DROVE FROM Jerusalem to Beit Jala the next day to witness this dramatic escalation in the Israeli-Palestinian conflict. As I neared the checkpoint on the Hebron Road, I could hear heavy shooting coming from the hillside village. I parked my car on the Jerusalem side of the border, strapped on my heavy black flak jacket with bright green "TV" tape on both sides, and walked unhindered across the checkpoint to a row of orange Mercedes taxis parked beneath olive trees. The eyes of all the drivers were fixed on Beit Jala, visible beyond an olive grove and the cinderblock huts of Aida refugee camp. Dense clouds of smoke billowed from old stone houses on the hill, the worst nightmare of the Christians become devastatingly real. A taxi driver agreed to drive me down the Hebron Road to Main Street, which slopes gently uphill and changes its name to Virgin Mary Street as it approaches Beit Jala's Old City. The gunfire was louder now. Dozens of Palestinians had gathered at the intersection. During a lull in the shooting, I persuaded another driver to take me up Virgin Mary Street as far as he could.

Beit Jala was a war zone. Barricades of burning tires, manned by Tanzim carrying M-16s and dressed in black, blocked the road. Members of the Palestinian security forces fought alongside the guerrillas, most of them armed with aging Kalashnikov rifles; two men carried on a stretcher the body of a National Security Force officer who had been shot in the head, they said, while firing on the Israelis from near Beit Jala's mosque. "It's hopeless to face the Israelis with these old weapons," one of the men told me. "But what else can we do? We have to defend our territory." Fifty yards up the hill, past the last Tanzim barricade, a Merkava tank squatted in Virgin Mary Street, its giant gun barrel pointing downhill. An armored personnel carrier was parked behind it, the face of an anxious Israeli soldier peering out through bulletproof glass. The scene had attracted a crowd of Beit Jala civilians, who stared with a mixture of fear and fascination. At that point in the intifada it was still difficult to believe that Israeli tanks would roll back into Palestinian territory. One teenaged boy spat on the ground in front of the tank in disgust.

I walked through the curving alleys of Beit Jala's Old City, lined with two-story houses of Jerusalem stone. I could hear sporadic gunshots in the distance, but it was mostly quiet. Another Israeli armored personnel carrier blocked the door of a handsome stone house, and the owner, a middle-aged Christian woman named Nicola al-Alam, leaned out the second-floor window when she saw me walk by. "They're holding us prisoner," she said matter-of-factly. Israel troops had commandeered the house as a base just after midnight, herding her entire family onto the top floor. As I spoke to Alam, shooting broke out all around me. The crackle of incoming M-16 rounds was met by a volley of tank fire; Israeli jeeps and armored personnel carriers raced up and down Virgin Mary Street. I ran around to the side of Alam's house and hid behind a cinderblock wall in the garden. I waited for fifteen minutes for the shooting to stop. Then an armored car packed with Israeli troops pulled up in front of the house. "You want to get out of here?" one soldier asked. I jumped in the back, squeezing onto his lap. With the rear door hanging open, the vehicle screeched through the streets, dropping me five minutes later at an Israeli checkpoint far from the fighting. "Have a nice evening," the soldier said.

ALL THAT NIGHT and the next day the shooting continued in Beit Jala. Atef Abayat, wearing a combat helmet and a flak jacket over a camouflage uniform purchased at a Bethlehem army surplus store, carried his .50-caliber machine gun into the fray, leading a company of 150 armed men. "Atef walked at the head of the group, and that gave us a lot of energy and confidence," Bandak told me. The Tanzim and the Palestinian security forces fighting alongside them refused to stop firing until the Israelis pledged to retreat, while the Israeli Defense Forces wouldn't pull out of Beit Jala until Atef Abayat's gunmen agreed to a cease-fire. Foreign intermediaries attempted to break the impasse. Alistair Crooke, the British Embassy's military attaché, had monitored the June cease-fire from a base inside Beit Jala and come to know many of the key players on both sides. In the predawn hours of Wednesday, August 29, Crooke made a dangerous trip across Israeli lines to meet with Palestinian security officials about solving the Atef problem. Walking from Israeli tanks to Tanzim barricades in the darkness, he arrived at the Beit Jala Municipality Building and was met by a dozen glaring faces; the men, in-

cluding the National Security Force commander Abu Baker Thabet, welcomed Crooke by slamming their Kalashnikovs on a table
in the conference room, gun barrels facing him. "They were very
concerned about losing face," Crooke told me. "They were not
prepared to ask the Tanzim to stop shooting without an agreement first from Israel to withdraw."

Crooke kept up the pressure on the security chiefs through
the following evening to persuade the Tanzim to declare a
"period of quiet." Yasser Arafat called periodically, checking on
progress. Atef Abayat remained intransigent. Israel now
demanded that he surrender his mortars before they would agree
to withdraw, but Atef refused to do so. He was backed by Salah
Tamari, who felt that the Israelis had unfairly singled out the
Tanzim chief. "Salah Tamari regarded Atef as an otherwise decent
young man who was just going a little wild and needed parental
attention and a man to tell him, 'Get yourself together,'" Crooke
told me. "He kept saying, 'Atef is not a problem.'" At last Arafat
overrode Tamari and personally ordered Atef to turn over his
heavy weapons to the National Security Force, and Israel pulled
out after a sixty-hour reoccupation. Just as the Israelis withdrew,
jeeploads of jubilant gunmen roared through Beit Jala's streets in
celebration, firing their weapons in the air. "It was like the Israeli
withdrawal from Lebanon," says Manuel Hassassian, who, like
most of Beit Jala's Christians, watched the Tanzim's display of
jubilation with mixed emotions.

ATEF ABAYAT BECAME a more awkward problem for
Yasser Arafat in the late summer and early autumn of 2001.
Shortly after the Israeli invasion, police found two young Christian sisters, ages eighteen and twenty-three, shot dead in their
beds in their Beit Jala home, and a confidential police report
stated that the killers had burned their breasts with cigarettes before executing them. Most Beit Jalans suspected Atef's men were
behind the crime, though Atef insisted that the perpetrators were

members of the security forces. One month later, after both local police and Palestinian intelligence, the mukhabarat, failed to turn up any leads in the killings—few crimes were solved in Bethlehem during these dark days—the citizens of Beit Jala faxed an open letter to Arafat demanding that he take action to avert "a civil war" between Muslims and Christians. The letter complained that a "government of the Ta'amra"—led, it claimed, by Atef Abayat, Ibrahim Abayat, Kamel Hmeid, and Abdullah Daoud, the new director of Palestinian intelligence, who was not in fact a member of the tribe—was terrorizing the community. The letter cited the murder of the two Christian girls, the shooting of Charly Shamieh and other Christian businessmen, the shakedowns of prominent members of the community, the firing on Gilo, and other crimes allegedly carried out by Atef Abayat and his men. "They kill the innocents in their houses during daylight hours and rob us of our money, for the only reason that we were born as followers of Jesus Christ," the letter stated. "We call upon you, President Arafat, in this critical period . . . to issue strict orders to the security apparatus to extinguish this phenomenon which might divide and destroy Palestinian unity."

Others pressured Arafat to act as well. In the wake of the September 11 terror attacks in America, the U.S. government renewed its efforts to obtain another Middle East cease-fire, a critical inducement to Arab states to join an international anti-terror coalition. At Gaza International Airport on September 26, Israeli Foreign Minister Shimon Peres and Arafat pledged to accept the recommendations of the 2001 commission led by former U.S. senator George Mitchell: the Palestinian Authority would make a "hundred percent effort" to prevent terrorist operations and punish perpetrators, while Israel would freeze all settlement activity and refrain from using lethal force in dispersing unarmed demonstrators. As a sign of compliance, Peres demanded that the Palestinian Authority arrest ten militants, including Atef Abayat. Two days earlier Atef's gunmen had carried out another sniper killing in the West Bank. They had shot dead Sarit Amrani, twenty-six, the mother of three small children, as she drove home from a Rosh Hashanah celebration in Kiryat Arba, a settlement near Hebron, to her settlement of Noqedim, located near Herodion on the border of the Judean desert; the Tanzim had gravely injured her husband as well. (The triggerman, I later learned, was Riad al-Amur, one of Abayat's most feared lieutenants.) The Palestinian leader at first resisted the demand. "Arafat assured me, 'He is perfectly secure,'" said Alistair Crooke, who was working with the Israelis and Palestinians on behalf of "The Quartet," made up of the United Nations, the United States, Russia, and the European Union. "And I said, 'I'm sorry. I do not believe that he is being detained.'"

After the meeting with Alistair Crooke, Arafat had one of his first direct phone conversations with Atef. "We are under a lot of pressure," he told the Tanzim leader, according to others present when the call came to the home of Kamel Hmeid. "Please understand, you are not considered a prisoner. Just go stay at the muqata [security headquarters in Bethlehem] for a few days as a guest of the Palestinian Authority."

Atef Abayat assumed his usual tone of informality. "Okay, *Amm* [Uncle]," he said. "No problem."

Kamel Hmeid rebuked him: "You are talking to the president, Atef." Atef apologized and told Arafat that he would turn himself in at once.

The following day, October 1, 2001, Atef Abayat reported as promised to Bethlehem's Preventive Security chief at the muqata and signed a document acknowledging that he had been placed under arrest. Once again, however, the Palestinian Authority was unwilling to challenge the power and popularity of the Tanzim leader. In fact, the security force provided Atef with a furnished apartment in Bethlehem and told him merely to "stay out of sight" until the furor died down. (It is unknown whether Arafat was aware of the arrangements.) Even Atef's own gunmen remained in the dark about the scheme, apparently part of an organized effort to fool the Israelis and the international community. As word spread of the "arrest," a crowd of Tanzim converged on the Bethlehem Hotel, where a security meeting was taking place between Fatah leaders and Palestinian Authority officials. Kamel Hmeid, who was in on the ruse, stood on the hood of his car and announced to the heavily armed fighters, "We are committed to the orders of President Arafat. Atef Abayat has agreed to go to prison." As local journalists filmed the confrontation, the angry crowd broke up the security meeting and then marched to Manger Square, firing their guns in the air and sending pedestrians diving for cover. Atef Abayat cruised around in a car with tinted windows, according to his brother, observing the scene in amusement. He then hid out in the comfortable apartment, which his custodians had fitted with a fax, telephone, and a computer with Internet access (though Atef had no idea how to use a computer). "Atef," Mazzin Abayat told me, "didn't spend a single minute in a jail cell."

Atef's house arrest lasted less than a week. On October 5 another violent incident brought an abrupt end to the charade and drew Atef back to the streets. That afternoon one of Atef's trusted lieutenants, Rami Kamel, received a new M-16 rifle with a laser scope and grenade launcher from an Arab-Israeli gun dealer in Jerusalem. The twelve-thousand-dollar weapon, partly paid for by Atef, arrived hidden in the trunk of a Mercedes taxi beneath boxes of tomatoes. A single grenade, wrapped in a white tee shirt and sealed with Scotch tape, accompanied the gun. At five thirty that afternoon Kamel, Ibrahim Abayat, and a few other Tanzim took the weapon to a field near Wadi Shaheen for a test firing. Kamel squeezed off a clip of M-16 bullets and then fitted the grenade into the launcher. As he pulled the trigger, the grenade exploded, blowing off his left arm near the shoulder. "I thought at first an Apache missile had hit me," Kamel later told me. "I looked at the stump of my arm and I screamed, and then I fell unconscious." Kamel's comrades rushed him to al-Hussein Hospital in Beit Jala; Preventive Security released Atef Abayat from his guarded apartment to be at his friend's bedside and he remained free from that point on. Kamel survived a seven-hour operation, but he remained in critical condition.

Kamel and Atef Abayat were convinced that the Israelis had booby-trapped the grenade, although they had no solid evidence that it was anything but a defective piece of weaponry. The Tanzim commander's old confidence faltered; the Israelis, he believed, were closing in. Yet he refused to return to the custody of the Palestinian Authority. A few days later, after Kamel had recovered enough to hold a conversation, Atef sat by his bedside and told him, "I feel, Rami, that I'm not going to stay for so long."

"What are you talking about?" Kamel said.

"Make sure this [intifada] goes on after me," Atef said. "Don't let me down."

"Don't worry about it," Kamel replied. "You are not going to die."

Atef blamed the media for exposing him; he regretted the many high-profile interviews he had given that had turned him into a household name in Israel. "Shaul Mofaz [the Israeli Defense Forces chief of staff] is talking about me now," he muttered one afternoon after hearing another Israeli TV report questioning whether he had really been arrested. Salah Tamari begged the Tanzim leader to move in with him temporarily. Tamari's main home was a villa that looked like a cross between a medieval chateau and a Malian mud mosque, situated at the edge of the Judean desert in Za'atara, an area still under the control of Israel. But the councilman had kept possession of his family's old house on Fawagreh Street, near the souk, or Municipal Market, in Bethlehem's Old City. "I wanted Atef to stay there, to keep a low profile for a while," Tamari told me. "But people told him, 'No, it would not suit you.' So he refused."

ON THE FIFTEENTH of October Atef's distant cousin and fellow Tanzim gunman Jamal Abayat, the leader of a car theft ring in Bethlehem, received a call from an Israeli with whom he regularly conducted business. The Israeli, who went by the name of Itzik, asked whether Atef would be willing to trade the stolen 2000 Mitsubishi Magnum he was now driving for a brand-new Mitsubishi Pajero, which he promised to deliver immediately. The Israeli auto insurance company that covered the Magnum, he explained, had refused to compensate the original owner for his loss, alleging fraud. Never one to refuse an automobile upgrade, Atef agreed to the trade.

On the morning of Thursday, October 18, a Palestinian associate of Jamal Abayat named Mahmoud Sabatin, from the Israeli-controlled village of Husan near Bethlehem, took delivery from Itzik of a 2002 white Mitsubishi Pajero at a gas station near the West Bank settlement of Betar Ilit—a frequent handoff point for stolen Israeli vehicles. Four hours later Sabatin dropped the Pajero at an entry point to Bethlehem with another go-between, who in turn delivered it to Jamal Abayat. Atef Abayat received the sixty-thousand-dollar sports utility vehicle from Jamal at three o'clock that afternoon at the home of his wife's uncle in Wadi Shaheen. He was delighted with the jeep, admiring the sleek gray leather interior—still wrapped in plastic—and noting with satisfaction that it had fewer than a hundred miles on the odometer.

An hour later Atef parked his new toy in front of the al-Hussein Hospital, strolled inside, and announced to the hospital staff, "I am going to take Rami Kamel for a drive." The nurses objected. Kamel remained in unstable condition, thirteen days after major surgery, and was hooked up to intravenous tubes. But Atef was insistent, lifting Kamel out of bed and guiding him down the hallway with the tubes still strapped in his remaining arm. As they emerged from the hospital onto Virgin Mary Street, Atef pointed out the new Pajero gleaming in the sun. Kamel stared at the vehicle and told Atef he wasn't going to step inside it. "My heart was beating hard," Kamel told me months later. "I had a bad feeling about it. I said, 'Look at my arm, Atef. The Israelis blew it off.'"

Kamel followed Atef in a separate car on a condolence call to the family of Ahmed Abayat, a member of the clan who had been fatally stabbed during a brawl in a Jerusalem nightclub the previous evening. As they sipped bitter coffee and mingled with Fatah political leaders and other Tanzim gunmen, Atef appeared to be in a good mood, momentarily distracted from his own troubles by the recovery of his close friend Kamel and his acquisition of the new vehicle. Kamel Hmeid greeted the Tanzim commander and asked Atef, "Did you make sure to check the jeep?" Atef brushed off Hmeid's concerns. "Don't worry," he assured him. "We only get the very best." Atef socialized at the condolence house for an hour, then left for a visit to an Abayat gunman who was recuperating at home in Beit Sahour after minor surgery. Atef was accompanied by his seventeen-year-old nephew Walid Abayat, who lived in the compound in Wadi Shaheen; Jamal Abayat; and another distant cousin and frequent hunting partner of Atef's named Issa Abayat.

Stepping outside, Atef pressed the remote control to unlock the vehicle, but instead of disengaging the lock, the device caused the directional lights to flash. Atef continued pushing the button, and the lights kept blinking. Jamal Abayat finally used his key, and the four climbed inside. Atef's distant cousin Nidal Abayat, who was to follow Atef in his own car with Rami Kamel, cast a suspicious look over the new Pajero. "I don't trust this thing, Atef," he said. He pointed his M-16 at Atef in a joking way. "Get out of the jeep," he said. Atef shrugged and drove away.

Walid settled into the rear seat, next to Issa Abayat. Atef, wearing new leather boots, a green shirt, and blue cargo pants, with a Browning nine-millimeter pistol stuck in his belt, sped past other vehicles on Manger Street. When they found themselves stuck behind Kamel Hmeid's car, Issa Abayat leaned out the window and yelled to the Fatah chief, "Open the road to your master!" Hmeid made way. Atef drove through Manger Square and past the Church of the Nativity, then turned down the steep slope that led to Wadi Shaheen. He stopped the vehicle at the base of the hill leading to the Abayat compound and ordered Walid to get out; he would not be invited to visit the recuperating fighter. Walid started to object, but Atef interrupted him. "Don't argue with me, Walid," Atef said. Walid obediently stepped out of the Mitsubishi. He watched Atef, Issa, and Jamal Abayat continue toward Beit Sahour.

Rami Kamel and Nidal Abayat followed the Mitsubishi. It was ten minutes before six o'clock in the evening. They chatted casually with Atef on the MIRS radio. Atef expressed his remorse about forcing Walid to leave, but said that the boy was still a teenager, still too young to be fraternizing regularly with the men of the al-Aqsa Martyrs Brigades. Nidal Abayat and Rami Kamel agreed. Nidal joked that they were taking a chance with the boy's life simply by giving him a lift home.

"Be careful of booby traps, Atef," Nidal said.

"Allahu akbar," Atef replied. Then the Mitsubishi exploded.

The force of the blast ripped off the doors and hurled the jeep in the air, expelling Issa from the rear seat. Atef's brother Mazzin Abayat, who was having his own stolen car inspected at a garage a block from the explosion, arrived at the scene thirty seconds later. Jamal and Atef Abayat sat side by side in the burning vehicle. The air bag inside the steering wheel had discharged, deflated, and twisted itself around Atef's neck. They were both still alive—barely. "Atef was lying back, his lips were moving, his tongue was sticking out," Mazzin told me. "He made gurgling sounds, then he died along with Jamal a few seconds later." Issa died an hour later at al-Hussein Hospital.

NINE MONTHS AFTER the death of Atef Abayat in the booby-trapped Mitsubishi, long after the grief and rage—and in many cases joy and relief—that enveloped Bethlehem in the wake of his killing had subsided, I made another journey to Ta'amra country. I had heard that Nasser Abu Sultan, a Ta'amra poet, had written a eulogy for Atef Abayat soon after he died, a poem that the al-Aqsa Martyrs Brigades commander himself had commissioned in anticipation of his demise. I found Abu Sultan in a Bedouin tent pitched behind his home in a parched and rocky field in the village of Darsala. Clad in a white dishdasha and ke-fiyeh, he invited me to sit on a rug, propped up pillows behind me, and poured me a glass of water from a tall clay jug. Abu Sultan had encountered Atef Abayat on October 15 at the office of the Bethlehem Petroleum Committee, which, until the reoccupation, worked with the Israeli government to coordinate the shipment of oil and gasoline to the area. "I'm upset at you, Sheik," Atef had jokingly told him. "You wrote a poem about the shaheed Hussein Abayat and you've written nothing about me."

Abu Sultan had laughed and said, "No problem, Abu Hussein. I will write you a poem when you die."

Atef had replied, "Sheik, keep your promise," and then he had continued on his way.

Three days later the sheik was smoking his *narghile*—water pipe—in his tent at dusk when he heard a loud explosion in Beit Sahour, two miles away. He told me that he had had a strong feeling that Atef was the victim. Immediately, he said, he fetched his notebook and jotted down a verse, which he recited at the memorial service held forty days after Atef's death. The sheik read the poem aloud to me as well:

> Oh Atef, how can I describe you?
> As determined as a lion on the hunt,
> Powerful like thunder in the skies.
> You are the pride of the people, the blade of the spear,
> A dagger in the heart of your enemies.
> You, who are washed by the tears of those who loved you,
> You, whose departure has caused pain to every mother,
> You, betrayed by the invisible hands of collaborators,
> As black as the darkest night,
> You did not die.
> For you left behind a small son named Hussein,
> An infant who is still feeding at the breast and unaware,
> But one day, he will seek revenge, and relive your glory.

THE GOVERNOR

∽∾

MOHAMMED AL-MADANI LEARNED THAT YASSER
Arafat had named him the new governor of Bethlehem in a two-
minute telephone conversation as he sipped Arabic coffee in the
office of the general director of the Palestinian Embassy in Amman, Jordan. It was October 4, 2001, and Madani had just arrived
in Jordan from Arafat's headquarters in the Gaza Strip to visit his
eldest son, Yafeh, who was finishing his master's degree in fi-
nance at a college in Amman. A former Fatah guerrilla and longtime aide to Arafat, Madani was paying a courtesy call at the
embassy when the urgent call came through the switchboard
from the presidential appointments secretary, Ramzi Khouri. The
promotion was effective immediately, Khouri said. "Come to Ramallah now," he ordered.

Madani, fifty-four, had been anticipating momentous developments ever since he had encountered Arafat in a hallway at the
Gaza City presidency two weeks earlier. "I am giving you an important post, Abu Yafeh," the Palestinian leader had told him,
then disappeared into his office without elaboration. Ever since
his return from exile in 1996, Madani had felt as if he had been
sitting on his hands, underutilized, and he was excited and a little awed by the appointment. As he stepped out of a taxi at the
gates of Arafat's presidential compound in Ramallah at six o'-
clock in the evening on Friday, October 5, Madani prepared himself for a lengthy meeting to discuss the specifics of the job. He
had never been to Bethlehem, knew nothing about the place, had

only a vague concept of the troubles caused by the Tanzim militiamen. He was looking forward to a heart-to-heart talk with
Arafat to determine how he should proceed.

The Force 17 bodyguards at the entrance to the muqata
saluted him and escorted him past parking lots and security-force
buildings to the presidential waiting room on the second floor of
Arafat's headquarters. A half dozen other guests sat in the chamber, all puffing on cigarettes on black-leather chairs beneath a
large sign that read "Thank You for Not Smoking." Casting an
eye on the portrait of Arafat that hung from one wall, Madani
went over again the questions he had for the president. Shortly
afterward, Ramzi Khouri called him into Arafat's office.

Arafat rose from behind his desk and greeted his old comrade
in arms with a traditional kiss on both cheeks. He studied his
aide in silence for a moment. Madani was a lean figure with graying hair and a slender, clean-shaven face. His thick brown eye-
brows, deep-set eyes, and strong jawline suggested a pugnacious
streak, which emerged only rarely behind Madani's gentle facade.
"This intifada is taking a toll on you, Abu Yafeh," the president
told him, his jaw quivering as he spoke. "You're becoming old.
Your hair is turning white."

Madani smiled self-consciously and thanked him for the appointment.

"So," Arafat asked. "When do you start?"

"Tomorrow, Abu Amar," Madani replied, calling Arafat by his
nom de guerre. "What are your instructions?"

"I have no instructions," Arafat replied. "Just behave sanely,
and follow your instincts."

Then the meeting was over.

THOUGH THE NEW assignment thrilled him, Madani's
instincts told him that he was stepping into a minefield. Madani
had been watching the Palestinian leadership closely during the
year since the intifada began, and—though he would never say so

publicly—he was dismayed about the direction in which they appeared to be leading their people. Madani was not skittish about violence; he had been a Fatah commander in Jordan, Syria, and Lebanon and had faced down Israeli tanks and 15,000 troops during the famous battle of Karameh in Jordan in March 1968, in which 120 Palestinian and 28 Israeli soldiers died. Eight years later he had taken shrapnel in the chest during heavy fighting against the Phalangist militia in Beirut and had fled with thousands of other guerrillas on a boat to Tunis in 1982. Yet Madani also believed that the time for armed struggle against Israel was long past. The arming of guerrillas under the nominal control of Fatah, the release of Hamas and Islamic Jihad terrorists from jail, the killings of soldiers and settlers in the territories and, increasingly, of civilians inside Israel struck him as a highly dangerous course. Israel, he knew, was a military behemoth that would cripple the Palestinian Authority and eventually crush the Palestinian resistance. In the wake of the September 11 attacks the United States, he believed, would probably give Ariel Sharon a blank check to put down the intifada under the guise of fighting Islamic terror. Madani remained deeply hostile to Israel—he believed that Arafat was totally justified in rejecting Ehud Barak's offer for a permanent settlement at Camp David in July 2000—and supported a campaign of civil disobedience against Israel at military checkpoints. But he felt that the intifada had begun to lose its way the moment the Palestinians picked up guns instead of stones. From the first days of the uprising he had made his opposition known in a subtle way. "Whenever anyone at meetings discussed violence, Madani would leave the room," a Palestinian Authority official told me.

Madani was closemouthed about what he knew of Arafat's role in fomenting the violence. Publicly he insisted that Arafat was not to blame, that certain members of his inner circle misled and exploited him. But Madani appeared to subscribe to a "don't ask, don't tell" policy, by which he deliberately avoided scrutinizing the Palestinian leader. He reassured himself that Arafat was dispatching him to Bethlehem out of a sincere wish to control the violence. But even if he had harbored doubts about Arafat's intentions, he wouldn't have turned down the assignment. After thirty-four years at Arafat's side he was a total loyalist, a man of his word. What's more, he viewed the Bethlehem job as a plum, both an honor and a challenge. Despite his misgivings he was determined to do the job, to stay the course, both because the president had asked him to do it and because he enjoyed a good fight.

MADANI SPENT THE night at the Ramallah apartment where his wife and the youngest of his three sons, Majd, seventeen, resided while he worked in Gaza. The next morning a presidential aide escorted Madani from tailor shop to tailor shop, where he purchased two suits, two sport jackets, six ties, three pairs of dress pants, and two pairs of lace-up black shoes. In all his years working for Arafat and the Palestinian Authority, Madani had never worn a suit or a tie. The new governor of Bethlehem left Ramallah at six o'clock on October 6, his fifty-fifth birthday, in a black Mercedes driven by an aide of Preventive Security chief Jibril Rajoub. Madani carried a single suitcase with his new wardrobe carefully folded inside. The driver followed a meandering course along West Bank back roads, switchbacking through olive groves and up and down steep hillsides to avoid potentially dangerous encounters at Israeli checkpoints after dark. Madani drifted in and out of sleep in the backseat. The Preventive Security man, wanting to engage Madani in conversation about his new assignment, started to tell him about the Abayat clan, the shooting at Gilo, and the growing lawlessness in the streets. Madani, weary, held up his hand. "I'll find out about the situation when I get there," he said. He thought about Arafat's mandate, "Behave sanely," and hoped sanity had a place in Bethlehem. He assumed he could count on Arafat's support.

The Hebron Road was dark and deserted when the Mercedes arrived in town after a two-hour journey. They drove to the muqata, the block-long two-story headquarters of the Palestinian security forces built during the British Mandate, where lights were still on in many windows after nightfall. There they picked up Ahmed Eid, the recently appointed local commander of the National Security Force. Eid was a tall figure with penetrating blue eyes whom Arafat had dispatched to Bethlehem under pressure to replace the hapless Abu Baker Thabet—the commander who had distributed bullets to Atef Abayat. Ahmed Eid guided the driver to a nearby presidential guest cottage off the Hebron Road, beside the hulking Ministry of Youth and Sport. Several of Bethlehem's other security chiefs, an uneasy collection of powerful rivals, had already gathered there for a get-acquainted meeting with the new governor. Madani knew none of them. Twelve independent security forces existed within the Palestinian Authority, many of them with ambiguously defined missions and often overlapping authority to make arrests. This was Arafat's way of turning competitors against one another and keeping his hold on power secure. It was also a recipe for chaos.

Over a simple dinner of fava beans, hummus, falafel, and pita bread, Madani assessed the men whose support would be essential to the success of his mission. Intelligence chief Abdullah Daoud, known to everyone by the nom de guerre Abu Qassim, was thin, forty years old, a longtime revolutionary, his brisk stride and glowering expression betraying a stubborn streak that put the governor on edge. Majdi Attari, the head of Preventive Security, was a balding figure with an enigmatic smile and a prominent mole above his upper lip. Madani would soon come to view him as being like Ahmed Eid, a potential ally; the Preventive Security people usually reflected the moderate views of their leader, Jibril Rajoub, a favorite of the United States government. Also in attendance were Hamido Bawab, the hulking director of Force 17, the personal bodyguard unit of Yasser Arafat, whose officers were often involved in the attacks against Israel; and Mohammed Seifi, the chief of the Naval Police, several dozen of whom had been reassigned from the coastal Gaza Strip to landlocked Bethlehem in the early days of the uprising. The final arrival was Kamel Hmeid, the local secretary general of Fatah, who enjoyed the closest relationship of all these men to Atef Abayat and his militia. Hmeid and Madani eyed each other warily.

MADANI WAS BORN in October 1946 in Kfar Sabit, a tiny olive-growing village between Nazareth and Tiberias, in the rolling hill country west of the Sea of Galilee. By a stroke of for-tune he ended up an Arab citizen of Israel rather than a refugee. During the war of 1948, Israeli forces attacked the village, and his parents fled toward Lebanon with three of their four children: Mohammed, then two, his seven-year-old sister, and his four-year-old brother. But as they neared the border, Madani's father had a change of heart. Instead of crossing into Lebanon, he led the family back to Kfar Sabit to search for his eighteen-year-old son, who had taken up arms against the Israelis. Madani's father found him lying dead in a field on the outskirts of the half-burned village. That evening he buried his son where he had fallen; two weeks later he died of a heart attack. Madani's mother moved with her surviving children to a nearby Arab village called Daburiya, which the Israelis had spared.

Mohammed al-Madani's father had been a prosperous landowner in Kfar Sabit, with three hundred dunams, or seventy-five acres, of olive groves and citrus trees. But the family had lost everything in the war and overnight found themselves reduced to refugees living in a one-room mud hut. To support her children, Madani's mother worked the harvest on the Israeli kibbutzim that were springing up across the Galilee. On one occasion she took Mohammed with her to pick olives on a kibbutz built over the ruins of Kfar Sabit and, weeping, showed him the half-destroyed house in which he had spent the first two years of his life. "I insisted that I wanted to drink from our well, and she took me there," Madani told me. "This is my first memory of the vil-lage in which I had been born."

When he was seven years old, Madani went to work, supplementing his mother's meager income by harvesting sunflowers and almonds during weekends and summer vacations on a moshav, or private collective farm, called Kfar Tabur. The Israelis at first rejected him, saying he was too skinny and small, but the Arab labor supervisor in Daburiya insisted that they hire him: "Take this one, he's poor, he's an orphan," Madani remembers him saying. "He doesn't even belong to this village. He's all alone. His father and brother are dead." He spent the next decade shuttling between school and farm work, trying to better the family's position in Daburiya. "We were outsiders to the village, refugees," he said. "I always felt, 'I don't belong here.'"

In 1965 he earned his high school degree, or *bagrut,* from a night school in Tel Aviv. But though he spoke fluent Hebrew and possessed the blue identification card allowing him to vote in Israeli elections, Madani always felt like a second-class citizen in Israel, he told me; he had formed no friendships with Jews, and soon after graduation he joined the Israeli Communist Party, drawn in by its advocacy of the right of return of Arab refugees. One day in Afula, after the Six-Day War, Madani and a group of shebab crossed paths with an Israeli woman who, he says, muttered "coward Arabs" and spat in Madani's face. It was a seminal moment. "When that woman spat at me, I took the decision never to speak Hebrew again," he told me. "I was lost, shattered. I could not handle the Israelis. I wanted to do something, but I didn't know what."

The answer came to him in August 1967. During a trip through the West Bank, which had opened up to Israelis following the Six-Day War and occupation, Madani fell into a conversation with a teacher in a Ramallah refugee camp. He shared his frustration about the Arab defeat and the Israeli conquest of the West Bank and Gaza with the teacher: "The teacher said, 'If you are talking about military resistance, I can help you. I can send you to Jordan or Syria for military training. Find me in this spot after three o'clock in the afternoon any day of the week.'" Madani returned to Daburiya and persuaded three close friends to join him. He paid his debts and told his mother he was taking a job on a moshav in the Negev Desert. Three days before the quartet was to leave, Madani's friends dropped out. One claimed to be in love with a woman in Nazareth; two admitted that they were afraid. Madani cursed them and called them cowards. "One told me, 'You won't go either.' It was a challenge I had to accept." On the last day of August 1967 Madani left his house at dawn, alone, bound for a life of exile.

The solitary journey that he took from Daburiya across the Jordan River led him to Karameh, a village in the Jordanian desert filled with Palestinian guerrillas, many of them as green as he was. He joined the Fatah movement and then carried a Kalashnikov in the bloody, house-to-house battle against the Israelis at Karameh in which a dozen of his friends were killed. Along the way, he told me, he learned a lot about courage and the art of choosing one's battles wisely. In November 1968 Madani led one of the first squads of Palestinian guerrillas into southern Lebanon. One of the guides was a hothead who wanted to attack the much more powerful Lebanese army. According to a member of Madani's force, Madani grabbed the man's gun barrel and placed it against his own chest, telling the guide he would have to shoot Madani first. "He was filled with hatred, and I was intent on avoiding a massacre," Madani said. "You have these kinds of people in all revolutions." After the Yom Kippur War in 1973 Madani realized that war against such a powerful enemy was fruitless; he accepted the fact that Israel was here to stay and that the Palestinians would have to achieve their state through negotiation rather than armed struggle. He pressed his view on Arafat, who replied, "You say whatever you want, I'll do whatever I want."

Madani took time away from the front in 1970 to marry a Palestinian refugee from the same village he had come from, Kfar Sabit, and managed to obtain his bachelor's degree in psychology at Arab University of Beirut a decade later, in the middle of the Lebanese civil war. In 1982 Madani fled Lebanon by boat for the Syrian port city of Latakia, then endured months of beatings and torture in a

Syrian prison camp during a violent split within the Palestinian Liberation Organization. Never wavering in his loyalty to Arafat, he befriended one of his Syrian guards, who allowed him to escape. He spent another decade working for Arafat in Egypt, Algeria, Libya, and Tunisia. Madani finally entered Gaza in 1996, hopeful—but not convinced—that a new era of peace had arrived.

IN THE FIRST WEEK after his arrival in Bethlehem in October 2001, Madani settled into his office in the modest governorate and received a near-constant stream of visitors from across the city's religious and political spectrum. The Latin patriarch Michel Sabbah, the representatives of the Armenian Orthodox, Coptic Orthodox, and Greek Orthodox churches in Bethlehem, the director of the Red Crescent Society, the heads of local Muslim and Christian charities, and delegations from Palestinian Authority ministries paid him courtesy calls in the governorate and visited him during the evenings at his guest quarters. Outgoing governor Jaabari, whom Arafat had unceremoniously fired, came to brief him; Madani consoled the man, bitter about his ouster, by assuring him that it was the result of forces beyond Jaabari's control. Days later Madani was provided with a clear indication of just how powerful those forces were. On October 18 Atef Abayat was blown up in his booby-trapped Mitsubishi Pajero. That afternoon ten thousand people gathered in the streets outside al-Hussein Hospital and crowded the morgue where Atef's charred body lay on a slab, the black air bag still twisted around his neck. Whipped into a frenzy by the sight of the corpse, the mob marched up the Hebron Road toward the muqata. The Palestinian Authority held three convicted collaborators with Israel, including Mohammed Deifallah, in the muqata's jail. With Atef Abayat's first cousin Ibrahim Abayat leading the charge, the crowd was now screaming for their blood.

Madani climbed to the rooftop. From that exposed vantage point he gazed at a roiling throng advancing up both sides of the median strip on the Hebron Road. Madani ordered one hundred policemen and National Security men to surround the building and form a cordon in front of the main gate. The mob's chanting grew more vociferous: "Death to the Palestinian Authority," they cried. "Death to the collaborators. Remember the shaheed Atef Abayat." Stones and chunks of concrete thudded against the walls and smashed through windows; several projectiles sailed past his head as he leaned over the roof. Mohammad Deifallah and his two fellow inmates waited terrified in their cells, expecting to be dragged into the street and shot. The security men fired volley after volley into the air, driving back the stone throwers. Finally Madani reached Kamel Hmeid and demanded that he disperse the crowd. Hmeid addressed the mob with a megaphone and urged them to leave. "We don't want another shaheed tonight," he told them. "Your real enemy is Israel, not the Sulta [Palestinian Authority]." Hmeid's speech seemed to turn the tide. After four hours and thousands of spent bullets but no injuries or deaths, Madani seized back control of the streets.

He lost it again a few hours later. That night the Tanzim launched their most furious attack yet on Gilo, firing from various vantage points around the city—a hilltop near Bethlehem University in the Madbasseh neighborhood, the Aida refugee camp—and overwhelming the security forces that Madani had deployed to stop them. One day later Israeli tanks and armored personnel carriers rolled down the Hebron Road and into Bethlehem, killing more than twenty Palestinians and occupying the city for ten days. Madani waited out the storm inside the presidential guest house. "I became aware then," he told me later, with characteristic understatement, "that I had been brought into a situation that wasn't normal."

I VISITED MADANI a few times during these difficult days and continued meeting with him through the summer and fall of 2002. Usually our encounters would take place in the early

evening in his one-bedroom apartment in Beit Jala, a sparsely furnished abode that he had rented after leaving Arafat's guest
house. Clad typically in a beige sweatsuit with rolled-up pants
cuffs and loafers, the governor would recline on a sofa and talk
quietly about his life and the difficulties he was facing in his new
position. Several times I would interview Madani over glasses of
dry red wine or a single-malt Scotch. Madani prided himself on
his secularism; he never prayed, never went to mosque, and felt
as comfortable among Christians as he did around Muslims, almost certainly one of the reasons that Arafat had chosen him for
the post. He lived a stripped-down existence in Bethlehem—his
only perk as governor was a chauffeur-driven Land Rover—and
that seemed to fit his personality, which was guarded, discreet,
and unadorned. It was difficult to have more than about fifteen
minutes of Madani's undivided attention, I soon learned: his cell
phone rang constantly, aides rushed in and out of the room with
communiqués for him to sign, and a stream of visitors, from security men to Ta'amra tribal leaders, would drop in unannounced
to pay homage, to gossip, or to beseech him for assistance.
Madani was like the calm in the storm, exuding quiet authority,
even as forces massed to take him down.

For Madani, the Israeli invasion was a traumatic rite of initia-
tion. In the aftermath of the ten-day operation, he realized that
Bethlehem would almost certainly face further incursions and
massive destruction at the hands of the Israeli Defense Forces
unless he quickly restored a sense of normality to the city. His
first priority was to rein in the militants. After learning about the
monthly subsidies being paid to the al-Aqsa Martyrs Brigades,
Madani summoned Kamel Hmeid, the Tanzim paymaster, and ordered him to immediately suspend all cash handouts to the
Abayat gunmen. Hmeid was furious, accusing Madani of treating
him with disrespect and of undermining the "national cause." He
threatened to complain to Arafat. But Madani called the president himself and urged him to stop the money flow, and, as Chris
Bandak confirmed to me, payments evaporated. Madani had

spent a lifetime in the Fatah movement, but now he believed that Fatah had gone astray, surrendering to the militant young Turks in the organization and increasingly placing itself at odds with the Palestinian Authority. He initiated a program to buy weapons back from the Tanzim and lured a handful of key gunmen away from the militias by giving them top jobs in the Palestinian security forces. When the leaders of the National Committee—an umbrella group formed at the start of the al-Aqsa intifada and made up of Fatah, Hamas, Islamic Jihad, and the Popular Front for the Liberation of Palestine—declared a protest strike in support of the intifada and told Bethlehem students to stay home, Madani appeared on local TV and ordered the schools to remain open. "I am the authority in this city," he declared, "and our students will not miss a day of class." After an Islamic Jihad activist verbally attacked Yasser Arafat during a rally of all the political parties in Manger Square, the police moved to arrest him, but Madani squelched the order, saying that even the Islamic militant enjoyed the right to free speech.

THE CHRISTIAN community knew little about Madani, but he quickly won their respect. Shortly after his arrival he held meetings with the clergy, mayors, and other civic leaders of Beit Sahour, Beit Jala, and Bethlehem, and told them that he considered the Tanzim's extortion and other criminal acts unacceptable. The Christians took heart; nobody from the Palestinian Authority had ever denounced the Abayat gang before. Christians became more hopeful when they learned about Madani's staunch secularism and his former membership in the Communist Party, which still enjoyed a modicum of support in Palestinian Christian communities. The governor pledged that he would pay the rent for people in Beit Jala who'd been forced to leave their homes, and he wrested money out of the Palestinian Authority to repair houses damaged by Israeli tank fire. Madani played the role of conciliator, a reassuring force for the beleaguered Christian community. On Christmas Eve 2001, when Ariel Sharon refused to allow Yasser Arafat to make his customary annual visit to celebrate midnight mass in the Church of the Nativity, Madani took his place. Smartly attired in a gray suit, the governor received a delegation of Palestinian Authority officials in front of the Peace Center and then knelt down and kissed the hand of the Latin patriarch of Jerusalem, Michel Sabbah. The gesture of Muslim and Christian solidarity went down well. "We are going to have a great Christmas, although the Israelis have done their best to destroy it," he proclaimed. Madani repeated the ritual on January 7, the Greek Orthodox Christmas, leading three hundred Roman Catholics and Muslims on a congratulatory visit to the Greek Orthodox patriarch in the Basilica.

Madani was not afraid to voice his disapproval of the al-Aqsa Martyrs Brigades, at a time when few ranking officials in the Palestinian Authority dared to challenge the Tanzim. The militants repeatedly threatened him, sometimes at gunpoint, but Madani refused to travel with bodyguards. Under Madani's rule the shooting stopped completely from Beit Jala, but the Tanzim found new roosts across the city, especially from the hilltop neighborhood of Madbasseh—the highest point in Bethlehem— and from Aida camp, engaging the security forces in a continuous cat-and-mouse game. The man behind the shootings, Ibrahim Abayat, Atef Abayat's volatile successor as head of the largest group among the al-Aqsa Martyrs Brigades in Bethlehem, quickly became Madani's bête noire in the city.

Ibrahim Abayat had come to power in December 2001, following an unsuccessful attempt to unite all of the Tanzim militias in Bethlehem's neighborhoods and refugee camps under a single leader in the chaotic aftermath of Atef's death. The battle to succeed Atef had been intense, with rival warlords arguing their merits late into the night at Kamel Hmeid's Bethlehem home. Hmeid's effort to broker a citywide deal fell apart, the Tanzim remained splintered, and Ibrahim Abayat assumed command of the Abayat militia. Yet many members of Ibrahim's own clan opposed his selection: the Tanzim considered Ibrahim Abayat a loose cannon, quick to anger, not in control of himself. During Atef's tenure Ibrahim had impregnated a sixteen-year-old Christian girl in Beit Sahour; he had paid for the abortion, but the word had leaked out, and the parents had been forced to move with her to Jordan because of the scandal. "Ibrahim was in need of psychiatric help," said Salah Tamari, who first met the Tanzim leader during his trial for the honor killing of Sara Abayat. "He was unstable. He could be influenced by anyone. He was desperate for attention." While Atef Abayat had assiduously cultivated Bethlehem's top officials, Ibrahim struck a belligerent tone with them. Early on the Tanzim commander made it clear that he would not respect Madani's authority. "The ones who stop us in the road we will kill," he declared at a rally in Manger Square, "and you are getting in the way."

In December Arafat replaced Bethlehem's ineffectual police chief with General Ala Hosni, a former comrade in arms in Jordan and Lebanon and the Palestinian Authority's former ambassador to Jordan. Hosni was a burly, no-nonsense figure who had served as the police chief of Nablus and led a crackdown on Hamas and Islamic Jihad militants in the mid-1990s. He made it known from his first days on the job that he shared the governor's disdain for the Tanzim. In early 2001 a woman in Beit Sahour whose fiancé had allegedly beaten her up asked Ibrahim Abayat for assistance. According to Hosni, Ibrahim Abayat handled the situation in his usual way: he broke the assailant's hands and feet with a metal rod and sprayed his car with bullets. Hosni summoned Ibrahim Abayat to his office. He ordered him to sit and confiscated his M-16. "You will stand trial for this," he promised. "You will go to jail and nobody will protect you." Ibrahim Abayat spent the night in a prison cell, then was taken to court for an arraignment. A half hour later, he was back on the street— released by a frightened judge. Ibrahim Abayat returned to the office of the dismayed police chief. "I'm a free man," he announced, grinning. "They couldn't touch me."

Abayat's release from custody made Ala Hosni realize that seizing back the streets from the Tanzim would be far more difficult than he had imagined. "It was a jungle of weapons," Hosni told me. "Lots of groups, no unified leadership, internal rivalries." The thorough intimidation of Bethlehem's judicial system was only part of the problem: only fifty of the four hundred policemen in his force possessed weapons, and those were aging Kalashnikovs. Most of the bullets that had been issued had been moldering in storage for two decades. Most important, he soon learned, the al-Aqsa Martyrs Brigades bore the imprimatur of the Palestinian leadership; they had a green light through Kamel Hmeid and Abdullah Daoud to continue the violence. At the once-weekly security meetings held in the muqata, Daoud announced in front of Ala Hosni and the other officials that he would keep providing the al-Aqsa Martyrs Brigades with money, guns, and ammunition regardless of Madani's directives, and he claimed he had support from higher-ups. After one of the periodic cease-fires declared by Arafat, Daoud told the astonished group, "I have instructions not to respect the cease-fire but to escalate the operations."

"I could have crushed [the militias] the first day. But without a political decision to stop the violence, I was powerless," Ala Hosni told me. He and the governor had come to Bethlehem "both expecting that we could control the situation completely," he said. But he soon realized that he had been deceiving himself. "Deep down inside I knew that [Arafat] didn't want to finish this off," Ala Hosni told me. "Arafat said or implied, 'Control it, but do not extinguish it.'" One senior Palestinian official close to both Hosni and Madani described the two men as pawns in a devious game: "I've known Arafat for a long time. He wanted a Kosovo scenario, with massacres and killings that would lead to calls for international intervention and increase the pressure for a Palestinian state. Then he could come back to the Palestinians and say, 'I brought you independence with my rifle.'" In public Madani still maintained that Arafat was on his side. He insisted

that the president was being sabotaged by conniving underlings
or that he had overestimated the power of the Ta'amra and there-
fore was reluctant to challenge them. But in private conversations, Palestinian sources told me, the governor admitted to
being as disillusioned as the police chief was.

IN JANUARY 2002, after a period of quiet ushered in by
Yasser Arafat's mid-December unilateral cease-fire, Madani
found himself tested anew by a crime that became a symbol of
the city's worsening anarchy and the hatreds unleashed by the
intifada. The victim was an American-born Israeli who lived in
Jerusalem, worked in Bethlehem, and for the first fourteen
months of the intifada had managed, despite the violence, to
move easily between worlds. The occasion was one of Madani's
lowest moments as governor—the moment when his authority
unraveled before his eyes.

Mohammed al-Madani had never met Avi Boaz, but he knew
him by reputation. Born in Brooklyn, New York, in 1930, Avi
Boaz studied architecture at Columbia University, joined a Zionist youth movement called Habonim Dror, and immigrated to Israel just after the Six-Day War. But his Zionist ardor soon
dimmed, his daughter, Idit Cohen, told me, and he found himself
drawn to the stark beauty of the West Bank and the warmth of
Palestinian society. In the fall of 1967 he began renting a room on
weekends in a quiet hilltop retreat in Beit Jala called the Everest
Hotel. Boaz spent his days hiking through the area and came to
know the Everest's owner, a Palestinian Christian named Jamal
Arjah. A friendship developed over their shared interest in sports
cars. In 1968 Boaz salvaged a gray twelve-cylinder Ferrari originally owned by King Hussein of Jordan that had been abandoned
in a wadi near Beit Jala when the Israelis seized control of the
area the previous year. Arjah and Boaz repaired the Ferrari and
spent weekends traveling around Israel, one time racing up the
coastal road from Tel Aviv to Haifa at 120 miles per hour. (Boaz

sent the Ferrari to be auctioned at Lloyd's in the early 1970s, but British customs agents spied the Royal Jordanian seal on the car and impounded it.)

Boaz crossed easily between Israeli and Palestinian societies. He married an American Jewish émigré, raised his daughter, Idit, as a Jew, and lived in a series of neighborhoods on the northern outskirts of Jerusalem that had been built on Palestinian land occupied during the Six-Day War. But he learned to speak Arabic far better than Hebrew, started an architectural design firm in Bethlehem, and returned with his wife and daughter often to visit Jamal Arjah and his family in Beit Jala. The bond between the American Israeli and the Palestinian grew stronger: after Jamal's older brother Ja'el Arjah, a militant with the Popular Front for the Liberation of Palestine, hijacked an Air France jetliner filled with Israelis and was killed by commandos at Entebbe Airport in Uganda in 1976, Boaz comforted the distraught Arjah. "Avi didn't consider himself a Jew," said Jamal Arjah's son Bashir. "He didn't consider himself an American. He was just Avi."

Boaz, an impish man with a boyish gap between his teeth and a pronounced limp he'd acquired during a childhood bout with polio, was a man of eclectic tastes. An incorrigible car buff, he often busted his budget importing pricey new vehicles from the United States and Europe; he loved tooling around in his 1996 British Rover convertible. At the height of the intifada he was waiting for delivery from the United States of a new Ford Mustang. He was a voracious reader whose tastes ran from the Talmud to Danielle Steele. He listened to classical music and jazz; a devotee of Frank Lloyd Wright, he incorporated the great architect's stylistic flourishes in his own modest projects in Bethlehem and Beit Jala.

He was also a creature of habit: every morning he rose at seven, combed his hair fastidiously, listened to the English-language news on Israeli Radio, rode a stationary bike for half an hour, ate a bowl of bananas and cold oatmeal, and then set out from his apartment in Ma'ale Adumim to his office in Bethlehem

and building sites around the West Bank. As the violence worsened and few Israelis dared to travel into the Palestinian territories, Boaz's yellow Israeli license plate became increasingly
conspicuous. But he shrugged off his family's concerns. "He
went to places we would never dream of going," Idit told me. "I
told him, 'Don't you know how dangerous these places are?' He
said, 'Nothing will ever happen to me. Everybody likes me.
Everybody knows me. I'm an American.'"

On January 15, 2002, Boaz started the morning with a visit to
the Everest Hotel, which is located at Beit Jala's highest point,
straddling the border with Jerusalem in Israeli-controlled territory. Boaz's wife had died of cancer only ten days earlier, and he
had arranged to move from Ma'ale Adumim, an annexed
Jerusalem neighborhood, to a smaller apartment in the twenty-
year-old hilltop settlement of Har Gilo, a few hundred yards
down the road from the Everest Hotel; the move would bring
him back to the region of hillside olive groves and undeveloped
wadis that he had fallen in love with just after his arrival in Israel
thirty-four years earlier. He and Bashir Arjah, Jamal Arjah's
thirty-one-year-old son, hung a mirror in Boaz's new apartment,
had lunch in the Everest's empty dining room, and then decided
to drive to Bethlehem to buy a table and chairs for Boaz's new
abode.

It was a tense time in the Palestinian territories. Two days earlier a remote-controlled bomb planted in the wall of a Christian
cemetery near his apartment blew to pieces Ra'ed Qarmi, the
charismatic commander of the al-Aqsa Martyrs Brigades in the
northern West Bank town of Tulkarm; the targeted killing by
Israel, which broke the longest lull in the violence since the beginning of the intifada, led to immediate calls by Tanzim factions
across the West Bank for revenge. Despite the threat of violence
against Israelis Bashir Arjah didn't feel any need for caution; Boaz,
he reasoned, was well known and liked in Beit Jala and Bethlehem. "He was one of us," Bashir says. Boaz got behind the wheel
of the Rover, with Bashir Arjah in the back and a friend of Bashir's

who was visiting from Amman sitting next to Boaz. They crossed the Israeli checkpoint into Palestinian-controlled Beit Jala at one o'clock and headed down the hill toward Bethlehem.

They didn't get far. A man with a Kalashnikov was standing in front of the Arab Orthodox Club, a few hundred yards past the checkpoint. He motioned for the Rover to pull over. Arjah thought he might be a policeman.

"Show me your ID," the man with the gun demanded.

"Who are you?" asked Arjah.

"Keep quiet," he replied.

He inspected the documents of the two Palestinians. Then he walked around the car to Boaz. The American, who still traveled with a United States passport, flashed him a friendly smile.

"*Shalom,*" he said. Boaz was just joking, as he often did with Palestinian Authority officials. But Arjah realized that Boaz had made a grievous mistake. The gunman shouted, "*Yehud!*"—Arabic for Jew—and called over several Tanzim lurking nearby. Arjah recognized one of them as Riad al-Amur, one of the late Atef Abayat's top lieutenants and the chief suspect in the shooting death of the female settler Sarit Amrani in September 2001. The armed men surrounded the Rover and one of them asked Boaz, "Do you have a gun?"

"Sure," Boaz replied, still not realizing the gravity of the situation. He extended his cane. "I have a gun right here."

Bashir Arjah tried to calm the militants. He showed them Boaz's blue U.S. passport and his New York State driver's license and explained that Boaz was an American businessman with connections to high officials in the Palestinian Authority. While Arjah was pleading, a jeepload of Naval Police passed by. "Is there something wrong?" one of the policemen asked.

"Get going; there is nothing wrong," one of the gunmen said, and the Naval Police obediently drove away.

One gunman climbed into the car with Boaz, Bashir Arjah, and his friend and ordered the American to drive to the Bethlehem Hotel. Four other cars filled with gun-toting members of the al-Aqsa Martyrs Brigades joined the convoy. Seated next to Boaz, Bashir whispered to him in English to speak no Hebrew and then tried to reason with the gunman, who was sitting in the rear. "Look," he said. "I'm from the Arjah family. We own the Everest Hotel. Let's go to the muqata. Let's go to Preventive Security. They all know me and they all know Avi."

The Tanzim guerrilla snorted derisively. "We'll go to *my* muqata," he replied. Bashir spotted his younger brother Anwar driving down the street in the opposite direction. Bashir waved frantically out the window and called to his brother. The gunman whacked Bashir in the back of his skull with his pistol, and Bashir slumped in the front seat. Boaz began to plead with him. "Please, my daughter will be asking for me," he said. "The police will be looking for me."

"We'll go to my police," the gunman said.

At the Bethlehem Hotel, a modern twelve-story building located at one of the city's busiest intersections, the Tanzim pulled Bashir Arjah and his friend from Boaz's car and at gunpoint forced them into another vehicle. Minutes later the gunmen dropped them on the roadside in Beit Sahour. "Anyone asks you what happened, you say you know nothing, understand?" one gunman said. Bashir nodded. But as soon as the car disappeared around a corner he began phoning his contacts at Preventive Security and Fatah, who passed the report of Boaz's kidnapping to Governor Madani. Madani dialed Arafat. "A crippled Israeli has been seized by the Tanzim in Bethlehem," he said. "Do your best to save the man," Arafat replied. The governor rushed to Kamel Hmeid's office. "What the fuck is going on?" he asked. Hmeid replied that he didn't know.

While Madani tried in vain to gather information about the kidnapping, the chief of the al-Aqsa Martyrs Brigades, Ibrahim Abayat, arrived at the Bethlehem Hotel. Accompanying him was Jihad Ja'ara, a former high-ranking officer with Preventive Security, now one of the al-Aqsa Martyrs Brigades' most ruthless killers. A compact figure with tousled black hair and a gap between his lower teeth, Ja'ara had joined the Tanzim thirteen months earlier, he later told me, after witnessing a checkpoint clash in Jericho in which Israeli soldiers shot several Palestinian youths dead. Ja'ara's Preventive Security unit had standing orders not to interfere in such clashes. But taunted by an eight-year-old boy, he told me, Ja'ara spontaneously opened fire on Israeli soldiers at the checkpoint, shooting one of them dead and injuring two others. Then he went into hiding, going first to Ramallah and arriving in April 2001 in Bethlehem, where he joined Atef Abayat's militia. In retaliation for Ra'ed Qarmi's assassination, he had decided to execute one Israeli; he had ordered that a trap be laid for Avi Boaz, who, he knew, worked in Bethlehem. "He was an Israeli, a Jew," Ja'ara told me. "He worked for Israeli intelligence and enlisted people to become collaborators."

Ibrahim Abayat objected to Ja'ara's plan; he thought that shooting a seventy-two-year-old polio victim who was a popular figure in Bethlehem would serve no purpose and would possibly harm the Tanzim's interests. Abayat pleaded with Ja'ara not to harm Boaz, but Abayat had never been able to command his forces with the same authority that his predecessor Atef had exerted, and Ja'ara ignored him. "This is not your business," Ja'ara replied. Ja'ara, Riad al-Amur, and a third gunman named Ismail Abayat commandeered the Rover, placed Boaz in the front passenger seat, and dropped Ibrahim Abayat in front of Kamel Hmeid's office. The Rover wound east toward Beit Sahour, following the edge of a barren wadi that was now vibrantly green from the winter rains.

Boaz was visibly frightened now. "Don't be afraid," Ja'ara, the driver, told him. "Nothing is going to happen to you." Ja'ara questioned Boaz about his relationship with the Shin Bet, the Israeli domestic intelligence service. Boaz denied having any connection to the agency. The Tanzim asked him if he owned property in Har Homa, the Jewish settlement still under construction on a West Bank hilltop just north of Beit Sahour and clearly visible from the car. Boaz, Ja'ara told me later, admitted to owning property there. "You're hurting the Palestinian people," Ja'ara said he told him. The car sped unhindered through a Palestinian Authority checkpoint—the cops manning the post later claimed they never saw the car carrying Boaz—and descended a steep path to a soccer field. Ja'ara stepped out of the car. He and the two other Tanzim with Boaz had already decided what they would do next. "Riad al-Amur and I walked ahead to the field," Ja'ara told me. "Ismail Abayat [a distant cousin of Ibrahim Abayat] got out and started walking too. Avi Boaz slid behind the wheel of the Rover and began to drive away. Then Riad raised his M-16 and sprayed his windshield with bullets." Avi Boaz was killed instantly; Palestinian police would later count nineteen bullet holes in the dead man's windshield.

Minutes later Madani learned that police had discovered Avi Boaz's bullet-riddled body in his car in Beit Sahour. Ala Hosni, the chief of police, who had spotted Ibrahim Abayat and Jihad Ja'ara in the Rover convertible fifteen minutes before Boaz's death—he hadn't realized Boaz was a prisoner in the car with them—now summoned the two Tanzim to his office in the Bethlehem Peace Center for questioning. Hosni was seated at his desk, eating a chicken and rice lunch, when Ibrahim Abayat and Jihad Ja'ara swaggered through his door. The two men helped themselves to bits of the police chief's meal.

"Did you kill Avi Boaz?" Ala Hosni asked them.

Ibrahim Abayat denied knowing anything about the murder, then turned around brusquely and walked with Ja'ara out the door.

THE PALESTINIAN Authority never arrested anybody for Avi Boaz's murder. Ala Hosni told me that the lack of forensic evidence, the power of the Tanzim, and resistance from the General Intelligence Apparatus made it impossible to pursue the case. Besides, a new crisis soon overwhelmed the governor and his allies. In the week leading up to Saint Valentine's Day 2002, Madani made a personal plea to the owners of Bethlehem's party halls and restaurants, asking them to open their doors for the occasion to the city's young couples. The city might be awash in violence, Madani argued, but it was important to demonstrate to the Tanzim that they could not disrupt normal civil life in Bethlehem. It was a well-meant but futile gesture. On Saint Valentine's Day Ibrahim Abayat and his Tanzim cruised around the city in jeeps, firing their guns in the air and threatening to attack any hall that remained open that evening; celebrations were inappropriate, they said, while the Israeli army was killing Palestinians every day. The terrified owners canceled all of the parties they had scheduled at the governor's urging. Enraged, the governor took to the airwaves as he often did in his running battle with the Tanzim, condemning Ibrahim Abayat and his men as cowards who were "trying to destroy our civil society."

Shortly after the governor's TV appearance, Ibrahim Abayat and forty gunmen paid a visit to the governor in his temporary office in the Peace Center. Pushing past a delegation of Italian peace activists, the Tanzim accosted Madani at his desk. Abayat brandished his M-16. "We are not cowards," he said. "We are fighters."

"Then you should be preparing for battle in a different way," Madani said calmly. "This is leading us nowhere."

"That is for us to decide," Ibrahim Abayat replied. "Not you." Abayat walked out of the room, followed by his entourage. Later that day, as the governor left the Peace Center for an appointment in Bethlehem's Old City, a soldier from the National Security Force approached him and suggested he escort Madani. The governor refused to depart from his long-standing policy of not being followed by bodyguards. "No thanks," the governor said. "I prefer to walk alone."

TWO WEEKS LATER I met Samir Zedan at the Saint George Restaurant in Manger Square for an interview with the Tanzim leader who had the entire city of Bethlehem in his grip. The restaurant was deserted, and the waiters hovered nervously by the entrance, waiting for Ibrahim Abayat to arrive. At one thirty in the afternoon five bodyguards bristling with weaponry, cellular phones, and two-way radios burst into the restaurant and took up positions by the door. Then five minutes later Abayat strode theatrically into the room, an M-16 rifle slung over his shoulder. He was a mesmerizing presence. A slim man with a military haircut and several days' growth of beard stubble, he wore a black leather bomber jacket, dungarees, brown leather boots, and a belt buckle that bore the insignia "U.S. Marine Corps." Abayat was sullenly handsome with fierce, glaring eyes. The guerrilla chief gave me a brisk handshake and sat down at the table, diving into the plates of hummus and tabouli that the Saint George staff had prepared for him. He chain-smoked L&Ms, barked orders over four mobile phones, fidgeted in his chair, and ate as if he hadn't had a meal in days. At one point when Tanzim scouts on the streets sent word via MIRS that Israeli helicopters were circling the city, Abayat dropped his silverware and ran outside for a look. Returning to the table, the al-Aqsa Martyrs Brigades commander told me that he kept a team of spotters posted around the city whose job was to watch for signs of imminent Israeli attack. "I'm on alert twenty-four hours a day," Abayat told me, scooping up a piece of lamb with a wedge of hot pita bread.

At the time of our meeting I was only partly aware of Ibrahim Abayat's life story—the honor killing of his first cousin, his trial and the aftermath, his narrow escape from the Israeli missile attack that killed Hussein Abayat, the death of his cousin Atef Abayat, the murder of Avi Boaz. But I could sense just from a few minutes in his company that he had a capacity for explosive violence: the intensity of his stare, the way he casually flicked his cigarettes on the floor, the nervous fidgeting all were deeply unnerving. Beside him sat Rami Kamel, Ibrahim's one-armed lieutenant and close friend, whose maimed, brooding presence seemed to heighten the sense of danger. Two weeks before our meeting, Abayat told me, Israeli soldiers had captured one of his

Tanzim underlings at a military checkpoint and sent him back to Abayat with a message: "You're next on our list."

Ibrahim Abayat freely admitted that his gang had staked out the nearby settlement of Efrat the previous week and on March 5—the day before our interview—had shot dead forty-five-year-old Devorah Friedman and injured her husband as they drove toward Jerusalem on the Bethlehem bypass tunnel road. "None of Sharon's operations can deter us," he boasted. "If we die, we are martyrs. And if we succeed, it's another nail in the coffin of the Israeli occupation." Moments later his Tanzim scouts contacted him again; an Apache helicopter, they told him, was hovering above Manger Square. I felt a surge of panic. Would the Israelis, I wondered, actually fire on the restaurant if they knew that the Tanzim leader was inside it? At that moment Ibrahim Abayat picked up his rifle, motioned to his bodyguards, and they all rushed out of the restaurant together.

IN THE WEEKS AFTER my first meeting with the Fatah guerrilla leader, Bethlehem seemed to be edging closer to all-out war. The crisis was not solely the work of Ibrahim Abayat and his gunmen. Ahmed Mughrabi, the twenty-seven-year-old commander of the al-Aqsa Martyrs Brigades in Deheishe camp, had—over Abayat's objections—escalated his operations from conducting guerrilla attacks in the territories to organizing suicide bombings across the Green Line, the informal administrative boundary that separates Israel from the West Bank. In early March a nineteen-year-old from Deheishe blew himself up at the entrance to an ultraorthodox yeshiva in the Beit Israel neighborhood of Jerusalem, killing ten Israelis, including five children. Palestinian intelligence agents working inside the camp had followed the Deheishe cell's planning, Madani told me, but had failed to intervene to stop the bombing, and had kept the governor completely in the dark. In response to the attack the Israeli army invaded the town's two largest refugee camps, Aida and

Deheishe, rounding up suspected militants and killing seven people. Then Ariel Sharon sent F-16 warplanes screaming over Bethlehem for four consecutive nights, flattening Palestinian security headquarters, the muqata, in a series of missile strikes—a signal to Arafat and the Palestinian Authority that Israel held them directly responsible for the violence.

The morning after the first attack, on March 8, I arrived in Bethlehem to find Governor Madani standing on the Hebron Road, gazing at the huge pile of collapsed concrete that used to be security headquarters. Wisps of smoke still rose from the remains of the two pancaked floors. A slab of what had been the roof teetered on its side, and charred bits of official documents papered the street like confetti. Madani had driven down to the wreckage at eight o'clock the night before, just after the first missile hit, and had been awake ever since, evacuating surrounding buildings and paying a condolence call on the family of a Palestinian watchman who'd been killed in the attack. "This is stupidity, a shortsighted policy," he was telling a small group of journalists and PA officials. "What's it going to accomplish?"

For four days Israeli tanks sealed off the entrances to the refugee camps, conducted house-to-house searches for Ahmed Mughrabi and his fellow cell members, and held positions throughout the city. Manger Square remained a safe haven for the gunmen, however, and dozens of Tanzim strutted about with their pistols and rifles. I spotted Ibrahim Abayat at the wheel of a silver Toyota Corolla. Looking suave in a black beret, he wasn't in the mood for a lengthy chat. "I've been on the run for the last couple of days," he told me, taking a deep drag on a cigarette. I asked Abayat whether he felt safe in Manger Square, and he assured me that there was no more secure place in Bethlehem. "The Israelis know that they can't come in here," Abayat said. "There are lots of alleyways and corners and rooftops where our guys can ambush them. Second, this is one of the holy Christian sites. It would be a propaganda defeat if they came in and shot it up."

*   *   *

After the destruction of the muqata most of the security forces disappeared off the streets, and in the vacuum they left behind, the Tanzim operated with impunity. At eight o'clock in the morning on March 14 I received a frantic call from Samir Zedan urging me to drive back to Bethlehem as soon as possible. Tanzim gunmen had seized two collaborators from jail and shot them to death on a street in Beit Sahour early that morning; at that very moment, Zedan told me, the gunmen were dragging the corpses through Bethlehem, intent on hanging them in Manger Square. One victim was Mohammed Deifallah, the convicted collaborator whom Madani had saved at the muqata five months earlier. The other was Mahmoud Sabatin, a middleman in the delivery of the booby-trapped Pajero to Atef Abayat. The man behind the lynchings was almost certainly Ibrahim Abayat.

An hour later Zedan and I drove down Wad al-Sawahra Street to the execution site in Beit Sahour. A witness who had watched the scene unfold from her second-floor window told me that two jeeploads of Tanzim had pulled up at two o'clock in the morning and hauled the two terrified prisoners onto the street. The Tanzim had chosen to carry out their act of vigilante justice at the very spot where Atef Abayat had died in the booby-trapped jeep five months earlier. "They stood them against the wall and made them repeat, 'There is no other God but God,'" the witness said. "Then they killed them with bursts of gunfire and hacked them with axes." Blood and bits of brain matter were splattered across the wall. The killers left the corpses where they lay but returned at seven o'clock that morning, she told us, tied the bodies by their ankles to the back of a jeep, and dragged them to Manger Square. When we arrived at the square, there was no sign of the murdered men. I later learned that Ala Hosni and a small contingent of his police had stood down the gunmen and prevented them from dangling what was left of Mohammed Deifallah and Mahmoud Sabatin from the clock that sits atop the three-story Bethlehem Shopping Center, in full view of the Church of the Nativity.

I found Madani later that morning in a crisis room he had set up inside the Peace Center. Surrounded by grim-faced security men, the governor looked exhausted; his hooded eyes were narrowed in rage and frustration. A few days earlier, it turned out, Governor Madani had presciently ordered his police to transfer the prisoners from the muqata to a secret jail cell, fearing that Israeli missiles would demolish the security headquarters. But intelligence agents had given away the location of the prisoners to the al-Aqsa Martyrs Brigades, and in the chaos of the latest Israeli incursion, the Tanzim had decided to exact their revenge. "Fifty people came to the jail, held guns to the heads of the police, and took the prisoners away. What could they do?" Madani asked, throwing up his hands. "There's no way we can execute the law with what's going on here. End the Israeli occupation. Give me some authority. Then I'll arrest the members of this lynch mob one by one." Madani was trying to use the few shreds of power he had left to find a burial place for the dead men, but even that was proving difficult. Just at that moment the phone rang: it was Dr. Peter Qumri, director of al-Hussein Hospital in Beit Jala, reporting that an angry crowd was threatening to burn down the building if the director admitted the corpses of the collaborators to the morgue. Procedure called for them to be autopsied and given death certificates there before they could be buried.

"The bodies are sitting in the parking lot," Qumri said. "I refused to let them through the door. The mob has cans of gasoline, and I think they mean business. What do you suggest that I do?"

"For the sake of human decency these bodies must be admitted," Madani said. "We are still the law. The mob is not the law."

These were empty words. Later that day as the standoff at al-Hussein Hospital continued, Madani ordered the police to bury the corpses secretly in the Islamic cemetery behind Rachel's Tomb. But the word leaked out, and when vigilantes from Aida refugee camp attacked the truck carrying the bodies, the police dumped them in the street and fled. Another police squad returned the corpses to the al-Hussein Hospital; the staff placed them in a boiler room. Mahmoud Sabatin's father finally claimed his son's remains the next day and received a *fatwa,* or religious decree, from the mufti of Jerusalem permitting him to bury his son in an Islamic grave. Mohammed Deifallah, who had already been convicted by a Palestinian Authority court and sentenced to execution by firing squad, remained a pariah in death. His corpse moldered in the hospital for three days while his mother and siblings tried without success to find a cemetery that would accept him. Madani finally paid a bulldozer crew one thousand shekels, or $220, to dig a hole in the earth in a junkyard in the village of Irtas and had Mohammed Deifallah interred in a secret grave in the middle of the night. "I can't tell you where he is," the governor told Deifallah's mother, "but trust me that your son is resting in peace." At least, Madani thought, somebody is.

THE CELL

৩৫৩

ON CHRISTMAS DAY 2001, AHMED MUGHRABI GOT married in a huge outdoor festival in Deheishe camp. After months of living underground, the chief of Deheishe's al-Aqsa Martyrs Brigades had decided to venture into the open for the celebration, reasoning that the Israeli troops ringing the city would not dare to mount an operation during the birthday of Jesus Christ. First came a photo session with his twenty-two-year-old bride-to-be, Hanadi Hammash, in the lush gardens of the French Hospital in Bethlehem. Then he and Hanadi, along with a wedding procession of hundreds of friends and neighbors, walked uphill through the warrens of the camp for an afternoon party at the Mughrabi home. The group sang Palestinian nationalist songs and danced exuberantly in the streets, but Mughrabi remained on edge during the procession. As they neared the top of the hill, a long line of Merkava tanks came into view at an Israeli military base on the ridge across the valley. Mughrabi called out a warning, and the men and boys who had been carrying him on their shoulders lowered him to the ground, then formed a protective cordon around him until they arrived at the house.

Wanted by the Israelis for shooting attacks against soldiers and settlers in the West Bank, Mughrabi was about to transform himself into something much more dangerous: the head of a clandestine cell that would dispatch six teenaged suicide bombers into Israel between January and May 2002 to kill eighteen Israelis, including ten in the single attack in the Beit Israel neighborhood of Jerusalem. One bomber was an eighteen-year-old female honors student named Ayat al-Akhras, whose deadly act four days before the Israeli invasion of Bethlehem on April 2 would symbolize to the world the lethal rage sweeping all strata of Palestinian society. If Ayat al-Akhras was the public face of martyrdom—her image splashed on magazine covers, her deed celebrated in the Arabic press and singled out in a press conference by U.S. President George W. Bush—then Mughrabi represented martyrdom's subterranean side. Lurking in the shadows, hidden from the outside world, Mughrabi was the master orchestrator. Driven by personal loss and religious conviction, he seemed to enjoy playing God—building bombs, recruiting volunteers, planning attacks, and saluting the bombers afterward with gunfire in the alleys of Deheishe. Mughrabi picked his bombers only after a series of lengthy face-to-face interviews, a twisted version of the process that Ayat al-Akhras was planning to undergo to gain acceptance to Bethlehem University for the fall of 2002.

AHMED MUGHRABI'S transformation into suicide cell leader was a slow and inexorable process, a lethal melding of personality and political circumstance. Probably it began long before the al-Aqsa intifada—in the bomb shelter of the Sidon refugee camp in Lebanon, in the desolate Third World military camps where he had spent his formative years. But it accelerated with his younger sibling Mahmoud's death at the hands of Israeli troops in December 2000. Ahmed insisted his brother had been executed, and from that point, family members told me, he was consumed by a single motivating impulse: revenge against Israel. During the first winter of the al-Aqsa intifada, the then–twenty-six-year-old construction worker lost his job on the Jericho cable car project and began preparing for war. He procured a dozen M-16 rifles from Atef Abayat and distributed them to a small circle of friends and neighbors in Deheishe camp.

Mughrabi's most important accomplice was a figure with long experience in the Palestinian struggle: Yihya Ibrahim Daamsa, a forty-year-old Deheishe explosives engineer who had met Mughrabi through a mutual acquaintance in the Palestinian intelligence division just days before Mahmoud's death. Technically sophisticated and endlessly inventive, Daamsa had been incarcerated in an Israeli prison between 1985 and 1994 for producing bombs for the General Command, a Syrian-backed breakaway faction of the Popular Front for the Liberation of Palestine that remained committed to the destruction of Israel. At the start of the second intifada Daamsa manufactured explosives for Mughrabi from fire extinguishers, propane gas canisters, and lead pipes. Ahmed Mughrabi and his cell planted devices on roads around Bethlehem, targeting settlers and military convoys. Daamsa also designed belt bombs, which were initially intended for use by Tanzim to blow themselves up if captured by the Israeli army. Mughrabi would soon put these devices to far deadlier employment.

Ahmed reembraced the life of prayer and regular fasting that he'd taken on before the intifada, and to that ascetic regimen he added a deadly new sense of purpose. Ahmed Mughrabi's wife, Hanadi, first encountered Ahmed during the Muslim festival of Eid al-Adha in March 2001, at a reception at his home in honor of his parents, who had just returned from the haj, the pilgrimage to Mecca. When she walked into the room, Ahmed was engaged in an impassioned argument with a woman whose son had died at Rachel's Tomb. "We don't need any more killing," the mother of the shaheed was saying. "We've had enough." "On the contrary," Ahmed replied, "this land deserves many more martyrs." A few weeks later Ahmed asked Hanadi to marry him, warning her that he was high on Israel's wanted list and considered himself "a shaheed with a suspended sentence." The tall, handsome guerrilla commander mesmerized Hanadi. She accepted his marriage proposal and assured him that the likelihood of his arrest or killing by Israel was of little consequence to her. "Neither of us can guarantee that we'll be alive or dead tomorrow," she said. "It is in the hands of God."

After their engagement Ahmed moved secretly into Hanadi's family's home and spent the six months before their marriage dividing his time between bloody encounters with the Israelis at clash points in and around Bethlehem and quiet domestic interludes with his fiancée and her parents. Two nights after Atef Abayat's killing and one night after the Israeli incursion into Bethlehem, Hanadi's future husband came staggering back to the house. He was bleeding heavily from bullet wounds in his pelvis and thigh received in a shootout with the Israeli army outside the Bethlehem Cinema. Hanadi brought him to the al-Hussein Hospital, where he underwent surgery, but the injuries plagued him and left him with a slight limp. "I never said to him, 'Where are you going? What are you doing?'" she told me. "It wasn't my place to ask. But when I saw him exhausted, I tried to make him forget his troubles."

Mughrabi's wedding was a brief diversion from the course of violence and isolation that he'd set out for himself. Seven hundred people turned out for the party on December 25, 2001. Although Deheishe residents still regarded the Mughrabi family as newcomers to the camp, the death of Mahmoud one year before had conferred upon them instant respect; everybody wanted to be part of their celebration. Among the invited guests was Ayat al-Akhras, a strikingly beautiful, green-eyed senior at the Irtas Secondary School. Ayat came to the wedding with her parents; her twenty-three-year-old brother Samir al-Akhras, who had employed Mahmoud as a tiler in his small construction company; and her older sister Zainat, who would later become engaged to Ahmed Mughrabi's younger brother Mohammed. "We wanted to help change the atmosphere of grief in the house," Ayat's mother later told me. "The father and mother were crying, still thinking about Mahmoud. It was a way of consoling them, of telling his mother, who had not lived here very long, 'You are one of us now.'" The affair was more conservative than most weddings inside Deheishe, reflecting the deep Islamic faith of Ahmed and his parents: the men and boys drank soda and juice and ate baklava and other Middle Eastern sweets on the bottom floor of the house, spilling into the street to dance with one another when the music began. The girls and women remained on the second floor, cut off from all contact with the males. Ayat al-Akhras, her older sister, and their mother stayed for only half an hour, just long enough to dance and congratulate Hanadi, who looked radiant in a borrowed white wedding dress; in the company of women Hanadi had lifted up the thick white wedding veil that she kept draped over her face whenever she was in the presence of men. During a break in the music, the bridegroom came into the room for a brief visit with his bride, shyly avoiding eye contact with the other women.

The last guests left at seven o'clock, and the immediate families of the bride and groom gathered for a post-wedding meal. As they sat down to eat, Hanadi recalled, they heard the whirring of helicopter blades. Rushing to the window, Yusuf Mughrabi, Ahmed's father, spied an Israeli Apache gunship hovering in the wadi three hundred yards from his house. "Take your bride and leave," he ordered. Friends ushered Ahmed and Hanadi, still wearing her wedding dress, into two separate cars and drove them into the darkness, following back roads to the Bethlehem Hotel. Ahmed and Hanadi registered there under assumed names. The newlyweds had planned to move into a rented flat immediately after their marriage, but Ahmed's fear of collaborators and of an Israeli incursion made it impossible to keep a fixed address. "We were always on the move, sleeping at friends' houses, my family's house, and other safe houses," Hanadi said. "It was like being in a war."

AS AHMED MUGHRABI began his new life as a married man, conditions in the Occupied Territories were deteriorating. From Bethlehem to Hebron, from Jenin to the Gaza Strip, the collapse of several cease-fires, the tightening of closure, and an escalation of

Israeli military incursions and targeted killings of Palestinian militants had deepened the mood of despair. Many Palestinians had cheered a succession of suicide bomb attacks carried out by Hamas and Islamic Jihad militants—including the Sbarro pizzeria blast in central Jerusalem in August 2001 that killed sixteen, among them five infants, and a Haifa bus bombing that killed fifteen in December 2001. Increasing numbers of Palestinians regarded such lethal acts as a legitimate means of evening the score, of inflicting pain against a much more powerful enemy. Palestinian polls during this period found that 78 percent of the population in the West Bank and Gaza supported suicide bombings, a far greater percentage than those who backed the peace process.

That winter the nature of the attacks changed. Islamic fundamentalists, young zealots drawn to martyrdom by visions of everlasting bliss in the afterlife, had carried out all of the suicide bombings during the first year of the al-Aqsa intifada. But as the violence in the territories worsened, the lure of—and opportunity for—martyrdom spread beyond the closed circles of the Islamic groups to the Palestinian mainstream. The relentless rhapsodizing about martyrs in the Arab press and in schools, as well as the gory images of intifada violence bombarding Palestinians over the al-Manar television network, owned by the Lebanese Shi'ite guerrilla group Hezbollah, and other stations, carried a deadly contagion through Palestinian society. Both boys and girls as young as eight spoke openly of becoming human bombs. "It became a kind of wish at school to go and conduct suicide operations," said Shuruq Awwad, a high school student from Deheishe camp and the best friend of Ayat al-Akhras. "This is revenge for the martyrs, for those who have died."

Many militants of the al-Aqsa Martyrs Brigades, the offshoot of Yasser Arafat's secular Fatah movement, had grown impatient with low-level guerrilla warfare and viewed the body counts being racked up by Hamas and Islamic Jihad with mounting envy. The al-Aqsa Martyrs Brigades executed their first suicide bombing in December 2001. Ten more would follow in the next three months. Though their political aims were different, the al-Aqsa intifada had united all of the militant groups around an immediate goal: to kill and maim as many Israelis as possible and demoralize Israeli society. The flood of volunteers made the work of the recruiters much easier. The indoctrination process once involved months of prayer, study of the Quran, addressing one's fear of death by lying in shallow graves, and systematic dehumanization of the enemy. Now in many cases the preparation time was cut down to weeks or even days.

The Tanzim even started a unit for female recruits. Hamas and Islamic Jihad operatives refused to accept women as suicide bombers, citing the Quran's prohibition on an Islamic woman's traveling outside her home without her *makram*—her husband, brother, or father. Sheik Ahmed Yassin, the spiritual leader of Hamas, cautioned several times that under Islamic law women should not carry out suicide operations as long as men remained available for such work. But the secular Fatah movement had no such prohibitions. Wafa Idriss, a divorced twenty-eight-year-old ambulance worker from a Ramallah refugee camp, became the first female shaheeda, blowing herself up at the crowded intersection of Jaffa and King George streets in central Jerusalem on January 28 and killing an eighty-year-old Jewish man. The Arab press idolized her. "The body of Wafa became shrapnel that eliminated despair and aroused hope," a writer in a popular Cairo newspaper proclaimed. Dareen Abu Ayish, a student at al-Najah University in Nablus, who was considered brilliant by her classmates, tried in vain to join Hamas early in 2002. After Hamas rejected her, she signed up with the al-Aqsa Martyrs Brigades and detonated her explosive belt at a checkpoint near the Jerusalem suburb of Modi'in in February of that year, killing herself and injuring five people.

Ahmed Mughrabi discussed with Hanadi the importance of women in the armed struggle against Israel. "Ahmed said that Palestine needs both men and women for jihad," she told me. Both agreed that women should encourage their men to be fighters and raise their children with a strong commitment to the

Palestinian cause—and, in the right circumstances, be ready to sacrifice their own lives. In this respect Ahmed's allegiance to the secular Fatah movement trumped his Islamic beliefs. Ahmed stated that women could be a powerful asset in the struggle: they could slip into Israel with far more ease than Palestinian males and insinuate themselves into crowds without drawing attention. The downside, he told Hanadi, was that if the Israeli army or police arrested them, they would be more susceptible to torture than men and would put the other members of the cell at risk. He also claimed to be concerned that if the Israelis arrested the female suicide bomber before she carried out her act, other Palestinians would consider her to be damaged goods, and she would be unable to find a husband in the event of her release from prison. "A woman in Palestinian society is like a piece of glass. She must not have a scratch on her," explained Hanadi. "If she is arrested, she is scratched forever. If she dies, then she ascends to heaven."

AYAT AL-AKHRAS grew up hearing stories about Israeli aggression and Palestinian flight. Both her parents were raised in the Majazi refugee camp in Gaza, to which they had fled with their parents from villages near Tel Aviv in 1948. After Israel occupied Gaza in 1967, they migrated separately to Deheishe, met up again while both were employed at the Mount of David Hospital in Bethlehem, and were married in 1970. Mohammed al-Akhras found a job working for an Israeli construction firm at the Jewish settlement of Betar Ilit, building houses for Jews as they secured their grip on the Palestinian territories. He built himself a four-story concrete house in an alley in the heart of Deheishe, and there raised his eleven children, four boys and seven girls, alongside hundreds of other families of the Palestinian dispossessed. Some residents of the refugee camp took a dim view of his working for the Israelis, but in a destitute community where 75 percent of the men have no regular work, they also recognized that his first priority was to take care of the needs of his family.

Ayat al-Akhras, the couple's third daughter, was a small child when the first intifada roiled through Deheishe between 1987 and 1991, but the violent upheaval touched her life. Mohammed al-Akhras's oldest son, Samir, was arrested twice and served a total of a year in jail for throwing rocks at Israeli troops. An Israeli soldier shot in the spine and paralyzed Ayat al-Akhras's first cousin, a militant with the Popular Front for the Liberation of Palestine. Like most other children in Deheishe, Ayat grew up believing Palestinians were victims, deprived of their rightful inheritance by the hated Zionists. "From water to water, it is all Palestine," her father, Mohammed, told me. "We do not deny Christians and Jews the right to live in Palestine, but all of these people from Russia, Poland, should go back to their places of origin. Even if we have to wait one thousand years, a generation will rise up to liberate Palestine."

Ayat received similar messages in the all-girls schools she attended, first a United Nations–administered institution in Deheishe camp and then, for the last three years of her life, a government-run school in Irtas. Six mornings a week she woke up at six thirty, prayed in her room, donned her green-and-white uniform, complete with white hejab, and either walked or took the public bus down the Hebron Road to the Irtas Secondary School, a hulking stone structure in which six hundred female students were enrolled. She distinguished herself among her peers: in her senior year, Ayat maintained an average grade of 86 percent, among the highest in her class, and aspired to attend Bethlehem University and become a journalist so that, her mother told me, "she could tell the world about Palestinian suffering." "Everyone at school was jealous of Ayat," her best friend, Shuruq Awwad, told me. "She was the most beautiful one in the class, with high manners and beautiful clothing and straight As."

But her standout scholarship did not accord her any special independence at home. As an unmarried girl in a traditional Muslim family, Ayat lived a life as carefully circumscribed as that of most girls in Deheishe camp. Ayat's mother expected her to return home immediately after classes finished at one thirty in the afternoon. When she ventured beyond the boundaries of home and school, her mother ordinarily served as chaperone: Imm Samir even forbade Ayat to shop for clothing alone in the souk. "I didn't want her meeting strangers," her mother explained. "And we do not appreciate the behavior of the young men in the souk." The family kept two salons, one for men and boys and one for women and girls, and Ayat was discouraged from venturing across the hall to show herself to guests of the opposite sex, even her first cousins. Casual discussions about men, except for the fictional characters they observed on television soap operas, were considered taboo for Ayat and her unmarried sisters. She spent Friday, the Muslim holiday, shut up indoors, preparing family meals—fried aubergines, tomatoes, and potatoes were her favorite dishes—and, during pleasant weather, socializing on the roof with her sisters and brothers. She rarely left Bethlehem, except for a school trip before the intifada to Haifa, Akko, and Ben Gurion Airport, and to visit the al-Aqsa Mosque for Friday prayers during Ramadan with her mother. Those pilgrimages were the times that she enjoyed most, her mother told me, and she insisted on going to pray at Haram al-Sharif even when the outbreak of the al-Aqsa intifada made traveling by bus across the checkpoint impossible and forced them to sneak around Israeli military posts and cross fields into Jerusalem.

Ayat's engagement, which took place just after Ramadan in 2000, when she was sixteen, followed the strict guidelines of a traditional Muslim courtship. Shadi Abu Laban, who worked as a tiler for her brother Samir, had taken notice of Ayat while playing cards at the al-Akhras home. He expressed interest in her, the parents of both sides became acquainted, the subject of marriage was raised, and Ayat told her parents that she liked what she had seen of Shadi but she would defer to their judgment. "You know him better than I do. You make the decision. Ask more about him. Ask my brothers," she told her mother. Her mother told her, "He's a religious boy, well mannered, but now what do you think?" Ayat replied, "I agree." Then came the *jaha,* the formal engagement, in which the extended families of both parties gathered in the al-Akhras home to finalize the terms of the contract. Ayat remained upstairs with the women of the clan. Downstairs the oldest male member of Shadi's family, an eighty-year-old great-uncle named Abu Sahid, made the formal proposal to Ayat's father, who in turn laid forth the conditions that Shadi would have to meet to take the hand of Ayat. In this case they included a copy of the Quran in lieu of money, a pledge that the groom would provide Ayat with clothing and gold jewelry, plus the promise of five thousand Jordanian dinars ($7,500) "compensation" in the event of a divorce. In a sign of independent-mindedness that set her apart from many other girls in the camp, Ayat had also made it clear that she would not consummate her marriage to Shadi Abu Laban and move into his family's house until she had finished her *tawhije,* her high school final exams, and unless she could continue her education at Bethlehem University. Ayat's father read the opening verses of the Quran. Then, after consuming chocolate, baklava, and coffee, the men poured out into the street, firing guns in the air in celebration. Shadi went upstairs to exchange gold wedding rings with the bride. Thereafter Shadi was welcomed into the al-Akhras family, visiting Ayat almost every evening—always under the close supervision of her parents. "We follow our Quran, which says that when a man and a woman are together in a room alone, the third person will be the devil," her father told me.

The devil was lurking a few blocks away. When the intifada erupted in September 2000, Ayat spent hours glued to graphic imagery of bullet-riddled children from the intifada that aired on al-Jazeera and al-Manar TV. "She was always the most outspoken one in the family about it," her mother told me. "She said, 'We Palestinians cannot be weak. We have to fight back.'" Soon the violence touched her family: she was horrified when three cousins, all members of Hamas, were killed in the Gaza Strip—a place that Ayat and her immediate family, lacking permits, remained unable to visit. Then Israeli troops shot and lightly wounded her oldest brother, Samir, near the settlers' bypass road; the family insists he was just an innocent bystander near an operation being carried out by Tanzim guerrillas. Like most people in Deheishe, the family was sympathetic to the militants who attacked settlers and soldiers in the territories—even though Abu Samir kept excellent relations with his Israeli bosses and commuted daily to the settlement of Betar Ilit. The apparent execution of Mahmoud Mughrabi by Israeli troops in December 2000 deeply affected the whole family, Ayat's mother told me. Samir and Mahmoud had been exceptionally close, and Ayat had met Mahmoud several times as well, despite the prohibitions her parents placed on her conversing with men outside the family. In the months that followed Mahmoud's killing, the eldest al-Akhras boy visited Yusuf Mughrabi several times to console him. "The death of Mahmoud brought our families together," Mahmoud Mughrabi's mother told me. The al-Akhras family paid a condolence call on the Mughrabi family and hung a life-sized poster of the militant on their living room wall. "I made the frame myself," Ayat's mother told me proudly.

ACCORDING TO AHMED Mughrabi's confession to Israeli intelligence officers, he and Yihya Daamsa collaborated on their first suicide operation on January 22, 2002: an attempted bombing of a southern Jerusalem shopping mall by a Deheishe teenager that was aborted due to a malfunction of the detonator. Six weeks later, on March 2, Ahmed handed a belt bomb to a nineteen-year-old Deheishe camp resident named Mohammed Daragmeh. The teenager crossed unnoticed into Jerusalem and positioned himself next to a group of women with baby carriages who were waiting for their husbands to leave a bar mitzvah ceremony in the religious neighborhood of Beit Israel. In the blast that followed, Daragmeh killed himself and ten Israelis, including five children, and injured more than fifty. As word spread about the attack, the streets of Deheishe camp erupted in exultation. Militants drove through the alleys in pickup trucks and gave out hundreds of tires, which the shehab doused with gasoline and set alight. The fiery celebrations marked Ahmed Mughrabi's coming-out party. "Ahmed Mughrabi bought chocolates and handed them out in Deheishe, basically proclaiming, 'I am the guy,'" Palestinian journalist Nasser Laham, a Deheishe resident, told me. "He told me, 'We need heroes. If nobody is in the open, there will be nobody to lead us.'"

Ahmed Mughrabi slipped out of Deheishe with the rest of his fighters days later as the Israelis prepared to invade the camp. Returning as soon as the Israeli Defense Forces withdrew from Deheishe, he cast about for new volunteers. A cell of devoted followers, including his youngest brother, Ali Mughrabi, then fifteen years old, assisted him. "Ali's hatred of the Israelis increased after Mahmoud's death, and he was willing to compromise himself," his brother Omar Mughrabi told me. "He had been a strong science student, but he stopped studying. From then on he never talked about his activities." The suicide cell made little effort to hide their preparations. "Neighbors called me and said, 'Come see what they're doing,'" Laham told me. "I went to a house in Deheishe and I saw white [acetone and phosphate] explosive material laid out to dry like dough on the floor. I said to Ahmed Mughrabi, 'Don't do this,' and he said, 'They are killing our people every day.'" Chris Bandak turned over his house near the Church of the Nativity to Mughrabi, Daamsa, and their cell for the manufacture of bombs. He told me that by that point he had become so deeply enmeshed in the al-Aqsa Martyrs Brigades that he couldn't refuse their demands, even though, he assured me, he opposed attacks on Israeli civilians inside the Green Line and recognized the potential consequences of abetting the bombers. Mohammed Laham, the longtime Fatah godfather and director of the Deheishe Popular Committee, confronted the al-Aqsa Martyrs Brigades leader several times in the street during this period. "I told him, 'Ahmed, it's your choice to perform this kind of work, but I want you to know that I am against it,'" Laham said. "Ahmed respected me, but my words made no difference."

Ahmed Mughrabi's wife, Hanadi, remained on the periphery of the suicide cell, often going days without seeing her husband. But she told me, "He talked to me about [the suicide bombings] all the time, and I accepted what he did. I was proud of him. I only wish that I was with him during all of [the planning]. I kissed his hands every day that I saw him." He was highly selective about the people he chose for his operations, she insisted. "Ahmed said, 'I refuse to accept children [under the age of fifteen], or people who come to me in a pretentious manner. I am not interested in people who want to commit suicide simply because they don't like this life. True martyrs love life, they love people, but they are called for a higher purpose. They are fighters. It's like going to war.'" Mughrabi spent hours interviewing candidates, testing their nerves and their ability to keep a secret. According to Hanadi, the most important qualification in his eyes was faith in God and a belief that such deadly operations were part of a holy mission to liberate Palestine. "He used to quote from the Quran," his wife told me. "'Be in awe of the insight of believers. They can see in the dark.'"

THE CULT OF martyrdom was drawing Ayat in, inexorably. The teenager and her family gathered inside their house for four days during the Israeli incursion into Deheishe that began on March 8, 2002. Almost all of the Tanzim had fled the camp in advance of the Israeli invasion, but the Israelis were still blowing down doors, breaking through walls, shooting heavily, and searching for militants house to house. On the evening of March 8, the family's neighbor Issa Zakari Faraj and his young daughter were playing with Lego bricks on the floor of their living room when an Israeli bullet smashed through their window and struck Faraj in the head. Ayat's brother Samir and a cousin tried to carry the wounded man to a nearby hospital, but he died in their arms. "When Ayat saw me and our cousin carrying Issa past the doorway, she screamed out, and I told her to go back inside," Samir told me. That same night Jad Salem Attala and Ahmed Ishaq, members of the al-Aqsa Martyrs Brigades and close friends of Ahmed Mughrabi, were blown up in their car in the village of Irtas in unclear circumstances; Attala died on the spot, while Ishaq succumbed a few weeks later in a hospital in Amman. The Israelis claim that a homemade bomb in their car exploded prematurely. Ayat believed the Tanzim's version of events: that they had been struck by an Israeli missile in another targeted killing.

Despite the worsening violence Ayat's life still seemed filled with promise in March 2002. She was anticipating admission with a scholarship to Bethlehem University. Her parents had planned a marriage feast for the summer, as soon as she finished her secondary school exams. They had composed a list of several hundred neighbors and friends they would invite to a bridal lunch at their home. They planned to slaughter fifteen sheep for the occasion, and were searching for a hotel for the evening reception. At her school in Irtas, Ayat remained a radiant, self-confident figure. "She did not change a bit in the last months. She would talk about the incursions, but she never hinted at what she would do," Shuruq Awwad told me. But Ayat brooded about the violence she had witnessed and she was apparently tormented by images of death. In early March Ayat awoke in her room in the middle of the night and told her sisters that she had dreamed that a huge white bird had swooped down upon her rooftop, terrifying her and her brother Samir. "Don't be afraid," the bird had said. "I am the spirit of Mahmoud Mughrabi." Ayat told her sisters that the significance of the apparition was clear: when a dead person appears to a living person in a dream, it means, she said, that "one thing from this household will be taken away."

Days after her nocturnal visit from Mahmoud Mughrabi, Ayat made the fateful decision that she had apparently been mulling for weeks. The teenager passed a letter to a member of the al-Aqsa Martyrs Brigades in Deheishe, instructing him to hand-deliver it to Ahmed Mughrabi. The letter requested a meeting with Mughrabi—a highly inappropriate request in Islamic society, where encounters between an unmarried teenaged girl and a man outside her immediate family under any circumstances are strictly taboo. Ahmed Mughrabi didn't respond to Ayat's letter, according to an account he provided me from Nafha Prison using a smuggled-in cellular phone. Over the following weeks, Ahmed said, Ayat sent him three more letters, each one filled with a sense of urgency. Ahmed began investigating Ayat's background, he said in the phone conversation from prison, discreetly gathering information about her religious faith, education, and character. Finally in late March Ahmed decided "that another attack should take place." At that point he sent for Ayat, he said.

The rendezvous was held in secret, in a hideout that Mughrabi often used deep in the warrens of Deheishe. Ayat stopped off on the way home from school and was still dressed in her pale green school uniform and white hejab when she met Ahmed Mughrabi one-on-one for the first time. "Why do you want to commit this act?" he asked her. "I want to deliver a letter to the Arab leaders," Ahmed Mughrabi said she told him. "I will tell them through this act that I am willing to sacrifice my life for the love of my homeland, my country, and my family." Ahmed listened quietly, intently, regarding the poised and confident eighteen-year-old from across the room. "He could see this girl was serious, genuine. He saw that she wanted to face her God the proper way, and he decided to go through with it," said Hanadi, who learned about Ayat's recruitment by her husband after the fact. "It had to be done quickly, with extreme secrecy, because she was a woman and Ahmed could not risk failure." Ahmed abruptly stood up and said, "I support you totally and I will prepare you." The attack, he told her, would take place in a matter of days. "Get going with my blessing," he said.

*   *   *

NOT A SINGLE PERSON, not even her fiancé, noticed any variation in Ayat al-Akhras's closely supervised routine or had any hint of what she was planning during her last few days. Life went on for Ayat exactly as it always had: mornings and early afternoons in school, shopping with her mother in the souk, preparing her homework in the evenings, often with Shadi by her side in the family sitting room. On March 28, 2002, receiving word that the operation would take place the next day, Ayat managed to steal away from the family to film her farewell videotape in a safe house in Deheishe. Ahmed Mughrabi wielded the video camera and would later, wearing a black mask, deliver copies of the tape to three Bethlehem TV stations. Backlit, with her head wrapped in the black-and-white checkered kefiyeh of the Fatah movement, she read in a subdued voice from a prepared statement. "I am the living martyr Ayat Mohammed al-Akhras," she proclaimed. "I do this operation for the sake of God and fulfilling the cry of the martyrs and the orphans, the mothers who have buried their children, and those who are weak on earth. I tell the Arab leaders, don't shirk from your duty. Shame on the Arab armies who are sitting and watching the girls of Palestine fighting while they are asleep. I say this as a cry, a plea. Oh, al-Aqsa Mosque, oh, Palestine. It will be intifada until victory."

That night Shadi dropped by her house as usual, spending an hour drinking coffee and talking with her family before returning to his nearby home in Deheishe. Mohammed al-Akhras remained awake until four o'clock in the morning, watching live television coverage of another suicide operation in progress: a Palestinian gunman had cut through the security fence at the isolated settlement of Elon Moreh near Nablus, killing a family of four and barricading himself inside their house for hours before being shot dead by Israeli troops. Ayat stayed up through the night as well, apparently studying on her bunk bed in the small room she shared with her four unmarried sisters. None of them detected anything unusual about her behavior that night. Palestinian schools are normally closed on Fridays, but because the students in Deheishe had lost two weeks during the Israeli army's incursion in early March, teachers had scheduled makeup classes for that morning. At seven forty-five in the morning Ayat gathered her books and hustled out the door to class. "She said, 'Please wish me well on my test today,'" Imm Samir told me. "Then she waved good-bye." Classes ended at noon that day. As the students walked out the gate of their school in Irtas, Ayat dropped the first hint of what she was about to do. "She said, "I'm going to pray at al-Aqsa, I won't see you anymore,'" remembered Shuruq Awwad. "I asked her, 'Are you going to do something? Are you going to do some operation?' But she said, 'No, no.'"

Ahmed Mughrabi had meticulously planned his operation. At one o'clock the suicide cell leader gave Ayat al-Akhras the ten-pound bomb in a woman's black leather handbag. A male accomplice of Mughrabi drove her to the earthen barricade at the western entrance to Beit Jala. She climbed over the muddy obstruction and rendezvoused on the other side with Ibrahim Sarahneh, a thirty-three-year-old car thief who lived in Deheishe camp and whom Mughrabi had recruited to drive her into Jerusalem. Sarahneh, described by his younger brother as apolitical until the second intifada began, possessed two attributes that made him an invaluable accomplice for Mughrabi: he had a Jerusalem identification card and a car with yellow Israeli license plates, which allowed him to move freely across the Green Line dividing Israel and the West Bank. Ayat said little at first as she got into the front seat beside Sarahneh and sat with the black bag containing her explosive wedged tightly between her legs. The thin, balding Sarahneh, who would ultimately drive four of Ahmed Mughrabi's suicide bombers on their death journeys—one twenty-year-old woman named Arin Ahmed would back out at the last minute—was on his first ever mission that day. He had selected the target in advance, a place where he had worked as a checkout clerk before the intifada: the Supersol market in the south Jerusalem neighborhood of Kiryat Hayovel.

The pair crossed the Israeli checkpoint before the tunnel on the bypass road without incident. Sarahneh eyed the attractive teenager sitting beside him, bomb wedged between her knees, and attempted conversation with her. Their dialogue, as recounted by Sarahneh months later from a prison visitors' room, was chillingly mundane.

"Where are you from?" he asked.

"Deheishe camp," she said.

"Really? I'm also from Deheishe. But I don't know you. What's your name?"

"Ayat al-Akhras. From the al-Akhras family."

"I see. I am Ibrahim Sarahneh."

Ayat al-Akhras nodded. "Yes," she said. "I knew you when you had longer hair. But now I don't recognize you."

Sarahneh drove through the Gilo neighborhood and then turned north toward Kiryat Hayovel. He studied Ayat al-Akhras again. "Look," he said. "There's no need for you to do this. Why don't I just take the bomb and throw it? Then you can go home."

Ayat shook her head. "I want to carry out this attack," she said. "I have eaten a full meal and I am ready."

They continued to make small talk as they wound through southern Jerusalem, passing the huge Jerusalem shopping mall, a soccer stadium, a tennis center. Again Sarahneh suggested that he throw the bomb, allowing her to return safely home. Ayat was resolute. "I'm not afraid," she replied. "I want to kill people."

Sarahneh dropped off Ayat near the Supersol store in Kiryat Hayovel, a drab neighborhood of high-rise apartment blocks in the shadow of the Jerusalem shopping mall. It was Friday afternoon and the Sabbath rush had begun; the streets were crowded with shoppers. Ayat walked calmly toward the market, shooing away two Palestinian women selling herbs and scallions on the sidewalk beside the entrance. What happened next occurred in the space of a few seconds. As she passed through the glass doors, a fifty-five-year-old security guard named Haim Smadar sitting just inside the entrance noticed her black bag—he may also have witnessed her conversation with the Palestinian vegetable sellers outside—and tried to block her path. "You are not coming in here," witnesses said the guard told her. "You and I will blow up here." At that moment a seventeen-year-old high school student named Rachel Levy entered the store, on her way to pick up red peppers and herbs for a Sabbath dinner with her mother and two brothers. It was ten minutes before two o'clock. Ayat pressed the detonator, and a powerful explosion tore through the supermarket, gutting shelves, shattering glass, and sending bodies flying. The blast instantly killed Ayat al-Akhras, Rachel Levy, and Haim Smadar and injured two dozen more. By then Ibrahim Sarahneh was already halfway home to Deheishe. He heard the wailing ambulances and smiled. He was happy, he later told journalists, knowing that Ayat had succeeded in her mission.

THAT SAME AFTERNOON, on March 29, Samir Zedan and I found our way to the rutted alleyway in the center of Deheishe where Ayat al-Akhras's family lived. It was a cold, rainy day, and the miserable weather exacerbated the sense of gloom and dread I felt as I approached the house. A huge Palestinian flag was draped over the façade of the gray four-story home, situated in the middle of a long row of drab cinderblock constructions. Although just a few hours had passed since the bombing, a handful of male relatives standing at the entrance welcomed us inside. As I entered the gloomy stairwell, I could hear women wailing on the second floor. Ayat's older sister, Samar, twenty-four years old, had fainted after receiving the news of Ayat's death, and several crying female relatives squeezed past me down the stairs, bearing Samar's unconscious form. Mohammed al-Akhras, his sons Samir, Fatih, and Ismail, and a half dozen other male family members were gathered around an electric space heater in the tiny second-floor sitting room, decorated with the large poster of Mahmoud Mughrabi. Ayat's father, a solidly built man with a thick gray mustache, looked stricken, yet he still managed to stand up and greet Zedan and me with a vigorous handshake. He had heard about the suicide bombing of the supermarket on the radio, he told me, but hadn't thought any more about it until a half an hour later, when Ahmed Mughrabi and a half dozen of his comrades stood before the al-Akhras family home and fired their M-16s into the air in salute. Now, in dull disbelief, he stared down into his lap at a photograph of his daughter, a studio shot showing Ayat posed before a fake backdrop of the World Trade Center twin towers. It was the first time I had seen a photograph of Ayat, and I was struck by her beauty. It was difficult, if not impossible, to reconcile that sweet visage with the act that she had just committed, with her nihilistic surrender to revenge and hatred. It was harder still when I later learned how clearheaded she had been as she prepared for her attack and was driven on her death journey. Ayat had not been swept up in the emotions of the moment; she had thought long and hard about what she set out to do. That was what made the crime all the more chilling. "There was no reason," her father was saying. "I supplied them with everything possible to give them a decent life."

The al-Akhras home was too small to accommodate the flood of people who came to pay their respects. The family had opened a garage across the alley to absorb the spillover, and a hundred men sat on plastic chairs or milled about the freezing room, sipping bitter coffee and talking about Ayat's death. The mayor of Bethlehem, Hannah Nasser, showed up, as did a delegation from Hamas and French activists from Clowns Without Borders, a pro-Palestinian solidarity group. A dozen other guests gathered in the alley, warming themselves around a wood fire burning in a metal drum. Here I met Shadi Abu Laban, Ayat's fiancé, a lanky twenty-three-year-old whose handsome face was frozen in grief. "It will be difficult for me to go on with life without her," he told me. "I grew up with this family. There were two years of affection between us." He was reliving every moment they had spent together, he told me, sifting for clues, but he'd found nothing to indicate the deadly course she had followed. "If she had only told me what she was planning, I would have stopped her," he said.

"May God forgive her for what she has done." Abu Samir came downstairs and threw a comforting arm around the young man he had welcomed into his family. They were two men joined together by loss and utter incomprehension of what had just taken place. "When this is over," Ayat's father told me, "I will be the first to ask another woman for marriage with my daughter's fiancé."

What was one to make of this scene? Ayat al-Akhras's abrupt transformation from promising high school student into suicide bomber had filled her father with grief. Yet convention called upon him to play a role: receiving the tributes of Islamic militants, displaying his nationalist credentials by hanging a huge Palestinian flag in front of his house, hosting a stream of foreign journalists who were trying to fathom the unfathomable. The tragedy had transformed al-Akhras, whether he liked it or not, into a potent symbol of the intifada: the father of a shaheeda. Many members of the crowd of neighbors, friends, and officials were there to offer consolation. But others had come to rejoice in his sacrifice and honor him. His private grief had been co-opted into a public spectacle.

It was after dark now, a cold drizzle was still falling, and most mourners had drifted away. Abu Samir stood alone beside the metal drum, his features illuminated by the glow of the dying embers. "Killing only begets more killing," he said. "We want our children to live together in peace."

A few hours after Ayat al-Akhras's murderous act, the Israelis stepped up their preparations to invade Bethlehem. Early that morning Ariel Sharon had launched Operation Defensive Shield, Israel's biggest military action in the West Bank since the Six-Day War; troops and tanks entered Ramallah, besieging Arafat's headquarters, and took positions at the edges of a half dozen other Palestinian towns. A force was gathering on the Hebron Road, just in front of the main checkpoint, and I drove down from my home in Jerusalem the next morning to have a look. The residents of neighboring Gilo had also come out to eyeball the convoy—twenty-five Merkava tanks, a half dozen D-9 bulldozers, and dozens of armored personnel carriers—exchanging subdued conversation with reservists from the Jerusalem Brigade, the same legendary outfit that had captured the Old City of Jerusalem and Bethlehem during the Six-Day War. Soldiers had brought their wives and children along to see them off, and they stood in little clusters beside the armored vehicles. Everybody knew that the invasion would happen soon, that it would involve hundreds of armored vehicles and thousands of troops, and that resistance from the militias was likely to be fierce.

Across the checkpoint in Bethlehem, the mood was just as apprehensive. On Manger Square in the gathering darkness on April 1, the militiamen of the al-Aqsa Martyrs Brigades were preparing for the battle. The bravado that I had seen in previous encounters was absent this time. Everyone looked grim, scared. They knew that they faced a massive force and that they would be lucky to survive. Ahmed Mughrabi, I would later learn, had already slipped out of Deheishe camp and gone into hiding; he thus avoided being caught up in the subsequent battle of Bethlehem and the siege of the Church of the Nativity. Anxious crowds had formed outside the few bakeries still open; people came away with armloads of pita breads stuffed in blue plastic bags to tide them over in the event of a long siege. One of those I met waiting in line was Ayat's father, who had fled his home in Deheishe camp in advance of the Israeli invasion. We talked for a bit, and he again expressed his sorrow for the "children of Israel and Palestine" who were caught up in this ugly war. But taped to the windshield of his car, I noticed, were a half dozen black-and-white photographs of his late daughter, swathed in a Fatah kefiyeh and brandishing a pistol. They were the same pictures, I realized, that Ahmed Mughrabi and his men had spread across the walls and windows of Deheishe camp—intended to inspire other martyrs to the cause.

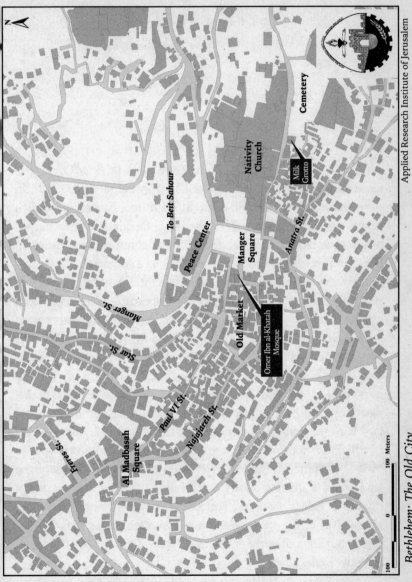

Bethlehem: The Old City

Applied Research Institute of Jerusalem

THE BATTLE

ෆ෫ව

AT THREE O'CLOCK THE FOLLOWING MORNING Captain Mike Aviad peered anxiously through a circular slot in the steel hull of an Israeli armored personnel carrier as it rolled down the road toward Bethlehem. A freezing wind whipped against his face as he struggled to find a comfortable position in the cramped vehicle, known in Hebrew as a Nagmash. Crouching with his feet on a metal bench and his helmeted head wedged painfully through the partially opened aperture, he rested a hand on the barrel of the Browning .50-caliber machine gun bolted atop the hull. A pair of gunners on both his left and right flanks aimed mounted French-made 7.62 assault rifles into the street. The dingy submarinelike interior was jammed with other members of the platoon he commanded, along with backpacks, weapons, and bags of ammunition. Aviad munched on a chocolate bar and swigged a can of Coca-Cola as the Nagmash rolled north at six miles per hour, the fifth in a long armored convoy led by a D-9 military bulldozer. He could see the headlights of the lead vehicles snaking up the Hebron Road, bathed in a miasma of dust. The Palestinians had scattered decoy mines here and there in an effort to frighten the soldiers—wooden crates, plastic jerricans—but the outskirts of the town were dark and deserted, and nobody fired a shot.

Aviad was a thirty-two-year-old Southern California–born Israeli who had immigrated to Jerusalem with his parents just after the Yom Kippur War in 1973. A week before the Israeli invasion of

Bethlehem he had been completing a degree in business administration at Hebrew University on Mount Scopus. But then a Hamas
terrorist had blown himself up at the Park Hotel in Netanya during
Passover, killing twenty-nine Israelis, the worst in a series of deadly
attacks that had spread fear and a sense of helplessness through
the entire country. On Friday morning, March 29, Aviad was eating
breakfast at home in Jerusalem's prosperous German Colony
neighborhood with his wife and eighteen-month-old son when
Ariel Sharon, in response to the Netanya attack, announced to the
nation that he was calling up twenty thousand reservists, the first
time Israel had placed itself on such a war footing in thirty-five
years. A fellow reservist in Israel's storied Jerusalem Brigade
phoned him a few minutes later: "They're calling us. Bring your
stuff. We don't know how long. Maybe a week or two." Aviad gathered his gear and caught a bus to a base on Jerusalem's outskirts,
arriving there just as word spread about Ayat al-Akhras's suicide
attack in Kiryat Hayovel. The Supersol market blast was the sixteenth suicide bombing in Israel in March, the most during any single month in the al-Aqsa intifada. Aviad spent two days training for
urban warfare and slept for two nights on an asphalt floor full of
gasoline stains in an old garage. On Monday Aviad's battalion
moved to the settlement of Neve Daniel, then began rolling toward
Bethlehem on Tuesday before dawn.

The Nagmash lumbered down the deserted Hebron Road. Its
destination was the "Palace" of Yasser Arafat, a seldom-used presidential quarters situated on a hill behind the now-destroyed
muqata. The battalion's mission was to surround and capture the
Palace and then await instructions. But when Aviad's convoy
arrived at the gates, they found the building locked and deserted.
Nobody moved on the streets. The police station was also shut
down. In anticipation of the Israeli invasion, the Palestinian
Authority's security forces had fled their posts and gone home.
"These guys obviously don't want to get killed for nothing," Aviad
thought. Then he and the others in the battalion climbed out of
their armored vehicles and waited out the frigid night in the road.

Aviad found it ironic that he was leading a platoon into combat against his Palestinian neighbors. Born in the affluent beach town of Santa Barbara, he was the son of an Irish-Catholic religion professor at the University of California and a Jewish mother who was also an academic. When Aviad was three years old, his father was invited to become a visiting professor at Hebrew University, and the family moved to Israel for what they expected to be a two-year stay. But Aviad's father became ill with cancer and died after returning to the United States for treatment, and his mother, Janet Aviad, decided to settle in Israel. In 1978 Janet joined Peace Now, the Israeli pacifist movement founded by 348 reserve officers and soldiers of the Israeli Defense Forces. Soon she became one of the group's most prominent leaders. Janet Aviad bought and renovated a handsome stone house in the German Colony, settled a century ago by German Templars, whom the British deported to Australia in 1938 because of their Nazi sympathies; after falling into ruins, the neighborhood came back to life in the 1970s as the thriving hub of Jerusalem's secular, liberal elite. Mike Aviad spent his teenaged years immersed in left-wing politics, accompanying his mother at Labor Party rallies, protesting the Israeli occupation of the Palestinian territories, and holding vigils in front of West Bank settlements. "I spent my childhood going from settlement to settlement," Aviad told me. "I grew up in a Democratic home, with a mother who admired people like Abraham Lincoln. I was taught that Arabs were people too, that Palestinians had basic human rights."

Aviad's military call-up when he turned eighteen coincided with the outbreak of the first intifada. As a second lieutenant in the Nachal Brigade, Aviad spent his three-year compulsory service dodging rocks and firebombs in Beit Jala, Bethlehem, and Hebron and trying to inflict as little harm as possible on the Palestinians he confronted. Like his mother he considered himself a Zionist, but he believed that the occupation had corrupted Israeli society. He cheered the signing of the Oslo Accords, mourned the 1995 killing of Yitzhak Rabin, and clung to the hope that Israelis and Palestinians could reach a final settlement by the start of the new millennium. But gradually the doubts set in. Aviad never really trusted Yasser Arafat—he was "a terrorist" to the core, he told me—and fretted over reports about the pace at which Palestinians were amassing guns and over the continued anti-Jewish rhetoric disseminated on Palestinian television and in newspapers and textbooks. "There was a point at which I realized that something was very wrong," he told me. Aviad argued with his mother about Arafat's intentions. When the Palestinian leader walked out on the Camp David talks in July 2000, and the violence broke out two months later, he saw the events as a confirmation that Arafat had no desire for peaceful coexistence. "We lied to ourselves for years," he said.

Aviad didn't vote for Sharon in the February 2001 Israeli election. But he felt that the old war hawk had performed reasonably well in the face of orchestrated terror. "I don't think that Ariel Sharon has done everything in his power not to be where we are now," he told me. "But over sixty percent is Arafat's fault." Janet Aviad, now fifty-nine, had no faith in either Arafat or Sharon; she and her Peace Now colleagues were demoralized, depressed, presiding over sparsely attended peace rallies and watching years of consensus building go down the drain. Neither mother nor son thought the Israeli military sweep through the territories was likely to accomplish much, but after the rash of suicide bombings, Aviad said, "something had to be done."

As the sun rose over Bethlehem, Aviad's commander assembled his officers in the dawn chill and gave them a new battle plan. All three battalions of the Jerusalem Brigade, about one thousand men in all, would enter the Old City from the Madbasseh neighborhood to the west and push the Palestinian militants through the alleys toward Manger Square. Aviad's 300-man battalion would take the middle path through the Old City, flanked on adjacent streets by the other two columns of troops. The soldiers studied black-and-white aerial maps of the quarter, each house and alley sharply outlined. Then they climbed back into their tanks and Nagmashes and continued north along the Hebron Road, turning east onto Pope Paul VI Street, a mile-long artery that petered out just before Manger Square. A half mile up Pope Paul VI Street they stopped and dismounted at Madbasseh Square, a small plaza dominated by the 110-year-old Evangelical Lutheran Christmas Church. At this point the streets became too narrow for a tank to pass. Aviad's 15-man platoon was to enter the Old City first—on foot. They picked up their rifles and ammunition but left everything else they had brought with them—flak jackets, coats, food, and water—inside the Nagmash. Expecting to be gone for two or three hours, the men had decided to travel light.

WHILE AVIAD AND his fellow soldiers kept vigil outside Arafat's Palace, Chris Bandak and forty other Tanzim fighters huddled in Manger Square against the cold, waiting for the sun to rise. The twenty-three-year-old Palestinian militant stamped his feet and shoved his hands deeper into the pockets of his heavy wool jacket. He wished that they could start a fire, but he knew that the glow of the flames would draw the attention of the enemy. In the distance the men could hear the rumble of Israeli armored vehicles; two Apache helicopter gunships hovered menacingly, like birds of prey, over Beit Sahour. Bandak looked at his watch: it was three thirty in the morning. Another three hours to go. He guessed that the Israelis would begin moving into the heart of Bethlehem at daybreak. He stroked the barrel of his MP5 submachine gun, a German weapon popular with NATO and counterterrorism forces around the world. Atef Abayat had purchased it for him six months earlier from an Arab Israeli arms dealer. It was a fine gun, accurate and easy to handle. Bandak had a half dozen magazines of ammunition—180 nine-millimeter bullets—and he was sure he'd use up his entire supply by the end of the day.

Bandak believed that the Palestinians had one advantage over

the Israelis: because the alleys of the Old City were far too narrow for heavy armor to advance, the battle would pit infantry
against infantry. In this case the Tanzim were fighting on their
home turf, with intimate knowledge of every passageway and
rooftop. Just in case, however, the militants had spent the last
few hours laying homemade pipe bombs and other explosives at
the entrances to Manger Square. There were mines in front of the
Peace Center, in front of the Municipality Building, and on Milk
Grotto Street beside the church. Thin red and white cables
snaked across the flagstones, each one linking a bomb to a hand-
held detonator controlled by a gunman standing by the Saint
George Restaurant on the square's southwest corner. The gunmen had also commandeered a bread cart, loaded it with pipe
bombs, and used it to block another alley leading into the square.
If the Israelis should advance this far, they would at least be
slowed by the blasts, Bandak thought.

At 3:45 A.M. Bandak's commander, Ibrahim Abayat, gave the
order over his MIRS radio to move out. Abayat had gathered a
small force on nearby Star Street; Bandak guessed that the
Tanzim fighters numbered about one hundred men in total. As
the militia moved up Najajareh Street—"the Street of the Carpenters"—they encountered a few armed militants from Islamic
Jihad and Hamas and a dozen of Abdullah Daoud's men from
Palestinian intelligence. The rest of the security forces had vanished off the streets. The gunmen walked single and double file
in the darkness past shuttered gold shops, tailors and bakeries,
and a passageway on the right that led to the outdoor Municipal
Market. Najajareh Street was a crooked alley, just wide enough
for a single car, lined with three- and four-story stone dwellings
with graceful arched doorways and windows, many of them constructed during the time of the Crusaders atop the ruins of
Byzantine structures. A quarter mile up Najajareh Street the men
passed through a thousand-year-old crumbling gateway known
as the al-Shaer Arch. Beyond the arch the alley curved to the
right and converged a few hundred yards further on with Pope

Paul VI Street at the Evangelical Lutheran Christmas Church on Madbasseh Square. The Tanzim gathered their forces in front of the church. The gunmen planned to wait at Madbasseh Square for sunrise, then fall back and engage the enemy in the warrens of the Old City.

AT SEVEN O'CLOCK on Tuesday morning Omar Habib stepped warily out of his old stone house at the end of a cul-de-sac off Star Street, a few blocks from Manger Square. He paused for a moment, shivering in the cold and listening for gunfire. Hearing nothing, he continued on his way to the family's favorite pharmacy on nearby Pope Paul VI Street, where he was to pick up injectable insulin for his diabetic mother. A seventeen-year-old honors student at the Franciscan-run Terra Sancta High School around the corner from the Church of the Nativity, Habib figured he still had time to buy a weeklong supply of drugs before the shooting started and the Israelis occupied the city.

Habib's family were Muslims who had lived in Bethlehem's Old City for more than a half century. His father, who had died a few years earlier, had built up a consumer electronics business that included a chain of retail shops in Bethlehem, one of which had burned down during the Israeli incursion the previous October. Habib's father had placed a high value on education, and almost all of Omar's ten older brothers had attended universities in the West Bank or abroad. One was an engineering professor in Jordan, another an American citizen living in San Diego. But the al-Aqsa intifada had begun to exact a toll on the family, luring several of Omar's brothers into armed resistance. Two months earlier Omar's twenty-three-year-old brother Ihab had been killed near the Bethlehem checkpoint by a bomb blast that blew off his arm and his leg; Israel claimed he was a Hamas terrorist who had been trying to sneak into Jerusalem when his bomb detonated prematurely. His family insisted he was just a shop owner killed by mistake. The Israeli Defense Forces had buried Ihab

Habib in a cemetery in Be'er Sheva designated for enemies of the
state, and at the time of the Israeli invasion his family was enmeshed in a legal battle to force the government to turn over
Ihab's remains. Three of Omar's seven surviving brothers—
Khaled, thirty-five, Ra'ed, thirty-two, and Ahmed, thirty—had
gone into hiding. Ahmed, a prominent Hamas militant in Bethlehem, was known to be on Israel's wanted list.

Omar Habib looked in both directions and then turned right
out of his house and headed toward the nearby Peace Fountain. A
large stone orb set in a star-shaped pool, the landmark stood in a
plaza where Pope Paul VI Street and Star Street converged, a one-
minute walk from Manger Square. Two steep flights of stairs and a
ramp in between led up from the fountain to Pope Paul VI Street.
He nodded to ten Tanzim fighters poised on the steps; all of them
wore flak jackets, their chests swathed with bandoliers of bullets.
Habib stopped at the first pharmacy, found it closed, then continued to a second pharmacy a little further up Pope Paul VI Street. It
too was shuttered. Habib could hear gunfire to the west, in the
direction of the Madbasseh neighborhood, and it was growing
louder. He was confused, a little panicky: should he keep heading
up Pope Paul VI Street and try to find another pharmacy? Or turn
around and go back the way he came—away from the gunfire?
Omar decided to continue. He brushed by gunmen and one shuttered shop after another. At this point Pope Paul VI Street had narrowed to a pedestrian path barely six feet across. He passed the
souk and then turned left into a narrow alley, Fawagreh Street,
that ran between Pope Paul VI Street and Najajareh Street. The
shooting was louder now, staccato bursts from machine guns
interspersed with tank fire that shook the neighborhood. Habib
spun around, collided in the alley with a group of fighters rushing
toward Najajareh Street, and fell to the ground. He felt disoriented: which way is my house again? he asked himself. The sky
had turned metallic; a few icy raindrops landed on his face and
dribbled down his thin cotton jacket. He counted about fifty fighters on Najajareh Street, jamming their clips into their M-16s,

preparing for battle. Habib turned left and headed down Najajareh Street, back toward Manger Square, hoping to reach home and shut himself inside before events really turned ugly.

CAPTAIN MIKE AVIAD waited breathlessly at the entrance to the Old City on Pope Paul VI Street with the fifteen young soldiers under his command. It was seven thirty in the morning. He had orders to seize the Evangelical Lutheran Christmas Church annex, an unfinished structure a few dozen yards down the road, and use the building as a base for deeper forays into the Old City. Aviad counted to three, then pulled a smoke grenade off his belt and hurled it down the street. Landing thirty yards away, it filled the narrow passage with a noxious gray cloud. Aviad sprinted toward the annex; the next soldier followed fifteen feet behind him, the next one ten feet further back, the rest similarly staggered. Then the wind blew the smoke back in their faces. As the last wisps dissipated, Aviad saw two Palestinian gunmen kneeling beside a car, their rifles pointed at him. "Oh shit," he said. He pulled up short, skidding on the slippery stones. The gunmen opened fire; the bullets ricocheted off the alley floor and the stone walls. Aviad took cover in the gated side entrance to the Lutheran Church, squeezed beside one of his men, a twenty-three-year-old Ethiopian immigrant. As the bullets whizzed past them, the Ethiopian shook with terror. It was his first time under fire. Aviad wrapped one arm around his shoulders and used the other to spray bullets from his Colt Commando semiautomatic rifle—a small, lightweight version of the M-16.

His men lined both sides of Pope Paul VI Street now, shooting down the lane; the Tanzim fired back from behind cars and from second- and third-story windows. Pinned in the entranceway, unable to break through the iron gate, Aviad radioed for support from the Merkava tank, which was waiting just behind them on Madbasseh Square. The tank rumbled down Pope Paul VI Street, but it couldn't quite make it through. Like an angry dinosaur, the armored hulk stripped off masonry and sheared through water pipes, sending water cascading into the street. What a goddam mess, Aviad thought. Amid ricocheting bullets he imagined the millions of dollars that the international community had poured into the city for the Bethlehem 2000 rehabilitation project—now all undone in a few minutes. The tank cannon fired two blasts, and the shells exploded up the street with a splintering of glass, stone, and cement. Then the Merkava advanced a bit further, shearing off a set of huge metal shutters covering an entrance to the annex that Aviad hadn't noticed before. Aviad dashed through the opening, adrenaline pumping from fear and excitement, followed by the rest of his platoon. The building was still under construction—half-finished interior walls, exposed wires and pipes, gaping holes instead of windows. Pipe bombs littered the floor; Aviad figured the Tanzim had been using the church annex as a munitions factory. The soldiers ran upstairs and from room to room, tossing grenades and spraying bullets in case Palestinians were lurking in ambush.

AS MIKE AVIAD and his battalion prepared to advance from Madbasseh Square, Chris Bandak and the other Tanzim were falling back from that square into the warrens of the Old City. Bandak, joined by Jihad Ja'ara, one of the murderers of Avi Boaz, hurried down Pope Paul VI Street, past the Evangelical Lutheran Christmas Church. Not far away they could hear the clatter and groan of tanks and armored personnel carriers. Ja'ara climbed onto the roof of a building opposite the Lutheran church and aimed his M-16 into the street. Bandak advanced another twenty yards and sought cover behind parked cars.

"Can you see them?" he radioed to Ibrahim Abayat. The al-Aqsa Martyrs Brigades commander was a few blocks away on Star Street with a force of a dozen Tanzim.

"I hear them," Abayat replied. At that moment Aviad's platoon pushed forward from Madbasseh Square down Pope Paul VI

Street, firing M-16s and rocket-propelled grenades. A grenade tore through a metal door a few feet away from where Bandak was crouching, sending deadly splinters of shrapnel through the air. Bandak stood, fired off a few bursts from his MP5 machine gun, and then retreated another dozen yards. He ducked behind another car and sprayed a full clip, then took cover in a doorway. Two fighters were shot in the alleyway in front of him; on the rooftops Tanzim hurled Molotov cocktails and pipe bombs at the Merkava tank that had pushed down Pope Paul VI Street, but the firebombs bounced harmlessly off the armored shell.

AT THE STAR HOTEL on Freres Street on a hilltop in Madbasseh, a few blocks west of the Old City, guests and staff alike huddled terrified inside the lobby. A dozen journalists and thirty delegates from the pro-Palestinian International Solidarity Movement sat immobile on the floor behind tattered sofas, hid beneath the reception desk, or crouched beside the bar. The densely packed hillside neighborhood around the hotel had become a free-fire zone, with Apache helicopters hovering overhead, tanks rolling through the streets, and frighteningly close bursts of machine gun fire sounding all around the hotel. The phone on the front desk rang constantly, bringing news—and rumors—from sources around town. One caller claimed that the Israelis had shelled the Santa Maria Church in the Old City and a priest, Father Jacques, had been killed. Another reported that nuns in the church had been raped. It was impossible to verify the stories because moving in the streets, even taking a step outside the lobby, was, under the circumstances, insane.

Hunkering down inside the hotel didn't guarantee protection either. At eight o'clock that morning I was sipping tea with a group of peace activists and fellow journalists in the hotel's fifth-floor panoramic restaurant, peering down at a convoy of armored vehicles rumbling down the street. A shot rang out and as the window shattered, a piece of glass lodged in the neck of an al-

Jazeera correspondent. "Get down!" shouted a French photographer. "They're shooting at anyone they see." Down in the lobby a few minutes later we watched as an Israeli platoon sprinted past in the direction of Manger Square, swiveling their M-16s threateningly toward the hotel windows. Richard Elias, the blond-haired Palestinian Swedish hotelier whose family owns the Star, was giving a telephone interview to a radio reporter in Europe when two Merkava tanks rumbled up to the front door. "I'm sorry, but I can't talk to you now," he said calmly. "I've got a tank cannon pointing in my direction."

The activists ranged in age between eighteen and seventy: they included a grandmother from Long Island, a quartet of French women in their early twenties, and an Australian man who had been hit in the leg by ricocheting bullet fragments during a confrontation at an Israeli checkpoint in Beit Jala the week before. They had been taking a tour of the West Bank when Operation Defensive Shield began, and now they found themselves trapped in Bethlehem and divided about their strategy. The leader of the group, a lanky and bearded American in his thirties, stood at the head of the table in the hotel dining room presiding over his third "general assembly" of the morning and trying to speak over a babble of agitated voices. Should they contact their embassies and request evacuation? he asked them. They had a moral obligation to remain in Bethlehem, an Irish woman argued. What about Palestinian suffering? What about the friends they'd leave behind? From the back of the room came a voice of dissent: "Somebody—please—call the Americans. I just want to get the hell out of here."

A HALF MILE AWAY, with gunfire crackling all around him, seventeen-year-old Omar Habib ran down Najajareh Street toward Manger Square, still hoping to return to his house. But as he approached the western edge of the square, he stopped in his tracks: an Israeli tank was parked in front of the Church of the

Nativity; the long steel cannon swiveled toward him and bobbed up and down like the snout of some primeval reptile. Trying not to panic, Habib retreated up the alley, not sure where he was heading. It was about nine thirty in the morning, and a steady cold rain had begun to fall. Outside the souk he encountered four teenaged friends from the neighborhood, including the nephew of Hussein Abayat, the assassinated militia leader. The five boys entered a pedestrian passageway in the hope of taking refuge in the souk. As they did so, an Israeli attack helicopter swooped in over the rooftops and raked the market with explosive bullets from its Vulcan machine gun. The boys fell to the ground in terror. "Where should we go?" Habib cried. They entered a passage too small for a car, raced down a flight of steps, burst through a pair of metal double doors, and sank to the floor inside the dark vestibule of an apartment building.

Habib squeezed his arms around his knees, shaking the rain from his soaking wet hair. He heard the chatter of machine gun fire, the shouts of Tanzim, the percussive blasts of tank shells smashing into walls. Habib soon realized he was famished. Creeping up the stairs, the boys encountered an old man in the corridor who invited them inside to dry off. Then, as the battle of Bethlehem raged, the old man fried up a slab of beef and tomatoes in his kitchen and served it to Habib and his friends with a handful of half-frozen pita breads. Habib thought it was one of the best meals he had ever had.

CROUCHING BESIDE a small window inside the annex of the Evangelical Lutheran Christmas Church, Mike Aviad fired his Colt Commando down Pope Paul VI Street. He and his platoon had checked the building for snipers, had found nobody, and now provided cover fire for other soldiers who moved down from Madbasseh Square. Soon forty Israeli troops filled the annex, all of them wet and shivering. Aviad set a cardboard box on fire, and he and his buddies luxuriated for a minute in the warmth. He cursed himself for leaving his poncho and his insulated flak jacket back in the Nagmash; he couldn't possibly recover them now.

The Merkava tank groaned down Pope Paul VI Street, crushing a half dozen parked cars beneath its steel treads. The armored vehicle quickly became wedged between the stone walls, and the Tanzim led fly another hail of pipe bombs from the windows and rooftops. One guerrilla hurled down a vial of sulphuric acid, which seeped into the cockpit and burned the face of the tank commander. The soldier cried out; the tank spun into reverse and laboriously backed out to Madbasseh Square, shearing off the bazooka shields around its treads.

AS THE THREE Israeli battalions surged through the Old City, Chris Bandak, Jihad Ja'ara, Ibrahim Abayat, and two dozen other fighters fled for their lives to the Municipal Market, their residual bravado of the early morning hours thoroughly extinguished. The two-level outdoor shopping arcade, covered by a wood-and-tin roof and reachable only by cramped passageways, was well protected from an Israeli ground assault. The guerrillas clustered beneath the roof for shelter from the rain, emerging to fire a few token shots down Pope Paul VI and Najajareh streets. At nine thirty an Israeli helicopter—the same one that Omar Habib had seen as he approached the market—dove toward the roof. Mazzin Abayat, Atef's younger brother, saw the Apache gunship and screamed for the fighters to take cover. The Vulcan gun's bullets tore through the wooden canopy, sending splinters and metal shards whizzing in all directions. A piece of shrapnel sliced into Mazzin's left knee and hurled him to the ground. The flying metal also injured ten other gunmen.

Mazzin Abayat limped into a house facing the upper arcade, where thirty other fighters, including Jihad Ja'ara and Ibrahim Abayat, had taken refuge. The exhausted gunmen gathered in the living room, devouring slices of avocado and ham provided by the family that lived there. A few minutes later, at ten o'clock, a gunman from the Palestinian mukhabarat burst into the house. Agitated, trembling, he told the men that a group of Tanzim were pinned down around the corner. And then he accidentally fired his Kalashnikov. A bullet from point-blank range tore into Jihad Ja'ara's lower right leg and lodged in his calf. Ja'ara stared, stunned, at the smoking wound and then fell to the floor moaning. Blood cascaded from the gaping hole. Ibrahim Abayat fashioned a tourniquet from a tee shirt and wrapped it around the wound. Outside more cannon fire from the Israeli gunship tore through the market roof. Soon the gunmen decided to evacuate the souk, one of them carrying Jihad Ja'ara, semiconscious from blood loss, over his shoulder.

AFTER FINISHING their beef and tomato breakfast, Omar Habib and his four comrades built a small fire in the building's foyer out of cardboard and scraps of wood. They warmed themselves for half an hour and then decided to make a move. Habib walked cautiously down Najajareh Street all the way to Manger Square; he was relieved to see that the Israeli tank had pulled out. He ran back up the street and told his friends that they ought to take refuge in the Omar Ibn al-Khatab Mosque, located across Manger Square from the Church of the Nativity. Finding the wooden front doors of the pink sandstone mosque unlocked, they rushed inside. The building was deserted. Removing their shoes, they curled up under prayer rugs. As rifle fire crackled through the nearby alleys, Habib and the others fell into a deep sleep.

AVIAD AND HIS platoon left the annex and resumed their progress down Pope Paul VI Street in a wintry downpour. They had been inside the building for three hours, holding it secure while other companies in the battalion advanced toward Manger Square. The men heard periodic sniper fire and gunfights breaking out on the parallel streets. The troops ran from shop to shop, kicking in doors and tossing grenades inside to kill any hidden Tanzim. Then a burly Russian-born Israeli private threw a grenade into a store that turned out to be packed with home-made gas balloon bombs; a huge explosion tossed the soldier six feet in the air and hurled him against the wall on the other side of the alley. He lay still for a moment as Aviad and his other com-rades rushed to help him up and grabbed his M-16. "What are you doing?" he yelled, regaining his senses. "Give me back my gun." He was uninjured, though the blast had driven into his eardrum a wad of toilet paper he had been using as an earplug, temporarily deafening him.

AT ELEVEN O'CLOCK Chris Bandak embraced Ibrahim Abayat in the marketplace and set forth with two other Tanzim fighters in the opposite direction from his commander. The fierce gun battles of the morning, in which a dozen of their comrades had been injured and three killed, had shattered whatever confi-dence Bandak and his comrades had left. The gunmen realized that they had no hope against the Israeli onslaught and now had only one objective: to live to fight another day. Bandak had grown up just around the corner from the Church of the Nativity, and he knew a perfect hideout in his neighborhood: the Roman Catholic cemetery off Milk Grotto Street, on the south side of the church. He led the other fighters across Manger Square, rain-slicked and deserted, then walked carefully along the long southern wall of the Church of the Nativity. There were no Israelis in sight. Past the Milk Grotto Church—a small Roman Catholic chapel built over a limestone cave where the Virgin Mary had supposedly first suckled the infant Jesus—Bandak turned right into an alley and entered the churchyard through an unlocked iron gate. The three fighters walked past row after row of marble crypts, stacked five or six high like filing cabinet drawers. At the rear of the cemetery, Chris stopped before three empty vaults about ten feet off the ground. The three men hoisted one another up and squeezed into the narrow slots, each one just big enough for a prostrate human being. They lay in the tombs, trying desperately to stay warm, as the freezing rain tumbled down and gunshots reverberated from the alleys of the Old City.

AVIAD AND HIS platoon swiveled their rifles toward the rooftops, peering cautiously around corners and engaging the Tanzim in fleeting firefights. Only two soldiers in his company had been injured during the battle: the tank commander who had been burned by acid and an infantryman who had been hit by a chunk of a statue blown apart by a tank shell in front of the Lutheran church. Aviad attributed the Israelis' good fortune to the Palestinians' terrible shooting and utter lack of discipline. But the men were still taking no chances. Soldiers ran up the stairs of apartment buildings overlooking the alley, commandeering strategically positioned windows and herding terrified Palestinian families into backrooms. By late afternoon the platoon had made its way to the edge of Manger Square, where twenty-five other members of the company had secured a third-floor apartment abandoned by its owners. Aviad and his fifteen comrades stumbled gratefully out of the rain. All of them were soaked to the skin, many shaking uncontrollably. The men tore off their helmets, put down their guns, and began searching the small one-bedroom flat for food and warm clothing. They found four thin wool blankets in an alcove behind a curtain and a few teabags in the otherwise empty cupboards. Aviad and his platoon brewed tea and then lay down together on the cold stone floor, huddled four to a blanket, trying to ward off hypothermia as evening fell and the temperature plummeted.

AT THE STAR HOTEL the electricity failed in the middle of the afternoon, and nobody was brave enough to venture down Freres Street to start the generator in the hotel's utility room.

Owner Richard Elias had drawn the curtains to prevent the Israeli troops from seeing inside, and with a heavy rainstorm deluging the town, the lobby was plunged into semidarkness. The television news crews, stoked on oversweetened Nescafé, were bored and restless and desperate for footage. As a tank rumbled past the hotel, a Sky TV cameraman peeled back the curtains and aimed at the lumbering vehicle. "Goddamit, get away from that window!" Elias screamed, the first time he'd raised his voice since the battle had begun. "Are you trying to get us all killed?" The Sky TV man backed away reluctantly, still filming as he retreated. Later the staff lit a few candles in the lobby and scraped together a decent supper—pasta and meat sauce, with a cucumber, tomato, and onion salad and pita bread—for their famished and exhausted guests. Two Italian girls from the pro-Palestinian group Ya Basta! scribbled postcards that they'd taken from a dusty rack by the front desk. An eighteen-year-old girl from Brooklyn wept quietly on a lobby sofa; her mother stroked her hand, assuring her that they'd be leaving soon. A consensus had built among the International Solidarity people: they had come to the West Bank to demonstrate, not to die in a war zone. It was time to call the United States Embassy and arrange to be evacuated as soon as possible.

AFTER SEPARATING from Chris Bandak, Ibrahim Abayat and the forty Tanzim who had taken refuge near the Municipal Market began searching for a new sanctuary. They crept down an alley behind the souk and descended a staircase leading to Star Street, one of the three main arteries of the Old City. Here they passed the oldest remnant of biblical Bethlehem: a sixth-century B.C. stone guard tower, known as Qus al-Zararah, that had loomed at the entrance to the ancient walled village. Star Street jogged left, right, and left again, joining Pope Paul VI Street in the plaza marked by the Peace Fountain and the twin staircases. At the top of the steps rose the Saint Mary's Syrian Orthodox Church, a towering pink sandstone edifice with large arched windows.

The door to the nave was open; the nuns and priests had fled. The Tanzim poured inside and slammed the door. Many removed their shirts and wrung them out on the cold stone floor. Men paced back and forth, confused, not certain whether they were out of harm's way. Ibrahim Abayat lay Jihad Ja'ara gently across a bench, where, groaning in pain, the injured fighter drifted in and out of consciousness. Mazzin Abayat, faint from his knee injury, collapsed in the corner. An hour passed. Then the Palestinians heard the crackle of radios, voices speaking Hebrew a few yards away, and a single warning shot. The Israelis had discovered them; many feared the enemy was preparing to attack.

One fighter hoisted Ja'ara onto his back. Then all forty Tanzim spilled back into the rain, clambered down a slippery metal staircase, and began to run, alone or in pairs, across Star Street. An Israeli patrol advancing down the street spotted the last group and opened fire, hitting one man in his hand. Crying out, he fell to the ground, but his comrade hoisted him up and they continued their flight. With Ibrahim Abayat leading the way, the men cut through a maze of narrow passageways, climbed a ladder onto a roof, and scampered down a metal staircase on the other side. Rainwater poured from rooftop gutters, sloshing across the narrow alleys. Abayat felt like he'd taken an ice-cold shower; he wiped the raindrops out of his eyes and kept moving, down flights of stairs, across courtyards, until he found himself on Manger Street, a usually busy commercial avenue that skirts the north side of Manger Square. The Tanzim stood still in the deserted road, listening for Israeli tanks. There was a burst of gunfire. "To the church!" Ibrahim Abayat cried. The men took off in two directions. Abayat and two dozen comrades entered the square and ran through the rain toward the Door of Humility, the three-foot-high portal that led directly into the fourth-century Basilica.

AT THREE THIRTY in the afternoon Omar Habib awoke with a start. Heavy shooting had erupted just outside the mosque, and

Habib could hear and feel the thud of bullets as they slammed into the stone exterior. The fighting had roused the other boys as well. The door to the mosque opened and an elderly man burst inside. "If there's anyone in the mosque, get out now," he shouted. "The Israelis are coming. Go to the church!" Terrified, Habib jumped to his feet and slipped on his shoes. He ran outside and caught sight of Ibrahim Abayat and the other Tanzim running across the far end of the rain-slicked square. Habib sprinted toward them, weaving through a dozen parked cars. From somewhere nearby he heard the clatter of steel treads on asphalt and the growl of a tank motor, which made him run even faster. A Palestinian Authority uniformed policeman stood in front of the church, beckoning people toward the fortress like a crazed crossing guard. The steel Door of Humility, Habib saw, was sealed shut. He was seized by momentary panic. But gunmen had shot the lock off the double metal-and-glass doors to the adjacent Franciscan monastery, and the portals hung invitingly ajar. Habib rushed into the cloister and sank gratefully to his knees before a marble statue of Saint Jerome.

THAT NIGHT I watched Bethlehem burn. In the darkened rooftop restaurant of the Star Hotel I squatted on the tile floor and peered cautiously through the window to avoid attracting the attention of Israeli snipers. I gazed across the skyline of church spires and TV antennas rising above tightly packed, dun-colored dwellings and saw that the Omar Ibn al-Khatab Mosque was on fire. It burned through the cold drizzle, emitting an eerie crimson glow. By now most of the fighters had either fled Bethlehem or had taken refuge inside the Church of the Nativity. I figured that Ibrahim Abayat must be in there, huddled inside the dark Basilica. Perhaps he was wounded, maybe even dead. My neighbor Mike Aviad was down there too, no doubt: Israeli tanks had advanced toward the square, and snipers were positioned on the surrounding rooftops. I had heard that Madani, the governor of Bethlehem, had gone to the church to investigate rumors that gunmen had seized priests as hostages. Now he too was trapped. Rumors swirled that the Israelis were preparing to storm the Basilica. The Vatican and the Greek and Armenian patriarchates pleaded for restraint. Fears grew of an imminent bloodbath.

The following morning, I summoned the nerve to leave the Star Hotel and make my first expedition into the Old City. Two colleagues and I donned our flak jackets and stepped cautiously out the glass lobby doors onto Freres Street. It was another cold and drizzly day, and a blanket of low-lying clouds hovered oppressively over Bethlehem. A hundred-yard walk downhill brought us to the corner of Pope Paul VI Street. Looking to the right in the direction of Beit Jala, I saw two Merkava tanks parked at a nearby intersection. We turned left toward the Old City, sticking close to the walls. The street was deserted; the electricity had been cut, and the only sound was the shrill continuous ringing of a burglar alarm. Soon we arrived at Madbasseh Square, site of the Evangelical Lutheran Christmas Church. A marble statue, blown off its pedestal by a tank shell, lay in fragments before the church door. Entering the Old City, we began to grasp the ferocity of the previous day's battle. Crushed vehicles lay everywhere, some of them pancaked like images from a children's cartoon. Water flowed from severed pipes into the street, cascading over a carpet of shattered glass and bullet casings. The glass crunched beneath our feet as we trudged past trashed shops, mangled metal shutters, sandstone buildings pocked with bullet holes or gouged by tank blasts. Another few hundred feet brought us to the alleyway, Fawagreh Street, that connected Pope Paul VI and Najajareh streets. Here some of the worst fighting had taken place. A biting wind howled down the casing-strewn alley. We climbed to the second story of a small mosque, where the corpse of a Palestinian militant sprawled on its back on the bare wood floor in semidarkness. His dark eyes gazed sightlessly at the timbered ceiling. His gray jacket was stained with something dark and sticky; it appeared he had bled to death.

The scene was worse a few doors down. Sami Yacoub Issa Abdeh, an unemployed forty-five-year-old souvenir seller, led us agitatedly through his family's small grocery store. Old women in hejab screamed and wailed beside the candy counter. In a small bedroom facing the alley, two corpses sprawled on the floor in a tangle of bedclothes. Both had been shot repeatedly as they cowered behind flimsy blue-metal storefront shutters during a fierce firefight in the alley between the Israelis and the Tanzim. Abdeh's sixty-four-year-old mother, Hajja Sumayya Moussa Abdeh, lay on her back. She wore a purple nightgown and a white headscarf, and her face was smeared with blood. Abdeh's thirty-seven-year-old brother, Haj Khalid Abdeh, slumped beside her, the top of his head blown off, his facial features grotesquely distorted, swollen and sagging like a week-old jack-o'-lantern. He wore black jeans and a blue denim jacket. His intact brain lay on the chair beside him.

Abdeh's mother and brother had been lying where they had been shot for the past twenty-four hours. The Israeli Defense Forces had refused to allow Palestinian Red Crescent ambulances to move about the city. But as we prepared to leave the house and make our way toward Manger Square, we heard the wail of a siren on Pope Paul VI Street. An ambulance screeched to a halt by Fawagreh Street. Abdeh beckoned excitedly to the crew, who told us that the Israeli soldiers had given them exactly thirty minutes to collect casualties. The team worked quickly, methodically, carrying out the Abdeh mother and son in blood-soaked blankets, along with the corpse from the mosque, and laying them in the rear of the vehicle. An old woman led them through a passageway to an airless bedroom where three injured fighters lay; two had been shot through the gut and another through the collarbone. The crew unfolded orange stretchers and took away the guerrillas. Then the ambulance sped toward the government hospital in Beit Jala, its siren blaring, its compartment jammed with both the living and the dead.

Armenian
Monastery

Manger
Square

Parish
Building

Applied Research Institute of Jerusalem

The Church of the Nativity

Greek
Orthodox
Church

Saint
Catherine's
Church

Franciscan
Monastery

THE SIEGE

ৼৢৢ৵

AT THE BREAK OF DAWN ON TUESDAY, APRIL 2, Chris Cardassos awoke in his small apartment in the Greek Orthodox monastery of the Church of the Nativity and brewed a cup of tea before heading downstairs to recite the *matina*, the morning prayer. The thirty-two-year-old priest from East York, Ontario, donned his black ceremonial robe and miter. Then he walked along a vaulted corridor and into the fourth-century Basilica, bathed at that early hour in near-total darkness. He ducked beneath the arched stone entrance to the Nativity Grotto, descended sixteen marble steps, and entered a labyrinth of faded silk tapestries, bejeweled icons, low-hanging silver and copper oil lamps, tapered candles, and carved stone columns. This was his second assignment in the Church of the Nativity—he had served as a deacon there a decade earlier—and he felt at home amid the sumptuous splendors of Jesus's purported birthplace. For the next hour Cardassos chanted, lit candles, and burned incense pellets in a silver receptacle containing a bed of charcoal and twelve tiny bells, each signifying the tongue of one of Jesus's apostles. He waved the incense fumes and rang the bells over a small hole in the marble floor fringed by a silver star, said to mark the exact place in the cave where the Virgin Mary gave birth to Jesus. As he climbed out of the Grotto to begin his morning chores, the priest heard the distant sound of gunfire, but he wasn't especially worried. Cardassos, known as Father Parthenius since his 1993 ordination at Jerusalem's Church of the Holy Sepulcher, had already been through one Israeli invasion the previous October, days after his arrival at the Church of the Nativity. With the exception of a single gunshot that shattered two windows high in the Basilica, the church had remained unscathed.

ACROSS THE CHURCH of the Nativity complex, in the Franciscan monastery, Father Amjad Sabbara was also beginning his priestly duties. The Palestinian cleric's morning schedule was usually packed with meetings with official Roman Catholic delegations and counseling sessions with members of his flock. Today, however, a ghostly silence prevailed in the monastery. In anticipation of bloodshed on the streets of Bethlehem, the forty-odd Franciscan, Greek Orthodox, and Armenian clergymen who dwelled inside the church complex had all agreed to lock the doors and to keep them closed until the crisis had passed. Father Sabbara, thirty-six, the parish priest of Saint Catherine's Church and the vicar of the house, still had work to do: keeping tabs on his parishioners in advance of an Israeli attack and arranging for the installation in Saint Catherine's of two new church bells that had just arrived from Milan as a gift from Pope John Paul II.

At ten o'clock in the morning, with the sounds of gunfire from the Old City coming ever closer, Father Sabbara was working in his office on the second floor of the three-story Parish Building when he heard loud voices coming from the rooftop. Climbing up the stairs to investigate, the priest encountered a dozen armed Palestinian youths trying to enter the building from the roof. The teenagers told Sabbara that they'd climbed into the complex from Milk Grotto Street, on the south side of the church, and made their way across the compound's walls to reach the Franciscan side. Sabbara asked them to leave. He led the fighters downstairs to the basement parking garage of the Casa Nova, a pilgrims' hotel that adjoined the monastery, unlocked the door, and watched them slip away into the street.

*   *   *

FIVE AND A HALF hours later, at three thirty in the afternoon, Omar Habib and his four friends joined Ibrahim Abayat, Jihad Ja'ara, and dozens of other Palestinian militants in a frightened rush across Manger and Nativity squares to the front doors of the Franciscan monastery. A previous wave of fighters had already shot open the locks, and the men and boys spilled into the graceful eighteenth-century Cloister of Saint Jerome. They swarmed through the arched corridors, which surrounded a small garden planted with lemon trees, and tried without success to enter the locked nineteenth-century Church of Saint Catherine, built by the Franciscans after the Ottoman sultan banned their holding mass inside the Basilica. They stared at the marble statue of Saint Jerome, the monk from Asia Minor who had translated the Bible into the Latin Vulgate in a basement cell in the Church of the Nativity and who died there in 420 A.D. Habib counted more than 150 fighters and civilians inside the rain-soaked cloister, and the flow of those seeking refuge hadn't yet stopped. The seventeen-year-old found a dark corner near the bathrooms and recited the afternoon Islamic prayer. Then he helped Ibrahim Abayat and a few of his men drag two huge wooden crates, containing the new church bells from the pope, in front of the shot-open doors to block the Israeli army from entering.

FATHER PARTHENIUS was in the midst of the afternoon prayer service, the final ritual of the day, when he heard a loud bang coming from the Franciscan monastery. Dropping his silver incense holder, he rushed up the sixteen stone steps from the Grotto to the transept of the church. At that moment a flood of bedraggled Palestinian guerrillas poured into the Basilica. The men were hyped up, terrified, disoriented. They circled around the ancient limestone columns, sank to the cold stone floor, stared wide-eyed at the gilded icons that decorated the Iconostasis, the ornate Greek Orthodox wooden screen that divides the nave from the sacred sanctuary, or altar, at the eastern end of the church. Parthenius, a boyish-looking man with wire-rimmed spectacles, a neatly trimmed black beard, and the ponytail worn by all Greek Orthodox priests, urged them to be calm. He asked them to remain to one side while he finished the service, then returned to the Nativity Grotto and, shaking, uttered the last words of the prayer.

Parthenius wasn't quite sure what to do. Six months earlier the Greek Orthodox patriarchate had transferred him to the Church of the Nativity from his previous position as superintendent and sole resident of the Holy Cross Monastery in Jerusalem. He hadn't been happy about the transfer—he regarded it as a step down in rank and responsibility—and his disgruntlement was intensified by the brutal atmosphere in the streets outside the church. Since his arrival Parthenius had had a few fleeting encounters with Palestinian militants while shopping in Bethlehem's souk, and he had always found them rude, disrespectful, and threatening. "They would walk past and I'd turn my head and walk somewhere else," he told me months later. Parthenius had tried to avoid taking sides in the conflict between the Israelis and the Palestinians, but he felt a visceral discomfort around the militants. Now he was face to face with many dozens of them, most of them, it appeared, heavily armed and agitated.

Despite his trepidations Parthenius felt obligated by his Christian vows to offer the gunmen sanctuary now that they had entered the church. Speaking the Arabic he had mastered during fifteen years of living and studying in the Holy Land, the priest assured the men that they could take refuge in the church but asked them to turn their guns over to the priests for safekeeping. He had an obligation to protect the Basilica, he explained, and he didn't want to run the risk that shooting would break out inside the holy site. The clergyman would store the guns and ammunition in a locked room in the basement until the crisis was over. But the Palestinians refused to surrender their weapons. The Israeli army might storm the church at any time, one of the fighters explained. They could not trust the Jews to respect the Basilica, he said. *"Fish din,"* he told the priest. They have no faith.

Parthenius drifted away from the fighters and helped his fellow Greek Orthodox priests remove icons and other sacred objects from the Greek chapel and the Nativity Grotto. Gingerly Parthenius and three other men carried away thousand-year-old gilded portraits of the Christ child, the Virgin Mary, and the Greek saints, and locked them behind the solid oak door of the treasury room. The Greek Orthodox archbishop, Ambrosios, a stern man in his early sixties, descended from his apartment to observe the commotion. Staring in disbelief at the mob in the Basilica, he turned to Parthenius in a rage and sputtered, "We cannot have guns in the church!" Parthenius tried to calm the archbishop, who had suffered a stroke four months earlier. Then he retreated to the basement refectory of the Greek Orthodox monastery and began preparing two hundred cups of coffee for his uninvited guests.

GOVERNOR MOHAMMED al-Madani had spent the night of April 1 and the morning of the second in the Manger Street law office of his friend Anton Salman, a prominent Palestinian attorney and the director of a Roman Catholic charity in Bethlehem. Madani's own apartment in Beit Jala was located beside a road that Israeli tanks wre certain to use, so the governor had decided to base himself near the Church of the Nativity, guessing that he would have more mobility. Instead Madani found himself pinned down like everyone else. Bethlehem had descended into anarchy: at eight o'clock Tuesday morning, April 2, Madani received a call from Majdi Attari, head of Preventive Security, informing him that Tanzim gunmen had pulled seven suspected collaborators from a makeshift prison near the Roman Catholic cemetery south of the Nativity Church and shot them dead. (Jihad Ja'ara six months later would admit to me that he was the killer.) Their bodies lay in a heap in the rain, and Madani tried, without success, to arrange for their collection by his security forces.

At eleven o'clock Abdullah Daoud, head of the mukhabarat, phoned to tell Madani that one of his fighters—Jihad Ja'ara—had been shot and was in danger of bleeding to death. Then several hours later Israeli Radio reported that armed Palestinians had entered the Church of the Nativity and had seized priests and nuns as hostages. Madani phoned Father Ibrahim Faltas, the Egyptian headmaster of the Franciscan-run Terra Sancta School and the Franciscans' keeper of the Status Quo, the complex set of regulations that governed the use of the church by the Greek Orthodox, Roman Catholics, and Armenians. Faltas confirmed that armed men had entered the church. Though he and the others didn't feel threatened, he believed that the situation was potentially explosive. Madani decided to assess the crisis himself, and he asked Anton Salman to join him.

The governor and the attorney walked cautiously down Manger Street through the still-heavy rain to the Casa Nova, encountering no Israeli troops or tanks on the short trip. Faltas let them inside the basement parking garage and guided them upstairs. The men crossed the Saint Jerome Cloister, greeting a cluster of nervous, brown-robed Franciscan friars, and ducked through the low door leading into the Basilica. Immediately a feeling of claustrophobia gripped them. The Basilica was steeped in semidarkness, the only natural light seeping in through ten barred windows located just below the high timbered roof on each side of the church. Centuries' accumulation of water stains and grime mottled the whitish walls. Madani could see, glinting through the murk high above the nave, fragments of Crusader-era frescoes restored by the British army after being used for target practice by the Ottomans during World War I. The great hall felt like an icy natural cavern. Palestinian men and boys paced around the two sets of twelve limestone columns that ran along each side of the hundred-foot-long hall. Others were sprawled on tattered rugs or on the stone floor. Madani spotted Jihad Ja'ara lying unconcious on a pink carpet in the transept of the church; a seventy-year-old Franciscan nun named Sister Lizetta tended to his injured leg with antibiotics and bandages. Madani made brief eye contact with his nemeses Ibrahim Abayat and Abdullah Daoud; how strange, he thought, to see them forced to take refuge in this holy place. Madani spotted Archbishop Ambrosios sitting rigidly on a chair on the southeast side of the Basilica, in the Greek chapel beside the Iconostasis, staring wordlessly at the armed throng. Madani bent down and kissed his hand. "We are your guests," he said. "Thank you for providing the church as a haven for the persecuted." The bishop grunted in response.

Madani looked out over a sea of men and boys—all of them, it seemed, soggy, dirty, freezing, scared, and exhausted. "Okay, you've made it alive," he told them, as he stood in front of the Iconostasis. "You are in the most sacred place in Bethlehem, and you have to preserve the holiness of it. Don't shoot from inside the church. Don't carry weapons around the church. Don't disturb the priests. And don't go wandering around the other buildings here. Stay inside the Basilica." After his short speech, the governor ducked through the doorway leading to the Greek Orthodox monastery and called Yasser Arafat in Ramallah. Arafat was then beginning his fifth day under a siege of his own at the muqata, surrounded in his office by Israeli tanks and armored personnel carriers. Madani reported to the president that the Basilica was calm, the priests didn't consider themselves to be hostages, and that he was preparing to leave. "Don't," Arafat said. "I want you to stay in the church to preserve order." Madani asked him for how long, and he was told it was an open-ended assignment.

AS EVENING FELL on Bethlehem, Omar Habib secured places for himself and his four friends on the floor of the lavishly decorated Armenian chapel in the Basilica's transept, beside the stairs leading down to the Nativity Grotto. Habib found four rolled-up rugs, which he gratefully spread on the ice-cold stone floor. A Palestinian cleaning woman who worked in the Greek monastery gave him a chunk of dry bread. Habib broke the bread into five pieces, distributed them among his friends, and ate the small wedge that remained. Soon the boys were joined in their sleeping area by twenty militants from Hamas, some of whom Habib knew through his older brother Ahmed.

As he wrapped himself up in one of the rugs for warmth, Habib realized that he had no idea what was going to happen to him. He couldn't hear gunshots, but he knew that the Israelis were in the streets and he believed that it was far too dangerous to go home. He watched Ibrahim Abayat pacing around the Basilica like a caged animal, chain-smoking and talking agitatedly on his cellular phone. The Israelis would certainly be hunting for the al-Aqsa Martyrs Brigades leader, and Habib sensed that his own fate was now inextricably linked to Abayat's. How long would he be in this place? he wondered. He was cold and hungry and missed his family. As night fell, the priests distributed tea and biscuits and tapered beeswax candles used for Christian rituals, and flickering flames danced across the drawn faces of the men and boys huddled on the floor. Habib joined the other Palestinians as they gathered for the evening prayer. The men stood in three long rows facing the south wall of the Basilica, in the direction of Mecca. Then, bowing between columns painted with long-faded images of the Virgin Mary, the Crucifixion, and Saint John the Baptist, they prayed to Allah to deliver them from the hands of their enemies.

THE INVASION OF the church by Muslim gunmen wasn't an unprecedented event. Ever since the caliph Omar ibn al-Khatab seized the Holy Land in 638 A.D. and began converting the local population, the Church of the Nativity has been an island of Christianity sitting uneasily in a spreading sea of Islam. The caliph guaranteed the integrity of the Basilica to the Greek Byzantine patriarch. But over the centuries a succession of Islamic rulers threatened to raze the great hall, and European warriors fought two Crusades in part to protect the Basilica, along with the Church of the Holy Sepulcher in Jerusalem (which was demolished under the orders of Caliph al-Hakim of Egypt in 1009 and rebuilt by the Crusaders during the next century). After the Ottoman conquest the sultan's horsemen invaded the church on a regular basis and shook down the monks and priests for protection money, as well as for "sugar, honey, wax, and linen," according to documents of the time. In the sixteenth and seventeenth centuries, Muslim pilgrims, venerating Jesus as a prophet, trooped down to Bethlehem to camp inside the then-derelict Basilica and pray in the Nativity Grotto. "It is a very unseemly thing that all the Turks who pass through Bethlehem should lodge in the great church, which is a great eyesore to Christians, who see their church made an inn for the infidels," wrote the Christian pilgrim Jean de Thevenot in 1658. "But it is above all troublesome to our Latin monks, whom they oblige to furnish them with all things necessary for diet and lodging."

The conflict between Muslims and Christians reached its climax in 1675, when the Greek Orthodox priests then in control of the church evicted the Muslim pilgrims and began renovating the great hall. Muslim leaders of Jerusalem appealed before the *kadi*, the Ottoman court. "In this site each of the dignitaries had his own place where he would sit and make himself coffee and things of this kind," the leaders complained. "[But now] the Greek Orthodox, who have seized this place and turned it into a shrine for saying their worthless prayers, do not let the Muslim visitors in." The fierce struggle for dominance in the Basilica ended with a definitive ruling from Istanbul that the church should be respected as a Christian shrine. "In a certain village there is a site upon which Christians say that Jesus, may he rest in peace, was born," the kadi declared. "They built upon it a church and placed within it images and statues. Is it permissible for a Muslim to enter that church for the purpose of pilgrimage or otherwise? The answer God knows best is: Entering into the church is reprehensible."

Tensions between Muslims and Christians have been only part of the church's turbulent history. For centuries the Greek Orthodox, Roman Catholic, and Armenian Orthodox churches have wrestled, sometimes bloodily, over the right to claim ownership of Jesus's purported birthplace. In 1099 A.D. one hundred French chevaliers rode into Bethlehem and planted the flag of the Crusaders atop the Basilica, evicting the Greek Orthodox priests who had assumed control of the church after the Great Schism and declaring the place the property of the Roman Catholic Church. The Greek Orthodox Church fought back, dispatching representatives to the sultan's court in Istanbul and matching their Roman Catholic rivals bribe for bribe: during one four-year period in the sixteenth century, the Ottoman rulers passed the keys to the Grotto back and forth four times between Greek priests and Franciscan friars, whom the Vatican appointed its official representatives in the Holy Land in the fourteenth century. The powerful Armenian Church entered the fray, persuading the Ottoman sultan in the 1640s to give it rights to place lanterns, burn incense, and hold masses in the Grotto. In 1757 the Greek Orthodox Church regained custody of the church, allegedly thanks to a huge payment made to the Ottoman sultan, and the so-called Status Quo that resulted remains in effect to this day, barring the Roman Catholics from holding mass in the Basilica but obliging all three churches to share access to the Grotto. Its intricate rules are codified in a three-hundred-page book that defines, for example, the positioning of oil lamps and incense holders inside the Nativity Grotto and the precise route through the Basilica's columns that the Roman Catholics must take during the funeral processions that wind through the Door of Humility into the Franciscan monastery.

Violence between the clergymen has erupted periodically, most recently a 1928 Christmas Day battle in the Grotto between Greek and Franciscan priests over who had the rights to wash the Basilica windows. Still, in recent decades the church has been an oasis of calm in a turbulent environment. In spite of their rivalry, the three Christian denominations have maintained cordial relations. And even as the second Palestinian intifada raged in the streets of Bethlehem, the violence stopped at the Door of Humility, the tiny portal lowered in the fourteenth century by the Egyptian Mamelukes to stop worshipers on horseback from desecrating the site. Now that Palestinian gunmen had stormed the church, however, the uneasy peace among all parties had been thrown into jeopardy.

IBRAHIM ABAYAT couldn't get to sleep. All through the first night the al-Aqsa Martyrs Brigades commander paced around the Corinthian columns of the Basilica, chain-smoking his stash of L&Ms and pondering his next move. Would the Israelis dare to storm the church? He couldn't believe they'd risk the international outrage that would certainly follow. Abayat was reasonably confident that the troops would withdraw from Bethlehem after a couple of days, under pressure from the United States government, the European Union, and the Vatican. Then he and the other fighters would be able to leave the church. But what if the Israeli troops stayed? He was anxious, adrenalized, burdened with his responsibilities as commander of the seventy al-Aqsa Martyrs Brigades militants who'd taken refuge inside. Abayat descended into the Nativity Grotto to check on the condition of his injured fighters; he gave some thought to his driver, Chris Bandak, whom he had last seen at the souk, and guessed he was either dead or in custody. He phoned Salah Tamari and asked him for advice. "Abu Hassan," Ibrahim said, "how long do you expect we'll be stuck in here?" Salah Tamari suggested that Abayat try to escape with his men before the Israelis really closed the net around the church. "Go into hiding; you've still got time," Tamari urged him. But Abayat believed that his best option was to remain inside the Basilica and let other parties negotiate with the Israelis for his freedom.

*   *   *

HALF AWAKE IN near-total darkness, Father Parthenius
stumbled down the steps from his apartment at four thirty in the
morning on Wednesday, April 3, and surveyed the Greek Orthodox monastery on the way to the Nativity Grotto. Parthenius, who
conducted the predawn incense-burning ritual in the Grotto in ro-
tation with the other Greek priests, was relieved to see that the
Palestinians had still not infiltrated the seventeenth-century residence. A three-story stone structure built around an arched courtyard, the monastery was dominated by a stately bell tower on the
northwest side that rose one hundred feet above the ground. Adjacent to the bell tower on the east side loomed Justinian's Tower,
nearly as tall, a four-story turreted monolith erected during the
twelfth century that contained the archbishop's residence and
several guest quarters. Parthenius dwelled in a two-room apartment on the second floor of the monastery with one small window that looked west toward the rooftops of Milk Grotto Street
and the Omar ibn al-Khatab Mosque on Manger Square; the priest
often studied or ate in his room to the sound of the muezzin calling the faithful to prayer.

Parthenius made a quick inspection of the food storage room,
down the hall from his apartment. At the time the siege began,
the priests had on hand five sacks of rice, a hundred-kilo bag of
beans, fifty pounds of pasta, plus hundreds of cans of meat,
lentils, and chick peas. Parthenius figured that, in a worst-case
scenario, the stocks were enough to keep the six priests in the
monastery fed for three months. In addition to that food supply
the Greeks maintained a garden on the east side of the residence
where they kept chickens and grew lettuce, cabbage, and cauli-
flower. Besides the archbishop, Parthenius's colleagues in the
monastery at the time the siege began included Father Visarion,
thirty years old, a relative newcomer; a twenty-three-year-old
church deacon; Father Elias, in his sixties; and eighty-four-year-
old Father Naofitos, who had spent more than half a century at
the Church of the Nativity. On the ground floor lived an elderly
Palestinian cleaning woman and her middle-aged daughter.

The priest unlocked a steel door on the ground floor of the monastery directly underneath his apartment and peered cautiously outside. Milk Grotto Street was deserted, Israeli troops nowhere in sight. For the next three days this door would serve as the church's single portal to the outside world. That morning Palestinian gunmen dispatched two teenagers to a pharmacy to pick up bandages, antibiotics, and other medicine for the injured and sick Palestinians; family members made frequent deliveries of cooking oil, food parcels, and cigarettes to the men inside. Parthenius played intermediary, escorting fighters to the door and helping them carry the bags of supplies back to the Basilica. The priest realized that he was becoming more involved in the fighters' predicament, against the wishes of the archbishop, who wanted to keep the Greek Orthodox priests completely segregated from the armed men. Parthenius also knew that he could walk out the door to safety at any time, but he had already decided to remain until the end, whatever happened. Besides feeling an obligation to guard the holy site, he had gotten an adrenaline jolt from being around the Palestinian gunmen, from being a part of history, and he couldn't bring himself to leave. "I'm an adventurous sort, and I was intrigued," he said months later. "I wanted to be there until the last minute."

ACROSS THE CHURCH in the Franciscan compound Father Amjad Sabbara listened to the ominous roar of Israeli tanks and armored personnel carriers in the Nativity Square, outside the Cloister of Saint Jerome. The siege, he knew, was getting tighter. Sabbara descended from Saint Joseph's Convent, home to fifteen Franciscan seminary students, sixteen priests, and four nuns, to a medieval grotto where the Franciscans kept their supplies. Unlocking the cellar door with an iron key, Sabbara stepped inside the musty chamber that had once contained the monks' cells and surveyed shelves stocked with vast supplies of macaroni, rice, canned meat, tuna fish, tomato sauce, and vegetables. There was enough to keep the thirty-five Franciscans and their two hundred uninvited guests fed for one to two weeks, as long as the priests carefully rationed the stocks. Carrying up sacks full of rice, macaroni, and sauce for the Palestinians, Father Sabbara knew he would have to keep the underground treasure a secret—or risk war inside the church.

SITTING WITH THE Hamas gunmen in the Armenian chapel of the Basilica, Omar Habib savored every mouthful of his soupy dinner. It was the first meal he had eaten since arriving in the church more than twenty-four hours earlier. Abu Ibrahim, a hulking gunman in his forties with a flair for cooking, had set up a makeshift kitchen with two portable gas stoves, given to him by the Franciscan priests, between columns on the north side of the Basilica. Abu Ibrahim doled out pots of macaroni and tomato sauce to the leaders of the different factions, who in turn distributed the food to the members of their groups. The great hall had quickly become a microcosm of the world outside: twenty men and boys from Deheishe camp occupied the western end of the Basilica, around the centuries-old wooden doors that led to the vestibule and the Door of Humility. Abdullah Daoud and a dozen men from the intelligence apparatus set themselves up at the opposite end, in the sanctuary behind the large Greek Orthodox altarpiece known as the Iconostasis. In normal times only members of the Greek Orthodox clergy were permitted inside this sacred alcove, which Parthenius and the other priests had stripped of all its priceless icons. The largest group, Ibrahim Abayat's militia, had settled on a thick red carpet that covered the nave directly in front of the Iconostasis. Fifty-six men from the National Security Force, plus smaller contingents from the Tourist Police and the Naval Police, were encamped between columns on both the north and south sides of the church. A dozen wounded and sick Palestinians, including a young postman suffering from acute appendicitis, lay in the warm Nativity Grotto, its low limestone ceiling blackened by centuries of accumulated soot from the perpetually burning oil lamps. As the men ate their meal, word was spreading that Israeli tanks had moved into Manger Square, and the news plunged Habib into a melancholy mood. That night Habib and his teenaged friends sat with the men from Hamas in a circle by candlelight, telling tales of Islamic prophets and wondering what the Israelis would do to them if they tried to escape.

FROM HIS COMMAND POST at the Peace Center one hundred yards away, Colonel Leor Littan stared across the rain-sodden square and pondered the risks of a commando raid on the church. Having arrived at Manger Square twenty-four hours after the siege began, the thirty-eight-year-old negotiator for the Israeli Defense Forces and veteran special forces operative found himself battling some of his fellow soldiers and their reflexive military urge for action. Hawks in the Israeli army were pushing hard for an immediate attack on the Church of the Nativity and the killing or capturing of all the Palestinian militants inside. But Littan knew the armed men had pipe bombs and booby traps, knew that the fortresslike Basilica was a tough building to assault, knew that any damage to the church or injuries to priests and civilians would cause an international outcry. At this point Littan was convinced that the priests and the civilians were hostages and that one wrong move might put them at grave risk of being killed by the militants. Littan had been to Waco, Texas, in the aftermath of the siege in which David Koresh and about eighty members of his Branch Davidian sect had died in a fire set by the group's leaders to avoid surrendering to the authorities. The failure of the Waco operation had stemmed, in part, from the SWAT team's decision to act unilaterally and attack the compound with pyrotechnic flares after the negotiators' efforts had stalled. Littan was determined to avoid that mistake: with Colonel Marcel Aviv, the military commander of Bethlehem, Littan had set up a joint command that would make sure that armed operations and talks with the men inside remained closely intertwined.

The slim, curly-haired Littan had spent fifteen years in the Israeli special forces, and he had long experience in hostage rescues and crisis negotiation; Littan had even shed blood on one of his missions. In October 1994 Hamas militants disguised as Hasidic Jews kidnapped a nineteen-year-old Israeli army corporal, Nachson Wachsman, and threatened to kill him unless Israel released the Hamas spiritual leader Sheik Ahmed Yassin from an Israeli prison. Littan was a member of a commando team dispatched by Israeli Prime Minister Yitzhak Rabin to extract Wachsman from a heavily guarded house in the West Bank village of Bir Nabbalah. In the shootout Wachsman and the Israeli commander, Captain Nir Poaz, along with all the Hamas kidnappers, were killed, and Littan was seriously wounded. Littan's most recent operation had had a more successful outcome: he had been the commander of a force that surrounded Preventive Security headquarters in the Ramallah suburb of Betunia for four days, forcing one hundred Palestinian militants holed up inside to surrender on April 2. A few hours after the siege ended, Littan had received orders to go to Bethlehem.

Establishing their base of operations in a ground-floor exhibition hall in the Peace Center on April 3, Littan and Aviv began drawing the net tightly around the gunmen. Israeli sharpshooters fanned out across rooftops and commandeered windows overlooking the complex. The troops transformed the neighborhood into a no-go military zone bristling with armored vehicles and sandbagged sniper posts. The Israeli Defense Forces erected two eighty-foot-high cranes overlooking courtyards and gardens in the church, each one mounted with a TV camera and a remote-controlled sniper rifle operated by a sharpshooter at the base. Littan's intention was to cut down on the Palestinians' breathing space, make it too dangerous to venture outside, deprive them of sunlight, dampen their morale. Soon after the cranes went up the army floated a white observation balloon over the complex, which would provide information about the movements of the armed men throughout the siege.

At the same time Israeli intelligence agents studied television footage gathered by the crane-top cameras and contacted inform-ers in Bethlehem, trying to determine who the men locked inside the church were. They quickly identified Ibrahim Abayat, Jihad Ja'ara, and Abdullah Daoud, all of whom were high on Israel's wanted list. Littan and his aides began calling them on their cel-lular phones, sounding out their moods. Littan found Ibrahim Abayat to be defiant and dangerously volatile. In some conversa-tions with the Israeli negotiator Abayat struck a hectoring tone, demanding that the Israeli Defense Forces withdraw from Beth-lehem and assuring Littan that the European Union, the Ameri-cans, and the Vatican would intervene on the Palestinians' behalf. At other points, when he was less sure of rescue, he ranted on about his role in history and vowed to die with his gun in his hand. "I cannot surrender. I don't have any options," he told Lit-tan. "I am the leader. I'm here to the end with my people." "We knew Ibrahim Abayat was the leader of the largest group, but he wasn't respected," Littan recalled months later. "He was impul-sive. He didn't have enough authority."

Palestinian intelligence chief Abdullah Daoud—suspected by Israel of complicity in the Beit Israel suicide bombing, an allega-tion he denied—was a different story. In speeches to the men in-side the church, Daoud, known by the nom de guerre Abu Qassim, also sounded antagonistic, frequently telling them, "You will resist. There can be no solution." But the Israelis sensed that his speeches were largely posturing. Littan believed that he might prove flexible, especially if offered the possibility of going into comfortable exile abroad, and was certain that Daoud com-manded far more respect than Abayat among the gunmen and se-curity forces. "His decision was worth much more than Ibrahim Abayat's," Littan said. The third figure, Jihad Ja'ara, was too inca-pacitated from blood loss and infection to talk to the Israelis at first. But as time went on, the Israelis would regard him as a weak link. His wound was in danger of becoming gangrenous, and Ja'ara knew time was critical. "He was a tough guy, but he was speaking about solutions," Littan told me. "His attitude became, 'I want to end this.'"

AT THE ROMAN Catholic cemetery south of the Church of the Nativity, Chris Bandak, Ibrahim Abayat's driver and comrade in the al-Aqsa Martyrs Brigades, was nearing the point of collapse. Except for grass and flowers foraged from around his tomb, the Tanzim gunman had not eaten anything in three days. His entire body ached from the cold and from being jammed inside the vault for most of the last forty-eight hours. On Thursday morning, April 4, at ten o'clock, he telephoned Ibrahim Abayat and asked him where the militia leader had ended up. Abayat was pacing around the Basilica when he received the telephone call. He dashed into the Cloister of Saint Jerome, where the reception was better. He was overjoyed to hear Bandak's voice. "Chris, are you still alive?" Abayat said. "I'm in the church. You should come as soon as you can."

The time had come, Bandak realized, to make a move. He and his two fellow gunmen clambered down from the vaults, stretched and massaged their stiff muscles, and then walked cautiously toward Milk Grotto Street. With Leor Littan's sharpshooters still not fully deployed around the church, the trip passed without incident. Bandak stopped at the home of a neighbor and picked up three packs of cigarettes and a pita bread filled with baba ganoush; after giving the signal to Ibrahim Abayat to open the door beneath the Greek monastery, Bandak and his two comrades dashed across Milk Grotto Street and collapsed in tears inside the sanctuary. Ibrahim embraced him; other Tanzim grabbed all his cigarettes. Abayat and his comrades guided the three new arrivals, the last Palestinian militants to take refuge inside, down the corridor and into the Basilica.

*   *   *

THEN AT ELEVEN FORTY in the morning on Thursday, April 4, an hour and a half after Bandak's arrival, all hell broke loose inside the church. Father Parthenius was brewing coffee in his kitchen when the floor beneath him shook violently and, he says, "everything turned red." Frightened and confused, Parthenius reeled out his door into the courtyard, and with the four other priests sealed himself inside the archbishop's quarters in Justinian's Tower. In the Basilica the Palestinian captives heard the explosion and assumed that the church was under attack; all two hundred of them poured panic-stricken through the doorway leading to the Cloister of Saint Jerome and spilled through the garden into the reception area of the adjacent Saint Joseph's Convent. Resting in his room on the second floor, Father Amjad Sabbara heard the blast and the agitated voices downstairs and was also certain the Israelis had invaded. He ordered all of the seminarians, priests, and nuns to remain in their rooms. But no Israeli soldiers appeared, and after an hour the Palestinians trickled back tentatively to the Basilica. Emerging from the archbishop's residence, Parthenius found a mysterious three-foot hole blown through the steel door leading to Milk Grotto Street.

The explosion changed the mood inside the church. Convinced that the Israelis were preparing a full-scale assault, Ibrahim Abayat and other militant leaders deployed their gunmen in doorways, windows, and steeples. Five Hamas militants occupied Parthenius's apartment and commandeered his window as a lookout post. The gunmen evicted the other priests from their rooms, took positions inside a small church called Saint George's—reached via a door behind the Basilica's altar—and overran Justinian's Tower. Archbishop Ambrosios was forced to vacate his apartment in the tower; he regarded the intrusion as the final insult. The aging leader, still shaky from his recent stroke, berated the men in the hallway outside his rooms: "You came to the church, we said all right," he said. "You came to the church with guns, and we accepted that. But now you want to enter our monastery? That's crossing the line." Ambrosios grudgingly joined

Parthenius and the other priests in guest rooms on the third floor of the monastery, facing away from Milk Grotto Street, which was now filled with Israeli snipers and highly dangerous. Parthenius gave a room to Governor Madani, who had heeded Yasser Arafat's order to remain inside until the siege was over.

Soon the tension grew too much for several clergymen. Five ailing Franciscan priests were spirited to safety through the Casa Nova basement; the rest remained concentrated in fifteen rooms in the seminary on the top floor of Saint Joseph's convent, forbidden by the church leadership—Sabbara, Faltas, and a German priest named Father Johannes—from entering the Basilica. The same day, Archbishop Ambrosios, the young Greek Orthodox deacon, and the Palestinian cleaning woman and her daughter left the church through the damaged doorway on Milk Grotto Street and were evacuated in an Israeli armored personnel carrier. Parthenius was relieved to see the archbishop depart; he had worried that the man might suffer another stroke. The young deacon too had been highly agitated, and Parthenius had feared that he might do or say something that would create trouble with the Palestinian militants. (Months later Leor Littan explained to me that the Israelis had not attempted to invade the church the morning of the explosion; Israeli sappers, or explosives experts, had detonated a car filled with booby traps just outside the Greek monastery, and the blast had ripped through the monastery door.)

AFTER A WRETCHED first night in the abandoned house in Bethlehem's Old City, Captain Mike Aviad recovered his warm clothing from the Nagmash, ate a full meal, and then settled with his men on military cots in a second-floor room of the Peace Center. The thirty-two-year-old reservist was shocked, and a bit ashamed, at the way his fellow soldiers had vandalized the Peace Center: some had rampaged through the underground parking garage, smashing the windows, slashing the tires, and scratching the bodywork of dozens of cars belonging to Palestinian Authority officials. Graffiti spray painted on one wall summed up the soldiers' bellicose mood: NO ARABS, NO GUARD DUTY. Other soldiers ransacked the second-floor office of Arafat's Tourist Police and carted away toys intended for Palestinian children, the gift of a European charity. Aviad thought that crossed the line, but he would later join in expropriations himself when his men made a foray to Arafat's nearby presidential office, the Palace. Stunned by the building's opulence—gold-plated faucets in the bathrooms, televisions in every office—he and his men helped themselves to new police uniforms, snowsuits, and berets—the spoils, he later told me, of "the enemy army."

Aviad and his fellow soldiers settled into a tedious routine of guard duty, interrupted by moments of drama. On the sixth night of the siege, Monday, April 8, Littan dispatched a team to plant eavesdropping equipment inside the Franciscan compound. Palestinian gunmen, hearing the Israeli commandos as they climbed onto the roof of the Parish Building, engaged them in a firefight. Two Israelis were shot and seriously injured; Aviad and his team raced up five flights of stairs and carried the bleeding soldiers on stretchers to safety. The gun battle ignited a fire in a top-floor reception hall of the Parish Building that burned out of control. Smoke poured into the Basilica. When a Palestinian fighter named Khaled Abu Siam clambered through the smoke-filled corridors of the Parish Building and came out on the roof to retrieve the weapons left behind by the injured Israelis, an Israeli sniper shot him dead. It was the first death at the Church of the Nativity since a mentally retarded bell ringer was killed the first evening while attempting to return to his home across Manger Square. The bell ringer's corpse had lain where he had fallen for four days, until Littan allowed a Red Crescent ambulance to take it away.

IN THE CANDLELIT Basilica the deadly possibilities of the siege had become real. Ibrahim Abayat and his comrades solemnly placed the corpse of thirty-six-year-old Khaled Abu Siam on the floor of the Armenian chapel, a few feet from where Omar Habib and his friends were trying to get some sleep. The men retrieved charred planks of wood from the burned room in the Parish Building, nailed together a makeshift coffin, placed Siam's body inside, and then sealed the gaps with candle wax. After dawn Chris Bandak ventured out of the Basilica and crossed a courtyard to the base of the Greek bell tower. He rang the bell dozens of times to commemorate Siam's death, a ritual that he would repeat each time a Palestinian was shot dead inside the church compound. Later that morning all two hundred Palestinians accompanied the coffin through the door of the Basilica to a small garden filled with lemon trees in the same courtyard. In the warmth of the sun, beneath the shade of a lemon tree, the Palestinian fighters began to dig a hole to bury Abu Siam's remains.

Father Parthenius was relaxing in the guest quarters in the Greek monastery when a Palestinian Christian teenager burst into the room. "They are burying a fighter in the garden, *Abuna*," he announced. The priest rose up, horrified: if the gunmen succeeded in interring their comrade in the Greek garden, he told Madani, that would give them the right, according to established precedent, to turn the grave into an Islamic shrine. Parthenius exclaimed that the men would bury their comrade there "over my dead body," and rushed outside with Madani, Father Visarion, and the Roman Catholic attorney Anton Salman, who was living alongside the Franciscans in Saint Joseph's Convent.

The Palestinians had gathered around the open grave; Ibrahim Abayat and three other Tanzim slowly lowered the makeshift coffin into the five-foot-deep pit. "Stop!" Parthenius shouted. Madani, in his customary role of conciliator, stepped forward and in a calm voice explained the priests' objections. The men reacted angrily; then Father Visarion came up with a solution. Beside the garden was a staircase leading to the Cave of the Innocents, a gloomy grotto containing the bones of children two years old and younger slaughtered by King Herod in Bethlehem after the birth of Jesus. Visarion proposed that the militants store Siam's body inside the cool, dark chamber until it could be removed from the church. The Palestinians accepted the compromise, and Parthenius unlocked the steel gate and helped to slide the coffin into the ancient reliquary.

THE FOOD KEPT flowing into the Basilica for the first few days, helping to ease the strain of captivity. Sympathetic Palestinians who lived near the Franciscan monastery threw hundreds of pita breads into the compound on several occasions. Across the compound, a woman who lived in a house on Milk Grotto Street stuffed linen bags with cigarettes, bread, bologna, and canned lentils, and tossed them onto the wall of the Greek Orthodox monastery after dark. At nine o'clock, after making the drop, she would call Chris Bandak on his cell phone and say, "It's here." Then a ten-man team would carry ladders out to the courtyard, creep along the wall, and retrieve the bags with hooks mounted on ten-foot-long rods. Huge cheers erupted inside the Basilica when the men and boys returned with their booty. But the siege was tightening: when Israeli surveillance cameras caught the operation on videotape after a week, the Israeli command stationed snipers near the drop-off point. On the fourth such foray a twenty-year-old was shot in the leg. The following day Chris Bandak made a sortie out the blasted door of the Greek monastery to try to get food and cigarettes from an abandoned grocery store just across Milk Grotto Street. Bandak shot the lock off the iron shutters with his pistol, then heard a shout and saw an Israeli soldier aiming his rifle at him from a dozen yards away. Bandak hastily retreated into the safety of the church.

With extra nourishment from outside becoming more and more difficult to obtain, the internal rations ran down quickly, and relations between the Palestinians and the priests began to curdle. Militants ransacked the room of Father Visarion, stealing his private six-month supply of canned bologna, beef, and vegetables. Gunmen broke into a chamber where Parthenius had stashed priceless icons, crosses, incense holders, and priestly garments. Although they left the icons alone, they took bread used for the Divine Liturgy and perfume with which the priests anointed worshipers during religious festivals. Furious, Parthenius warned the governor that if the men broke in again, he and the three other Greek Orthodox priests would leave and abandon the fighters to their fates. Gunmen smashed through a window on the roof of the Parish Building and descended into the basement kitchen of Saint Joseph's Convent, carrying off fresh vegetables and other supplies as terrified nuns watched. (The larger stocks in the grotto remained undiscovered.) Father Sabbara confronted a "commission of seven" that had formed early in the siege, made up of Abdullah Daoud, Ibrahim Abayat, and representatives of Hamas, the Naval Police, and the Palestinian National Security Force. "You must stop them coming in," Sabbara pleaded. "We want to give it to all of you equally."

Mealtimes grew increasingly tense, with one group of militants often accusing another of grabbing a disproportionate share of the food. Some gunmen hoarded cans of meat and vegetables that they had ransacked from the priests, hiding them beneath blankets or inside clothing and devouring them in secret; Parthenius discovered empty cans, marked with Father Visarion's initials, discarded inside the Grotto. The law of the jungle seemed to be taking over, Parthenius thought. He fed several weaker boys in the privacy of the monastery, out of sight of the gunmen.

Food shortages were only part of the punishment. Ten days into the siege, the Israelis cut the main water supply, forcing the captives to begin drawing brackish water from four abandoned wells. Omar Habib pulled up one pail and, to his horror, noticed red worms wriggling in the brownish liquid; from that point the men used white sheets as filters. Two nights later the electricity shut down. When an electrician named Hassan Quan tried to run extension cords from the Basilica across the rooftops of the Franciscan monastery to the Casa Nova pilgrims' hotel, which had a separate power supply, he was shot in the chest by an Israeli sniper. His comrades dragged him back to the Basilica in his death throes. Omar Habib watched him writhing on the floor of the Armenian chapel, surrounded by distraught friends. "I have pain," he cried. "Mother, oh, Mother, I'm so cold." Quan gasped, gave a final shudder, and then lay still. Parthenius and Visarion placed his body alongside that of Siam in the Cave of the Innocents.

Moving almost anywhere outside the Basilica had now become a potentially deadly excursion. With the exception of the Cloister of Saint Jerome, every outdoor courtyard and garden lay within the sights of remote-controlled guns or Israeli snipers perched in buildings that ringed the church. Drawing water from the wells or using the still-working toilets on the second floor of the Greek Orthodox monastery required a dangerous sprint across exposed territory. (The Greeks drew an emergency water supply from rain reservoirs on the roof of the monastery; the plumbing, which ran on a gravity system rather than electricity, kept working throughout the siege.)

Chris Bandak discovered just how dangerous the church had become after Ibrahim Abayat assigned him guard duty with a half dozen other Tanzim in the most exposed corner of the compound: Father Visarion's old room, located in a courtyard between the second floor of Justinian's Tower and the Basilica, directly beneath a crane mounted with a remote-controlled sniper rifle. Because the courtyard was the site of both a guard post and one of the four wells in the church complex, a stream of pedestrian traffic passed through it: nine Palestinians would be killed or injured in that one spot during the siege. One day an exploding dumdum bullet hit Bandak's fellow guard in the stomach as he ran the ten yards from the stairwell to his post in Visarion's apartment. Bandak and other fighters dragged the groaning man back to the Basilica and laid him in the Armenian chapel. Sister Lizetta, the Franciscan nurse, stuffed his intestines back through the gaping hole in his side, shot him full of antibiotics, stitched the opening, and then poured honey over his wound to keep the bacteria away. But his organs festered, and militants, to mask the smell of decomposition, sprinkled him with perfume used for Greek Orthodox religious rituals.

TWO UNITS OF Israeli sharpshooters now surrounded the Church of the Nativity. One unit was an elite intelligence squad who manned the remote-controlled sniper guns and television cameras and who were specifically supposed to identify wanted Palestinian militants. They would relay names of suspected "terrorists" to the Israeli military command, and the commanders would decide quickly whether or not to shoot them down. The other group consisted of ordinary reservists based in windows and on balconies and rooftops. Although their rules of engagement stated that the troops could fire only when they felt directly threatened, the soldiers interpreted the rules loosely. Captain Mike Aviad says that his men followed a simple rule: "Anyone armed gets shot," he told me. "Anyone crawling around gets shot."

Behind the scenes the efforts of intermediaries to find a solution to the standoff were going nowhere. During the first week of April officials at the United States Embassy in Tel Aviv began holding secret talks with the leaders of Egypt, Jordan, Tunisia, and Yemen about giving asylum to wanted Palestinians inside the church. At that point Israel was using a figure of "2 percent" of the men inside—five or six militants—that the government wanted to see stand trial in an Israeli court or be deported. But those delicate discussions collapsed after Prime Minister Ariel Sharon gave an interview to CNN on April 14 during which he announced, misleadingly, that Israel and the United States had coordinated their positions and were working hand in hand. The Palestinians pulled out of the talks, not wishing to appear to be dancing to Israel's tune. Monsignor Sambi, the Vatican's ambassador to Israel and its representative to the Palestinian Authority; the Anglican Church representative Andrew White; and the

Swiss ambassador to Israel all offered to mediate between the Israeli government and a committee of Palestinians. But the Israelis refused to accept third-party involvement. "The problem must be ended with the people inside the church, not with people outside," Littan told Governor Madani and Salman, his principal contacts inside the church. Littan even rejected repeated entreaties by the International Committee of the Red Cross to bring food and medicine to the church and evacuate the wounded.

The Israelis prepared for a standoff that would last weeks, perhaps months. Seeking to demoralize and to divide the men inside the church, Littan placed a military telephone outside the Door of Humility and, via megaphone, urged those who wanted to leave to call the Israeli army for help. A screeching dissonance of dog barks, cat fights, grinding tank treads, explosions, and orders to surrender began to blare over loudspeakers mounted on a platform. Chris Bandak would often ring the church bells in response, a futile effort to drown out the noise. For two nights the Israeli troops hurled messages into the Greek monastery inside plastic Evian bottles. "Come out. Don't depend on others. Depend on yourselves," the notes urged. "Your families, your wives, your children are waiting." One day Littan sent an armored personnel carrier to the home of Ibrahim Abayat's family in Wadi Shaheen and brought his mother, Imm Khaled, to the Peace Center. The colonel urged her to phone her son and press him to surrender. But when she reached him, she encouraged him to be strong and keep resisting.

Littan knew that the Palestinians inside the church fell into three groups: The most defiant were militant leaders, including Ibrahim Abayat and Abdullah Daoud, who understood they faced exile or imprisonment if they surrendered to Israel and who seemed determined to hold out at any cost. The second group consisted of fighters of the al-Aqsa Martyrs Brigades, Hamas, and the mukhabarat, who had pledged loyalty to their commanders but didn't have as much at stake as the leaders did and might be persuaded to give up. The third group comprised Palestinian security men and a few dozen civilians who had been swept up in the chaos of April 2 and had no desire to remain inside. But this group was also unwilling to break ranks—at least for the moment. Despite the Israeli army's assurances that they wouldn't be harmed, most of the Palestinians believed that stepping outside to face a cordon of Israeli snipers and tanks would be suicidal. And those who contemplated braving the ring of troops knew that they would have to answer to their Palestinian confrères. The message from the militants was explicit: anyone who left or tried to leave would be branded a coward and a traitor to the cause—a possible death sentence in highly politicized Palestinian society.

The Palestinian security forces were frustrated by their predicament. Many had thrown down their weapons and retreated to the church when the Israeli tanks rolled into Bethlehem, and they wanted only to return home. "We've got kids, we're not wanted men, we're caught in here by mistake," they frequently complained. But as Chris Bandak later told me, "They didn't dare leave, because it would have been considered treason." Teenagers such as Omar Habib felt the same way. Mohammed al-Madani meanwhile found himself caught between Israeli negotiators and the militants. One day Littan pressed him to organize the evacuation of the dozen teenaged noncombatants in the Basilica. "They're starving in there," he told Madani. But Madani had no desire to be seen as cooperating with Israel, was outraged that the Israeli Defense Forces were surrounding the church, and believed that keeping the entire group together would strengthen the Palestinian Authority's bargaining position. Madani ended up, ironically, supporting the interests of the two men who had been his biggest enemies during the intifada: Ibrahim Abayat and Abdullah Daoud.

One morning two weeks into the siege, Madani gathered the teenagers, including Habib and his friends, beside a pillar in the Basilica and told them the Israelis were ready to accept a limited release of the youngest civilians. "The Israelis say that you are hostages," the governor said. "I am prepared to let those leave who want to leave. I will open the door." Bored and hungry—he often found himself shortchanged during mealtimes—Habib greeted the news of his impending liberation with relief. Then the governor appended a caveat: "I want you to know that whoever leaves the church will be considered a traitor and a lowlife," he told them. "Those who stay will be heroes."

Madani asked those who wished to go to raise their hands. Despite the governor's warning, all twelve boys thrust their hands in the air. "They want you to leave so that the Israelis will come in and kill your brothers," Madani said. "If you stay, I promise you I will give you a job in the governorate when this is over." Madani wore them down: eleven teenagers agreed to remain in the church. Habib would not give up so easily. He pursued the governor to the entrance to the Greek monastery.

"Can you open the door for those who want to leave?"

"Are you sure about this?" Madani asked him.

"I accept that I'm a lowlife," Habib replied. "Just open the door and let me out. I'm very hungry. My mother and sister are alone in the house. Everyone else is in hiding or in jail."

"Stay here," Madani said. "If you go out, everyone else will look down on you. Stick it out. Your family has a big business in Bethlehem. If you leave, you will be harming the reputation of your family."

By now Habib suspected that the governor had no power to coordinate a safe release anyway. "Okay," he said. "I'll stay."

The governor hugged him. "I have three sons, living all alone," he told him. "I'm suffering along with you."

The campaign to keep everyone together was effective. For the first seventeen days of the Church of the Nativity siege, the only Palestinian who left was a sixteen-year-old from Deheishe camp named Jihad Abu Qamil. He attempted to scale the outer wall of the Greek monastery's garden on April 14 to retrieve a carton of cigarettes for Ibrahim Abayat. An Israeli sniper ordered the teenager, who looked about twelve, to freeze, then placed him under arrest. He was taken for interrogation in the Peace Center—Israeli military intelligence was disappointed to learn that the suicide-cell leader Ahmed Mughrabi was not inside the Basilica—and then sent home.

DESPITE HIS INITIAL misgivings Father Parthenius was drawing closer to the men inside the Basilica. The priest was aware that Israel considered dozens to be terrorists, knew full well that there were murderers among them. But thrown together with these men under extreme circumstances, Parthenius began to sympathize with their plight and their political views. Early in the standoff Parthenius provided a room in the monastery to Jihad Ja'ara, perhaps the most prolific killer among the Palestinians, and slowly nursed him back to health. The priest brought Ja'ara extra rations, talked to him about his family, gave him chocolates from the priest's private stash. "I got to know these 'terrorists,'" he told me months later. "They have feelings. They're human beings. They're not lunatics. Some of the younger ones were swaggering around, showing off. But anyone who was over, say, twenty-five or twenty-six, you could see they were fighting for a cause."

While most priests isolated themselves from the men in the Basilica, Parthenius relished the interaction with the trapped Palestinians. One day he found two large drums of olives in the Greek monastery's storage room and passed out dripping handfuls to the grateful men. After the Israelis cut the electricity to most of the church, Parthenius helped the gunmen string extension cords from the Greek Orthodox bell tower, which had a separate power supply, to the Basilica and provided them with power strips that allowed them to keep charging their cellular phones eight or ten at a time. The Israelis shut that source as well, leaving the entire church complex with no power for forty-eight hours. Parthenius learned that a room formerly occupied by the elderly Palestinian housekeeper also had its own current, and, to the cheers of the Palestinians, he restored electricity again.

Parthenius often entered the Basilica by night to wander through the columns and utter reassuring words to the anxious men. Candles pilfered from the Greek storage room flickered across the floor, bathing haggard and unshaven faces in an eerie yellow light. Thick smoke and flame billowed from a huge saucer filled with wax mounted on a tripod in the center of the Basilica. It was near a large aperture in the floor created in the 1930s to expose mosaics underneath that dated from the original fourth-century church commissioned by the Empress Helena, mother of Constantine. The odor of aromatic candles mixed with the sickeningly sweet smell of perfume that the men had begun applying on their clothes to cover their worsening body odor; it often mingled with the scent of burning oregano that the cigarette-deprived captives had picked from the garden and rolled in notepapers to smoke. The fighter with the gut wound lay moaning on the floor in the Armenian chapel, tended to by Sister Lizetta. Parthenius would often find the Palestinians lined up three deep along the south wall, engaged in their Islamic prayers; it was a practice that at first disturbed him but that he soon came to accept.

Parthenius tried to maintain his usual routine in spite of the deprivations and the violence. Most mornings Parthenius and Visarion ventured into the large garden to feed the chickens and cut roses, talking in loud voices, shaking their keys, and stamping their feet as they stepped through the doorway to avoid surprising the Israeli sharpshooters perched on surrounding rooftops and balconies. The snipers would lay down their guns and signal with little waves that the priests could move around safely. While the Franciscans and the Armenian Orthodox priests rarely entered the Basilica, Parthenius and his fellow Greeks continued their rituals and prayers there throughout the ordeal. During the Annunciation of the Virgin Mary in mid-April, Parthenius, Visarion, and the two elderly priests, Father Elias

and Father Naofitos, donned red robes and carried icons and pro-
cessional crosses among the fourth-century columns, as the
Palestinians watched in respectful silence. Most days Parthenius
attended to the chores handled by the Greeks as part of the Status Quo: sweeping the Basilica, cleaning the windows, polishing
the floors of the Nativity Grotto, and soaping down the silver star
above Jesus's purported birthplace.

The priests ate their meals with Madani in the monastery's
dining room, carefully rationing their waning supplies of cheese,
beans, macaroni, canned meat, and tomato paste. They also
parceled out food to the Palestinians: a daily ration consisting of
one large can of beans and one can of tomato paste. Two or three
times a week the Greek patriarchate in Jerusalem tried to ship
cartons of chocolate spread, sliced bread, bologna, olives, and
other food to the priests through the Israeli military. But, fearing
that the priests would share their food with Palestinian militants,
the soldiers confiscated almost all of the packages. (Weeks after
the siege ended, Parthenius would discover boxes of food sent
from the patriarchate moldering in an abandoned house on Milk
Grotto Street.) The Israeli Defense Forces offered to feed the
priests—so long as they left the church and ate their meals at the
Milk Grotto Church, the small Roman Catholic house of worship
200 yards down Milk Grotto Street. But the Franciscans were unwilling to make the journey, which would have required them to
cross the Basilica in front of the two hundred ravenous Palestinians, and the Armenians and Greeks declined the Israeli offer too
in a gesture of solidarity.

At night as the Greek priests slept on couches in the salon
they had converted into living quarters, gunfire and explosions
jolted them awake. Certain sound effects were taped—part of Israel's "psy ops"—but other times they were all too real. The oc-
togenarian Father Naofitos was nearly struck by a bullet that tore
through the window of his quarters facing Milk Grotto Street
when he went to retrieve clothing. During the worst shooting
Parthenius often comforted Madani, who suffered from a moder-

ate form of diabetes exacerbated by the poor diet and whose nerves had been stretched thin by the siege. When a bullet smashed through the window of the guest room in which Madani slept, the petrified man moved in with the priests. He would lie awake at night on a mattress on the floor, trembling and drenched in sweat, certain, he told Parthenius, that the Israelis were about to storm the church.

Small gestures helped to relieve the grimness. One night two weeks into the siege, Parthenius produced a bottle of *tsuika*, a clear Romanian liquor distilled from grain, like arrack. Gathered in the salon, the four priests and the governor drank the powerful intoxicant in tiny glass cups, and then as the governor watched, the clerics broke into Greek folk songs and little jigs. "Viva freedom!" they sang in Greek. "Better an hour of freedom than forty years of slavery." Father Naofitos suggested that all five of them climb to the top of the bell tower and perform the Dance of Zoloka, a ritual that had originated during the 1821 Greek revolution, when Greek mothers and their children danced off cliffs one by one into the Aegean Sea rather than allow themselves to be captured by the Turks. Naofitos headed for the door, only to be restrained by Parthenius and Visarion. The younger men put the old priest to bed on the couch, wishing him sweet dreams.

SWEET DREAMS WERE difficult for Captain Mike Aviad and the other soldiers bunked on thin mattresses in the Peace Center. The men were bored and stressed and couldn't wait for the ordeal to end. During down times Aviad and his men talked politics while one reservist played melancholy jazz riffs on a grand piano. "Everybody was depressed," Aviad remembered a few months later. "We all believed that this operation was okay, that something had to be done. But nobody really believed that it would change anything." Brief flareups of violence punctuated the monotony. One night Aviad and his men engaged Palestinian militants keeping watch in Justinian's Tower in a two-hour gun battle; Aviad shot a flare that ignited a fire on two floors of the Crusader-era fortress. As smoke and flame billowed from the building, his men teased Aviad relentlessly. "What would your mother say?" they joked. The son of the left-wing peace activist Janet Aviad shrugged and said nothing in reply.

Littan, meanwhile, tried to leaven his harsh tactics with occasional humanitarian gestures. After the inferno in the Greek monastery—another black eye to the Israelis, who faced fierce criticism from the Vatican, the Greek and Armenian patriarchates, and other sources—the Israeli command agreed to permit its first evacuation: the injured fighter whose infected abdominal wound had imperiled his life. The Israeli colonel sent word to Anton Salman, by now Littan's favored contact, that he could carry the wounded guerrilla through the Door of Humility and hand him over to the Israeli Defense Forces.

FATHER PARTHENIUS escorted the Roman Catholic attorney to the thick steel door on the afternoon of April 17. As mandated by the 1757 Status Quo, the Greek Orthodox were the official keepers of the key to the Door of Humility, and only they had the right to open and close the portal. Fifty Palestinian militants, armed with loaded assault rifles and homemade pipe bombs, crowded the vestibule behind the two men. Ibrahim Abayat had given the command that if the Israelis attempted to storm the church after Parthenius opened the Door of Humility, the Palestinians would "go down fighting." Seized by fear for the first time since the Palestinians burst into the church on April 2, Parthenius inserted a foot-long iron key into the huge keyhole, turned the key in the lock, and then slowly swung the portal toward him. Sunlight streamed through the tiny doorway. Palestinians surged around the opening, eager for a look. "Don't shove, don't push," Parthenius shouted over excited voices. "None of us are allowed outside."

Edging in front of Parthenius, Anton Salman ducked down and yelled, in English, "Don't shoot! I'm coming out." He and the Greek priest gently eased the fighter with the gut wound through the door and into Nativity Square. Parthenius squinted into the sunlight and stared down the barrel of an Israeli tank cannon aimed at the Door of Humility from fifty yards away. Beside the door, he noticed, was an old army field telephone, placed there by the Israelis in the improbable event that somebody wanted to call in an offer to surrender. Parthenius gave an involuntary laugh at the sight of it. As Parthenius retreated to the vestibule, Salman hoisted the wounded militant on his back and tottered across the square to the Israeli army. One down, Parthenius told himself, and 239 to go.

FOR BOTH SIDES the pressure to negotiate was growing. On the one hand, Leor Littan knew that the longer the siege dragged on, the weaker and more eager for an end to their misery Ibrahim Abayat and the other men would become. The escape into Israeli hands of eight Palestinians just after Salman brought out the injured man—three fled from the Franciscan monastery, another five, all from the Tourist Police, leapt from the Greek bell tower into the Armenian compound and then through the gate leading into Nativity Square—sent a signal to Littan that his tough tactics were having an effect. At the same time the Israelis knew that the men had explosives and that prolonging the siege would increase the chances of damage to the church. By refusing to talk to the other side, they also risked the possibility that the militants might harm the civilians trapped inside with them or decide to shoot their way out in desperation.

Yasser Arafat and other top officials of the Palestinian Authority also felt the time had come to try to break the deadlock. United States Secretary of State Colin Powell had come and gone in mid-April without resolving the Church of the Nativity crisis. The Israeli Defense Forces had withdrawn from all Palestinian-controlled territory except for Bethlehem and the area immediately around Arafat's muqata in Ramallah, but they made it clear they were in no rush to complete the pullout. "We stayed thirty years in Bethlehem and we are prepared to stay another thirty years," an Israeli military spokesman announced during the third week of April. Days after Salman's excursion the Palestinian Authority dropped its demand for third-party participation in talks, and on Tuesday, April 23, Littan and Aviv agreed to meet with a negotiating committee established by Yasser Arafat. Salah Tamari, former guerrilla commander turned Palestinian Legislative Council delegate, led the team. The other members included Bethlehem Mayor Hannah Nasser; Mitri Abu Ita, the Palestinian Authority's minister of tourism; Imad Natsheh, director of the District Civil Liaison Office in Bethlehem; and Anton Salman, representing those inside the church. (Littan had made it clear he preferred Salman to Madani as a negotiating partner.) Alistair Crooke, the chief military attaché to the British Embassy in Tel Aviv, who played go-between during the Beit Jala invasion, served as the Palestinians' unofficial adviser.

On the afternoon of April 24 Tamari and his team were taken in a white Israeli Lantra jeep through the deserted streets of Bethlehem. Riding past the cordon of tanks and snipers ringing Manger Square, they pulled to a stop in front of the Peace Center. At the same time, Anton Salman ducked through the Door of Humility and walked across the square, casting a wary eye upon the Israeli tank cannon pointed in his direction. Colonel Leor Littan and Colonel Marcel Aviv, accompanied by nine military aides, cordially greeted their Palestinian counterparts in a shabby ground-floor meeting room littered with cigarette butts and Styrofoam coffee cups. Then the discussions began. Tamari demanded the Israelis stop the sniper fire. The Israelis said the shootings would only cease if the Palestinians stopped moving about the church with their guns. The Palestinian asked Littan to let him carry a large supply of food into the church. "You can't expect starving people to think or act reasonably," he argued. The

Israelis agreed in principle to a delivery of food, but first insisted on deciding the fates of the most dangerous gunmen. Littan demanded a complete list of the men inside and suggested that they would cull between five and seven people from that list, including Ibrahim Abayat, Abdullah Daoud, and Jihad Ja'ara. Those few would then either be jailed in Israeli prisons to await trial or dispatched into exile overseas. Tamari refused to provide a list of names—"I won't be an informer. That's a job for Israeli intelligence," he told them—and he ruled out any deportations abroad. Tamari understood well the painful connotations for Palestinians of exile, with its echoes of the Israeli-Arab wars of 1948 and 1967 and the flight from their homeland of hundreds of thousands of refugees. "I left Bethlehem in 1963 and I stayed away for thirty-two years," Tamari told Littan and Aviv. "I will not agree to send other Palestinians into exile. This is a taboo in our society." Instead he proposed the Gaza Strip as an alternative. The meeting ended without any issues being resolved, but the men agreed to continue their dialogue the following day.

Ibrahim Abayat led a mob of two hundred Palestinians around Anton Salman as he walked back through the Door of Humility. Holding court in front of the Iconostasis, the attorney laid out the Israeli demands for the exile of "five to seven wanted men." Confronted for the first time with the hard prospect of banishment to Gaza or an undetermined foreign country, Abayat and Daoud left the meeting in a fury: the al-Aqsa Martyrs Brigades commander called Salah Tamari, shouting that he would not be sent to Gaza to be "targeted by Apache helicopters." "You'll go anywhere I tell you to go," Tamari replied. Ibrahim Abayat spent the evening pacing among the columns, smoking his carefully guarded cigarettes and brooding in silence. A mood of melancholy fell over the men inside the Basilica. "After this I felt, 'The siege is not going to end any time soon. It's going to be really tough,'" Parthenius told me later.

Ibrahim Abayat's options were narrowing, and the guerrilla commander swung between self-pity and defiance. He called

Salah Tamari frequently, begging him to send food into the church. "For God's sake, help us, Abu Hassan!" Abayat pleaded. At other moments he gave bellicose phone interviews in which he vowed that he would never surrender. Tamari chastised him after one such interview; he thought Abayat's speeches only antagonized and hardened the position of the Israeli command. "What are you doing? Keep your mouth shut," he said. "It's the last time, Abu Hassan, I promise," Abayat replied. Abayat roamed restlessly through the church during the night, napping in the sacred altar behind the Iconostasis during the daytime. He could be jovial one minute and threatening the next. He denounced the five members of the Tourist Police who leapt over the Armenian compound wall as "collaborators" and warned the rest of the Palestinian Authority security men not even to consider fleeing the church. He conferred with Mazzin Hussein, the policeman turned Tanzim militant, about the possibility of breaking through the Door of Humility and shooting their way to freedom.

OMAR HABIB, awakening in the Armenian chapel just after dawn on April 25, steeled himself for another day of tedium and hunger. The seventeen-year-old had been inside for twenty-three days, and he barely had the energy left to stand. There would be no food today, Habib knew: to make their dwindling stocks last longer, the Palestinian committee of seven in the church had declared that each Monday and Thursday would be a day of fasting for the Muslim men and boys. At ten o'clock Habib caught sight of Madani descending from the Greek monastery. For the second time in two weeks the governor assembled Habib and eight others under the age of eighteen, some of them skeletal and sick after weeks of deprivation. The previous day Leor Littan had asked Salah Tamari to arrange a coordinated release of civilians to prove that they weren't being held as hostages, and Abdullah Daoud had agreed to let nine boys under the age of eighteen depart.

"Okay," the governor told them. "Get ready to leave. You're getting out today." Habib didn't believe him; he assumed the Israelis wanted to keep everyone inside so the food supplies would be stretched as thin as possible. He thought Madani was just testing the boys again.

Habib was returning to his bedroll when Parthenius and Visarion entered the Basilica, carrying white sanitary masks. The priests asked for volunteers among the teenagers to remove the coffins of Khaled Abu Siam and Hassan Quan from the Cave of the Innocents; the Israelis had agreed to their evacuation along with that of the teenagers. Minutes later, the Door of Humility swung open, and Habib stumbled nervously into the sunlight, bearing with three others the crude wooden coffin containing the corpse of Abu Siam, dead for seventeen days. Holding his breath against the stench of decomposing remains that seeped through the wax-sealed wooden box, Habib stared fearfully at the Israeli snipers perched behind pillars and trees and on rooftops and terraces. Israeli troops positioned around a jeep in Nativity Square motioned for him to keep moving. Habib slid the coffin into a Red Crescent ambulance and then staggered into the Peace Center. There he was interviewed by Mike Aviad, then transferred by bus to a further interrogation by Israeli military intelligence officers in the settlement of Gush Etzion—a violation of the agreement made by Salah Tamari and Leor Littan that stipulated that the boys would be sent directly home. At last, in the early evening, Israeli troops dropped the exhausted seventeen-year-old in front of the family home on Star Street. After twenty-three days trapped in the Basilica, Omar Habib was finally free.

The Palestinians left behind could only dream about freedom. Meals now consisted of a few tablespoons a day of rice or macaroni, along with whatever else the Franciscan and Greek priests could spare—a few olives, a can of chick peas. For the first time fistfights broke out over the dangerously dwindling food stocks. Palestinians risked death by creeping into the gardens behind the church, under the guns of Israeli snipers, to forage ferns and leaves from lemon trees, which they boiled into a tart soup. One night the group ate wild lettuce stained with the blood of a man who had been wounded by a sniper while picking it in the garden behind the Church of Saint George. The Basilica was growing ever more fetid: garbage lay strewn about the columns, and the odor of unwashed bodies and decay hung like an infectious miasma. Men desperately looked for a way out: on Sunday, April 28, Parthenius heard loud noises coming from underneath the Greek monastery. Descending to the basement to investigate, Parthenius discovered two militants armed with shovels trying to burrow a tunnel from the disused olive press to a house across Milk Grotto Street. The pair had succeeded in loosening a huge boulder built into the wall—which, if removed, might have caused the monastery to collapse. Parthenius called Madani, who persuaded the men to stop their excavations.

The threat of death still hung heavily over the compound, and a momentary lapse of attention could be fatal. At ten o'clock the next morning Parthenius was drinking his last remaining coffee in his third-floor room when he was jolted by a single gunshot. Emerging into the outdoor corridor, he looked across the courtyard and saw a dozen agitated fighters gathered around the Icon of the Nativity, a black Madonna mural painted on the second floor. A lanky, bearded gunman whom Parthenius recognized as Nidal Abayat—the same Nidal Abayat who had been driving behind Atef Abayat when his booby-trapped Mitsubishi exploded—lay dead beneath the icon, surrounded by his fellow fighters, in a spreading pool of blood. Moments earlier, Parthenius learned, Nidal had finished taking a shower in the second-floor bathroom, the only working shower in the church complex, and was heading back to the Basilica with his M-16 slung over his shoulder. Instead of sprinting across the exposed corridor as he usually did, he had walked—and a sniper manning the robot rifle in the crane above the courtyard had shot him in the heart.

Parthenius later learned that Nidal Abayat's father had dreamt the night before that his son had appeared to him draped in a white *jelabiya*—a sign that he was a visitor from beyond the grave. The old man had awoken in a sweat and called the church that morning, asking the militant who answered the phone whether anything had happened to his son. "He is sleeping now," the militant had answered. "Shall we wake him?" Nidal's father said no. A half hour later Nidal was shot dead. Now as Chris Bandak rang the bell in the Greek tower, signaling another fatal shooting, Parthenius helped carry the gunman's body on a stretcher to a waiting ambulance in Nativity Square. Parthenius had become fond of Nidal during his weeks inside: the militant had come to the priest's room daily to share his food with Parthenius's cat and they had chatted from time to time about their families, religion, and the Palestinian struggle. Parthenius had to battle to suppress his anger as a team of Israeli soldiers coolly took fingerprints from the dead man. "He was very kind, very respectful," Parthenius remembered months later. "When the Israelis told me, 'He's a terrorist,' I said, 'I don't believe you. You're lying.'"

The priests' own sense of solidarity with one another was showing signs of strain. For most of the monthlong standoff Parthenius had maintained cordial relations with his Franciscan and Armenian colleagues, joining them for morning coffee and commiserating over the damage that the monasteries had suffered. But as the siege dragged on, ancient tensions bubbled to the surface. Problems began a week after the Roman Catholic Easter, when the Greek Orthodox priests informed the Franciscans that their failure to remove Easter ornaments from the Grotto violated the Status Quo. During a phone conversation with the Israeli military command shortly after Nidal Abayat's death, the Franciscan priests Father Faltas and Father Sabbara requested permission to exit through the Door of Humility to visit an aging Franciscan priest who had been holed up incommunicado in the Milk Grotto Church for weeks. Littan approved the request, but Parthenius overruled him. Again citing the Status Quo, he reminded the Franciscans that the Door of Humility be-

longed to and was intended for the exclusive use of the Greek Orthodox Church; the only occasions during which the Franciscans
were permitted to pass were funerals. Relaxing the rules, he said,
would establish a dangerous precedent. He offered to let Faltas
and Sabbara exit through the Greek monastery, but the Franciscans, grumbling, claimed that that route was unsafe. Hours later,
however, Sabbara and Faltas quietly opened the portal using a
duplicate key kept without the Greeks' knowledge by the Armenians, and slipped away to Milk Grotto Street. Quickly learning
of their secret departure, Parthenius ambushed Faltas and Sabbara when the Franciscans returned from visiting the church.

"What are you doing with that key?" Parthenius asked.

Faltas, holding the cast iron duplicate, sputtered that the Armenian priest had given it to him.

"This is a serious violation of the Status Quo," he told the
Franciscan. "The patriarchate will know about this and it will go
all the way to the Vatican." The Armenian priest, Father Qad,
begged Parthenius to let the matter rest. Faltas and Sabbara, saying little in response, retreated to the safety of their monastery.
Later that week the Greek patriarch made a formal complaint to
the Vatican; relations between the Greeks and Franciscans stayed
cool for the rest of the siege, and when the standoff was over,
Parthenius changed the lock on the Door of Humility.

ON THE AFTERNOON of April 27 Salah Tamari and the
British military attaché Alistair Crooke drove through the tense
Qalandia checkpoint into Ramallah for their first meeting with
Yasser Arafat since the beginning of the standoff. In exchange for
arranging the release of the nine teenagers, Leor Littan had permitted Tamari one encounter with the besieged Palestinian
leader in the muqata. For Tamari the meeting was vital. Tamari
needed to know that he had Arafat's backing, that he should continue rejecting Israel's demand for overseas deportations and
strictly limit the number of Gaza Strip exiles to seven. The fifty-

eight-year-old Fatah war hero regarded his role in the church siege as a historic opportunity to face down the Israelis, rescue men he regarded as freedom fighters, and further his own political ambitions. It was a delicate task: according to one close friend who met with him during this period, Tamari believed that making too many concessions, failing to bring food into the church, or being perceived as weak in any way could wreck his political career. "Salah is a guy who works with an abacus in his brain," says the friend. "He is always calculating his relationship to his colleagues, his constituents. During the church siege, he always considered what they would think of him in the church. You could see the abacus going every single minute."

An Israeli armored vehicle escorted Tamari and Crooke from Qalandia to the edge of the partly demolished muqata, which was surrounded by a ring of tanks. The men advanced on foot from building to building, under the escort of an Israeli Defense Forces officer, until they reached the sandbagged entrance to Arafat's three-story headquarters. Inside Tamari and Crooke encountered a netherworld: the electricity was out, the Palestinians had drawn all the shades as protection against Israeli snipers, and through the near-total darkness Crooke and Tamari could see filing cabinets and overturned furniture blocking the stairwells. People slept on the floor; bullet holes pocked the walls and windows. A group of European and American peace activists clambered over the debris to guide the two visitors down a corridor by flashlight. The men squeezed past more filing cabinets and entered Arafat's office, where the president sat at the end of a long table sifting through papers by candlelight and eating from a box of biscuits. Arafat seemed distracted, preoccupied by his own predicament; the Palestinian leader was immersed in negotiations mediated by the United States government to end the siege of the muqata by handing over four alleged killers of Israel's former tourism minister Rehavam Ze'evi to the custody of United States and British police, who would guard them in a Jericho prison. Arafat said little as Tamari briefed him for ninety minutes on the siege and his dialogue with the Israelis. Then the Palestinian leader rose from his chair. "Abu Hassan," he said, "I trust your judgment."

Tamari returned to Bethlehem resolved to stay the course: he would maintain his opposition to the overseas deportations demanded by the Israelis. But the same morning that Tamari was visiting Arafat in Ramallah, an incident had taken place that hardened the Israeli position and forced the Palestinian side on the defensive. Gunmen cut through the perimeter fence of the West Bank settlement of Adura, shot dead four Israelis in their beds, including a five-year-old girl, and then escaped. Both Hamas and the Popular Front for the Liberation of Palestine claimed responsibility for the attack. At the meeting in the Peace Center the next day, Littan sat silently for the first twenty minutes of the discussion.

"Why are you so quiet?" one member of the Palestinian team asked him.

"I'm so boiling inside that I'm afraid I will say harsh things," Littan replied. "I was in Adura yesterday and I saw the bloody bed of the child murdered by Palestinian terrorists. This was the fifth time I have seen such things during this intifada. So let's assume for a moment that one of those murderers is trapped inside the church. What should be his destiny? As a soldier I think he should be dead. But as a negotiator I know I have to settle for a less severe punishment. We need to focus on the ninety percent of the people inside who are innocent. Let's get this over with."

After ten seconds of silence in the room, Tamari asked for a short break. A few minutes later the Palestinians' chief negotiator returned. The fierce resolve that had stalled progress in the discussions for the last five days was absent. Reluctantly, Tamari told his Israeli counterpart that he was ready to discuss overseas deportations.

AFTER WATCHING seven men shot in front of him, two of them fatally, Chris Bandak had reached the limits of his endurance. He was starving, fearful of being arrested by the Israelis, and concerned that the mounting desperation of his fellow fighters might drive them to do something rash. Bandak had already cased the compound for an escape route and recruited four men to join him. On the night of May 1, the thirtieth of the siege, he conferred quietly in the Basilica with Abdullah Daoud and Ibrahim Abayat, telling them he was determined to break out the next day. Bandak urged them to keep his plans a secret: he was convinced there were informers among the Palestinians in the church. The Palestinian intelligence chief pleaded with him to abandon the scheme. "The Israelis are everywhere. You will almost certainly be killed," Daoud told him. Bandak asked Ibrahim Abayat to join him, but the al-Aqsa Martyrs Brigades commander replied that his obligation was to remain behind with the rest of his men. He would be, he told Bandak, the last one to leave the church. But he encouraged Bandak to make a run for it.

Abayat's willingness to let Bandak slip away marked a significant change from his previous resistance to anyone's breaking ranks. There were several reasons for this change of heart: Abayat had received assurances from Salah Tamari that the Israelis would not storm the church, so it wasn't really a question of safety in numbers anymore. He had largely reconciled himself to the fact that he would be banished overseas, but he didn't want to compel other wanted men—particularly close friends such as Bandak—to remain inside the church until the end of the siege and suffer a similar fate. Besides, conditions inside had grown so dreadful that he could fully empathize with anyone's wanting out. Not everybody was so understanding. Abayat's fellow Tanzim Rami Kamel and Jihad Ja'ara could not forgive Bandak for what they viewed as his act of desertion; months later they told me, "we all should have stuck together."

Bandak caught a few hours' sleep in the Basilica and awoke at seven o'clock in the morning, while everyone else was still dozing. He shook awake his four comrades. "Let's hit it," he whispered. The men crept into the altar behind the Iconostasis and entered Saint George's Church. In the early morning light they stepped silently over the huddled forms of a dozen Palestinian fighters and descended a staircase leading to the basement refectory of the adjacent Greek monastery. Earlier in the siege fighters had sawed through a barred window here that led to a garden behind Saint George's, and nearly every day the most courageous among the Palestinians ventured through it to forage lemon leaves for soup. Israeli snipers on surrounding balconies and rooftops ringed the garden. Two Palestinians had been shot and seriously wounded here during the standoff.

Bandak and the other escapees squeezed through the window, dropped into the dirt, and crawled for thirty yards across the garden until they reached a high stone wall. It was here that Bandak believed they'd be most vulnerable, but nobody shot at them as they clambered, terrified, over the top and jumped into a larger church garden on the other side. Still unseen, they slithered through high grass past a grove of almond and lemon trees, their branches picked clean by the hungry Palestinians. Two hundred yards farther east through the trees Bandak could see their destination: the eight-story tan stone Russian Hotel at the bottom of Milk Grotto Street, the former Tanzim gathering spot where he had once worked as a security guard. Early in the siege Israeli snipers had occupied the pilgrims' inn, but Russian President Vladimir Putin had complained to Ariel Sharon, who ordered the troops out. Bandak was grateful to the Russian leader; his escape would have been impossible, he knew, if the Israelis had still been in the building.

The five men crept across the garden, well camouflaged by grass and weeds. Peering through the foliage Bandak could see Israeli snipers in surrounding buildings; he drew himself lower to the ground. They kept crawling, inch by inch, until they hit a second stone wall marking the edge of church property. The men scaled the wall, landed in another field, slithered beneath a barbed-wire fence, and found themselves at the bottom of Milk Grotto Street, beside the hotel. The street was deserted. Bandak still had a key to the front door. Breathless, hand shaking, he turned the key in the lock and entered the abandoned lobby. Numbly the five men descended a staircase, half expecting to run into Israeli troops still lurking in the building. But the hotel was utterly empty. They walked out the basement door, hugged one another, and then disappeared into the streets of Bethlehem. Bandak had no plan, no idea where he could safely go. But something, perhaps an urge to tempt fate, compelled him to circle back to Bethlehem's Old City and head for an Israeli military barricade set up for the press at the end of Star Street. Mingling anonymously with the journalists and other spectators, Bandak smiled at the soldiers standing guard at the barricade and gazed at the stone facade of the Church of the Nativity, the white surveillance blimp hovering overhead, and the sniper cranes looming above the courtyards. Then he made a cell phone call to Ibrahim Abayat.

"It's Chris," he said. "I made it."

"*Hamdilullah,*" Abayat said. "Tell me how you escaped."

Bandak explained the route. "It's safe," he said. "It's easy. You have to try. With God's help you'll stay alive."

Abayat promised to think about it. But a few hours later he called back. "If I could go out, I would," Abayat said. "But I'm the leader here, Chris. You know I can't."

THE NEXT MORNING at ten o'clock, the last—and bloodiest—firefight of the siege broke out in the apartment where Bandak had been living for four weeks. Father Parthenius, polishing the oil lamps in the Grotto for the Greek Orthodox Easter, heard gunshots and shouts coming from the direction of Father Visarion's quarters. With Visarion and Father Sabbara, he rushed up the staircase to the second floor of Justinian's Tower and tried to cross the courtyard to Visarion's apartment but was driven back by heavy shooting. "What's going on?" Parthenius shouted. Palestinians inside yelled back that a sniper manning the remote-controlled gun above the courtyard had wounded two men, one apparently fatally. From the refuge of the stairwell, the priest phoned Anton Salman and asked him to tell the Israeli sniper to cease firing so they could retrieve the casualties.

Salman called back a minute later. "He says stay where you are," Salman told Parthenius. "Do not come out or you will be shot." A half hour of sporadic sniper fire followed before the men received permission to cross. Inside Visarion's front room, one gunman lay writhing in agony on the floor, soaked in blood: a dumdum bullet had smashed through his shoulder, torn through his torso, and exited his testicles. "Kill me," he was screaming. "I can't take the pain." Sabbara grabbed his head and shoulders, Parthenius took him around the belt, and Visarion held his feet, and together the men wrested his six-and-a-half foot frame through the doorway. They handed him off to Ibrahim Abayat and a small group of his lieutenants waiting on the staircase, who swiftly brought him to the Basilica. The second fighter was slumped against the wall with a bullet wound in his chest. "He still has a pulse," one Palestinian was saying. "He's still breathing. He's still alive." Parthenius, his hands and clothing now slippery with blood, dragged the unconscious man with Sabbara across the courtyard and passed him to another group of fighters. In the Basilica the gunmen dressed and bandaged the two fighters' wounds while Salman begged the Israelis to send an ambulance—a procedure that had become routine since the start of the face-to-face negotiations. On this occasion it took forty minutes before the vehicle arrived at the Door of Humility. By that time the fighter with the chest wound was dead.

THE CROWD of international media gathered at the entrance to Manger Square had been growing steadily through the siege, and by the first week of May it numbered well over one hundred. The Israeli Defense Forces had pulled back their barricades to the very end of Star Street, and from the edge of the narrow alley one could obtain a clear view of the fortresslike facade of the Church of the Nativity and the Door of Humility. The freezing rain and wind of early April had given way to balmy breezes and cloudless skies, and one could bask in the sun for hours while waiting for a breakthrough in the talks. A phalanx of photographers perched on ladders, aiming cameras at the tiny portal; a rotating crew of Israeli spokespeople trotted from the Peace Center to spin the latest developments. Israeli sharpshooters crouched behind pillars and cars in Manger Square; overhead the white surveillance blimp hovered, looking at once ungainly and sinister.

At times the Star Street stakeouts took on the air of a carnival. Family members of trapped militants, European peace activists, and priests of all denominations milled around the Peace Fountain on Star Street, eagerly offering quotes to journalists. A quartet of Japanese monks in saffron robes banged their drums and chanted Buddhist mantras, praying for an end to the siege. Tempers flared among competing news agencies: one morning a CNN producer demanded to know why the Israelis had allowed Fox TV's Geraldo Rivera to position his crew just yards from the Door of Humility while forcing everyone else to remain behind the barricades. The French-born press liaison promised to look into the matter but never responded, and Rivera continued to enjoy his privileged perch.

ACROSS THE SQUARE in the Peace Center the Israelis and Palestinians inched toward a resolution. Leor Littan and Salah Tamari had spent many hours together at the negotiating table, bonding over their shared background as warriors. Tamari had told Littan about his days kept in chains, deprived of food and water, in solitary confinement in the Ansar prison camp in southern Lebanon; Littan had responded with his own story of being wounded in the failed commando raid to rescue Nachson Wachsman from Hamas kidnappers. Now after two weeks of deadlock both Littan and Tamari believed that they were on the verge of a breakthrough. Tamari had dropped his objections to deportations abroad. The Israeli negotiator had agreed to allow Tamari to enter the church carrying fifty trays of meat, fresh vegetables, and bread—to be shared by the 125 famished men who remained inside. In return Tamari would emerge with at least a partial list of names, from which the Israelis would cull the militants it would send overseas. At that point the numbers remained vague, but Tamari believed that Littan was still talking about seven.

Other figures worked to undermine Tamari and Littan. For nearly a month the United States government had remained on the sidelines of the church negotiations, after Ariel Sharon's CNN interview, in which he said that the United States and Israel operated as a team, undermined its status as an honest broker. But the Americans remained busy on other fronts: on April 30 U.S. negotiators persuaded the Israeli government to pull back its tanks and end Arafat's imprisonment in his headquarters in Ramallah. In return the Palestinians agreed to surrender to joint British and American custody the four suspected killers of Rehavam Ze'evi and a fifth man, Fouad Shubaki, one of Arafat's financiers and the chief suspect behind the shipment of arms to the Palestinian Authority aboard the vessel known as the *Karine A* in January 2002. As a reward for withdrawing the tanks from the muqata, the White House granted Ariel Sharon a long-sought meeting with President George W. Bush in the White House on May 6. With the muqata standoff resolved, United States Ambassador to Israel Daniel Kurtzer now aimed to tackle the stalled church negotiations and conclude a deal before Sharon's trip. "This was the last thing holding up our ability to say that the Israelis had withdrawn from all Palestinian territory," a United States Embassy official explained later. "We pushed our way back [into the negotiations]."

Salah Tamari had jealously guarded his role as the Palestinians' sole negotiator: he had warned the U.S. ambassador several times that violence would erupt in the church if the Americans pushed him aside. "The militants will see it as an act of bad faith," he said. But Kurtzer had grown impatient with Tamari and doubted that he had the flexibility to make a deal happen. The day after the United States concluded the muqata negotiation, the ambassador authorized embassy officials including the CIA station chief in Tel Aviv to contact Mohammed Rashid, a Kurdish-born top adviser to Arafat who had been with the Palestinian leader through the muqata siege, and tell him in the strongest terms that the United States wanted a deal to end the church standoff done within twenty-four hours. At the same time, Sharon pushed Aviv and Littan aside and empowered his Israeli Security Agency, the Shin Bet, to negotiate with the CIA and the Palestinians. The Shin Bet had taken a hard line in the siege, believing that the only possible solution was to starve the men into submission.

TWO DAYS LATER, on Friday, May 3, Tamari and the rest of the committee—still unaware that they were now irrelevant—were driven to the Peace Center in an Israeli jeep. They carried dozens of cartons of cigarettes, antibiotics, aspirin, bandages, and diabetes and asthma medication. By prior agreement the Israelis were to give Tamari the fifty trays of meat and vegetables and allow him to enter the church with the rations. But when Tamari entered the meeting room, he was ambushed by a new participant in the talks: an Israeli intelligence officer he didn't recognize. "No food will be going to the church," the Shin Bet man announced. Tamari, confused, turned to Littan and Aviv, both of whom appeared distraught.

"I'm afraid he's right," Littan said.

"You can go into the church under one condition," the intelligence man said. "You provide us with a full list of the names of those inside."

"That's unacceptable," Tamari replied.

Deeply humiliated, Tamari stormed out of the meeting and phoned Arafat, who was in the middle of his midafternoon nap.

The committee leader spoke instead to Nabil Abu Rdeneh, Arafat's closest aide, and tendered his resignation from the negotiating committee.

THE ENDGAME was fast approaching. At eight o'clock on the morning of Saturday, May 4, General Haj Ismail, commander of the Palestinian Authority's National Security Force, called Abdullah Daoud from Arafat's side in Ramallah. "The leadership wants the names of everybody inside the church," he told the intelligence chief. According to sources inside the church, Ismail promised that the names "will be sent only to Arafat's office." Abdullah Daoud was disappointed and perplexed, but he was also an Arafat loyalist. He dutifully set up a table on the southern side of the Basilica, beside an icon of Saint George and the dragon, and ordered the 125 men who remained to write their names on a sheet of yellow paper.

An angry murmur spread through the church. For weeks Salah Tamari and other Palestinian officials had warned the militants that they should never commit their names to paper, because doing so would give the Israelis vital information and a precious advantage in the negotiations. "Will this paper go to Israel?" demanded Mazzin Hussein, the policeman turned Tanzim militant who was still nursing a scheme with a small group of other fighters to break out of the Door of Humility. Abdullah Daoud repeated what the leadership had told him: only the Palestinian Authority would receive a copy. Both Jihad Ja'ara and Ibrahim Abayat backed Abdullah Daoud; at that point the commander of the al-Aqsa Martyrs Brigades and his wounded lieutenant had come to believe that exile abroad was an acceptable option. The leaders of Hamas denounced the proposed list as "an Israeli and American plot" and announced defiantly that they would refuse to sign. Anton Salman voiced his reservations. But Abdullah Daoud informed the men they had no choice; the alternative, he said, was to die of starvation or under Israeli gunfire.

The grumbling died down; the names were collected and placed in an envelope. At seven o'clock that night Alistair Crooke received the envelope from Anton Salman at the Door of Humility. Crooke then delivered the list to Palestinian intermediaries, who carried it to the muqata. As the men in the church had feared, the Palestinian Authority, pressured by the U.S. government, was obliged to share the list's contents with the Israelis.

The fate of the Palestinians was sealed at the King David Hotel in Jerusalem on Sunday, May 5, in an emotional all-day meeting between Israelis and Palestinians, with American and Egyptian officials in attendance. Before the officials began their discussions Shin Bet had pored through the names on the list and matched them against those they had pieced together from their own intelligence. Ambassador Kurtzer's team urged the Israelis to show restraint. "We were using the number 'low teens' to impress on Israel, 'Don't go after every Tom, Dick, and Harry who's in the church, because almost everyone in there with a gun was probably guilty of something,'" a U.S. diplomat told me. The Israelis had come up with a far bigger number of Palestinians: thirty-nine. They remained inflexible on the point, and U.S. officials eventually dropped their objections. But the Israelis agreed, as a compromise, that they would dispatch to the Gaza Strip those they deemed guilty of lesser crimes. Thirteen militants, including Ibrahim Abayat, Abdullah Daoud, Rami Kamel (Abayat's one-armed lieutenant), Jihad Ja'ara, and Mohammed Said (a member of Ahmed Mughrabi's suicide cell in Deheishe camp) faced banishment in Europe. Sitting across from the Israelis in the King David Hotel conference room, Mohammed Rashid listened to their demand for thirty-nine deportations with disbelief: he had assumed all along that the total number would be about a dozen. Angry Egyptian officials urged him to reject the Israeli demand, as did Alistair Crooke, whom Rashid phoned during a lunch break. But with the U.S. government bringing its will to bear on Arafat to conclude an agreement immediately, the Palestinians had no alternative but to consent.

At four o'clock in the morning on Monday, May 6, two Palestinian Authority officials entered the church to confront a sea of hungry captives, their haggard faces illuminated by the fire burning in the large vat of wax in the center of the Basilica. The Palestinians rushed Arafat's men: Did they bring any cigarettes? Any food? The officials apologized and said they had come only to inform them of the details of the agreement. The Palestinians listened silently as the emissaries read one name after another from the list—thirty-nine men condemned to an indeterminate sentence away from their homeland. The roll call seemed to stretch on interminably. Men hugged one another, collapsed in tears, swore they'd been betrayed by Yasser Arafat. Ibrahim Abayat, despondent yet resigned, tried to console his fighters. Mazzin Hussein, who learned that he would go to Gaza, kicked a pillar in despair. "Thirty-five days we've endured in this place and we've got nothing!" he exclaimed. "Nothing!" Mazzin Hussein and many other militants had vowed never to surrender and had even contemplated a suicidal charge through the Door of Humility. But starving and abandoned, surrounded by an implacable enemy, and faced with a choice of deportation or death, the thirty-nine Palestinians realized that they had no choice but to accept their fate.

FOR FATHER PARTHENIUS the days felt endless now, broken only by a few moments of spontaneity and surprise. The priest was reading upstairs in the Greek monastery on May 3 when he heard a commotion in the Basilica. A delegation of European peace activists, he discovered, had dashed across Nativity Square under the guns of astonished Israeli soldiers and poured into the church through the Door of Humility—swung open on cue by Ibrahim Abayat. The starving Palestinians fell gratefully upon the eleven activists, who had brought bags filled with sardines, hamburgers, canned meat, chocolate milk, spearmint gum, lollipops, and cartons of Marlboro Lights. Several of the Europeans began videotaping the Palestinians and peppering them with questions: "Where are you from?" "Are you with Hamas or Fatah or Islamic Jihad?" "What are you accused of?" After the captives consumed the food, the mood turned ugly. Rumors percolated through the Basilica that the new arrivals were Israeli spies, and Anton Salman suggested that the group leave as quickly as possible. But the Israelis had tightened the ring of tanks and snipers around the church, and escaping was out of the question. Parthenius tried to calm jangled nerves by passing out two boxes of halkum, a candy similar to Turkish delight that the ravenous fighters ate in minutes. The eleven activists settled on the floor, watched over by the priests and eyed warily by the suspicious gunmen.

The Greek Orthodox Easter also brought Parthenius relief from the monotony of the last days of the siege. On Saturday, May 5, the day before Easter Sunday, the Israeli command permitted Parthenius, Visarion, and the Armenian Father Qad to travel by car to the Church of the Holy Sepulcher in Jerusalem to participate in the ceremony of the Holy Fire, one of the most sacred rites of the Orthodox calendar. Resplendently attired in a green-and-gold ceremonial robe, Parthenius joined a throng of Greek, Armenian, and Coptic priests in the gloomy eleventh-century church built on the site of Golgotha—the seventh station of the cross. As the priests looked on, the Greek Patriarch Irineos, wearing a gold crown studded with emeralds and rubies, entered the rose-colored marble edicule, the small interior shrine built in the fourth century containing the stone-hewn tomb of Jesus. Through a hole in the edicule, a hand appeared at that moment holding a fiery torch, said to be delivered directly from God and to represent the resurrection of the Savior. Parthenius and other clerics swarmed around the patriarch, each extending bundles of thirty-three tapered candles to be lit from the torch—each bundle representing the years of Christ's life. As the bells of the Holy Sepulcher rang triumphantly, the clerics bore the Holy Fire out the great iron door to churches and monasteries in Jerusalem and beyond.

Exhilarated crowds lined Virgin Mary Street in Beit Jala as Parthenius entered a small monastery beside the Church of Saint Nikolas and passed the Holy Fire to the bishop. Then he resumed his homeward journey to the Church of the Nativity. As Parthenius burst through the Door of Humility, the blazing candles in his hand, the 125 remaining Palestinian fighters cheered and shouted words of encouragement from both sides of the Basilica. Parthenius proceeded through the nave, descended into the Nativity Grotto, knelt before the altar, and touched the flame to dozens of candles spread around the Silver Star. Then he broke out his secret supply of lemonade—twenty bottles—and shared it with the Palestinians and peace activists in the Basilica. At eleven that night Parthenius returned to the Grotto for the Greek Orthodox equivalent of midnight mass—the Divine Liturgy celebrating the resurrection of Jesus. Attended by his three fellow priests, two Christian gunmen, and Madani, Parthenius illuminated every oil lamp and, with the Grotto flooded with golden light, chanted prayers from the twelve gospels describing the Passion of Christ. "Christ has risen," Parthenius wrote in his diary before dawn on Easter Sunday, after sharing a stale cake and a bottle of rosé wine with the priests and the governor. "Indeed, he has risen."

PALE, PLAGUED BY migraines, hungry, and weak, Ibrahim Abayat paced the stone floor, a mobile phone in his hand. Gone was the confidence of the gunman who had once strutted around Bethlehem, who had vowed to go out "either a winner or a martyr." Now Abayat was feebly pleading for exile. The rumor circulated that Abayat's destination would be Italy, and in an interview I conducted with him from Imm Khaled's house in Wadi Shaheen shortly after the Holy Fire celebration, he said I should tell the world that he would gladly move there. "They've got spaghetti there," he told me, "so I'll be okay." Moments later Abayat's mother took the telephone. "Abu Atef," she said, "may

God bless you. You still haven't received food? We hope God will send you a table of food like he did to the Prophet Moses in the desert." When Abayat told her that his last meal had been two spoonfuls of macaroni, eaten the previous day, she began to weep. Her son calmed her, then begged her to let him hang up. "I'm too weak to talk," he said.

THE DEAL HAD not yet come together. Ambassador Daniel Kurtzer left Israel for Washington on Easter Sunday, May 5, with Prime Minister Ariel Sharon, all but certain the church siege would end within hours. The Italian ambassador to Israel, Giulio Terzi di Sant'Agata, had called Kurtzer just before the trip and told him that Prime Minister Silvio Berlusconi was close to agreeing to accept all thirteen Palestinian militants whom Israel had ordered into exile. As the U.S. ambassador boarded his plane at Ben Gurion Airport, Terzi di Sant'Agata phoned again, this time assuring Kurtzer that he had talked to all the right people in Berlusconi's office and the deal was just about done. By the time Kurtzer arrived in Washington, however, the Italian government was in an uproar: Berlusconi, facing criticism from Jewish groups and from influential pro-Israel figures within his government, said he had never offered the militants an invitation. Kurtzer was dismayed: the Italian ambassador, he assumed, had either jumped the gun or been misled by someone close to the Italian prime minister. Kurtzer turned to Miguel Moratinos, the European Union's special envoy to the Middle East, and asked him to find a solution—fast.

Moratinos, a Spanish career diplomat, began working the phones. On Monday he called the President of Cyprus, Glafcos Clerides, and pressed him to offer his Mediterranean island as a refuge to the thirteen men. The following day, May 8, Sharon returned to Israel, his visit to the United States cut short by a suicide bombing in a crowded pool club in the Tel Aviv suburb of Rishon Lezion that killed fifteen Israelis. Arriving at Ben Gurion

Airport with Sharon early Wednesday morning, Kurtzer learned to his chagrin that the Cypriots had still not responded to Moratinos's request. From a car heading to Tel Aviv, Kurtzer telephoned Donald Bandler, the U.S. ambassador to Cyprus, and asked Bandler to call the Cypriot president directly. "Do it," he said, "and I'll get you instructions from Washington." Two hours later, under U.S. pressure, Clerides agreed to accept all thirteen Palestinians on a temporary basis.

One last complication arose as the Americans prepared to evacuate the church. Israeli officials demanded that the Palestinian militants and security forces submit their weapons to ballistic tests: they would return only those guns that the Palestinians had not used to carry out attacks against Israelis. The Palestinians rejected the demand. After many hours of haggling, the CIA station chief proposed an acceptable compromise: as they left the Basilica, the men would deposit their guns in a booth in the vestibule used by the church's security police. Then the men would pass through an airport-style metal detector to ensure that they were unarmed. The CIA would assume custody of all arms until the adversaries could reach a permanent agreement.

THE ISRAELIS dismantled their sniper cranes, and the Palestinians spilled into the gardens and courtyards, soaking up the sun. The cordon of tanks and troops around the church loosened up as well, and cigarettes, lentils, rice, meat, and chocolate bars began pouring through the door on Milk Grotto Street. Anticipating the confiscation of weapons at the door of the church by the CIA, the fighters wrapped their M-16s and sidearms in plastic bags and buried them in the church gardens, hid them behind stones from the ancient walls, and submerged them in the wells of the Greek Orthodox monastery. One Hamas militant removed the tiles from the doorway of Parthenius's apartment, planted his pistol and cartridges in the dirt, and carefully replaced the tiles while the priest looked on. Others secreted their guns inside

Parthenius's washing machine, video player, and television. (The fighters and the relatives of those sent into exile showed up the day after the siege ended to reclaim their cache.) At a hearty final dinner of lentils and rice—with extra portions for everybody—on Thursday night, those who were staying in Bethlehem embraced Ibrahim Abayat and the thirty-eight others destined for exile, murmuring comforting words. The fighters held hands and kissed each other; Parthenius suppressed tears as he bade farewell to men whom Israel had deemed its most vicious enemies. One militant after another hugged the priest good-bye.

"*Abuna*," a few assured him, "when we go out and this is over, we'll bring back our children to the church and we'll sit and have coffee together."

With nearly everyone too anxious and excited to sleep, the vigil continued through the night. The peace protestors, who had by now convinced the Palestinians that they were not agents of the Israelis, circulated with video cameras, recording the event for posterity.

Just how posterity would view the Church of the Nativity siege was, in those last hours, still murky. As the men prepared to depart the Basilica, both sides could lay claim to victories. The Israelis had forced the Palestinian Authority to surrender to international custody dozens more militants than the leadership had originally been willing to hand over. They had achieved that result without causing physical damage to the holy site or irreparable harm to their relationship with the Vatican and the Greek and Armenian Orthodox churches. Israel had decapitated the leadership of Hamas and the al-Aqsa Martyrs Brigades in Bethlehem and banished, perhaps permanently, nearly all its deadliest enemies in town—figures such as Ibrahim Abayat, Abdullah Daoud, Mohammed Said, Rami Kamel, and Jihad Ja'ara.

The Palestinians could also find cause for satisfaction. Although Arafat had broken a long-standing taboo by sending men into exile, he had denied the Israelis the accomplishment of their original goal: to kill or capture all of the besieged militants and try those they arrested in Israeli courts. The Palestinian gunmen remained, to a certain extent, free—and might someday be able to return to their homeland. An American political consultant who knew Arafat well confronted the president at the muqata in Ramallah weeks later. "You crossed a red line by agreeing to deportations," he told Arafat. "That's your red line, not mine," Arafat replied. "My red line is surrendering men to Israeli prisons, because then I have to negotiate to get them out."

But the Palestinian Authority had not fared well on other counts. The storming of the holy site by armed Tanzim had exacerbated the ill will felt toward the Palestinian leadership and its cadres by the Arab Christian community. Many Christians believed that Fatah's use of the church for tactical purposes and the gunmen's insistence on carrying weapons inside the holy site constituted outrageous acts of contempt. They resented the fact that the militants had forced the clergy to provide them with protection, and condemned the thuggish behavior of some gunmen: at one point late in the siege several Palestinians had robbed and terrorized an aging Armenian monk and rifled through every room in the Armenian monastery looking for food and valuables. The Palestinian leadership had tried to present the siege as a shining example of Christian-Muslim cooperation. But it was cooperation enforced at gunpoint, and the Christian community remained bitterly cognizant of that fact.

The United States and the European Union could feel a measure of gratification at the way they had resolved the standoff. After several false starts, the Americans and Europeans had forced two bitter adversaries to the bargaining table, had achieved a compromise that all sides could live with, and had maintained their standing as honest brokers. The impasse had not ended without bloodshed: Israeli snipers had shot fourteen Palestinians over the course of the siege, seven of them fatally. But the negotiators had managed to avert a Waco-style catastrophe and had proven that outside intervention could make a difference in the Israeli-Palestinian conflict. Even so, the end of the Church of the

Nativity siege was a cause as much for grim reflection as for relief. It had taken thirty-nine days and the full weight of the international community to resolve what was, in essence, a relatively minor dispute. Bridging the ever-widening abyss of distrust and hatred that separated the Israelis and the Palestinians seemed, in this context, a more formidable challenge than ever.

GOVERNOR MADANI and Anton Salman left the church before the militants in the gray light of dawn on Friday May 10. Then a security team from the United States Embassy was deployed in front of the church to oversee the transfer of the Palestinians from the Basilica to Israeli buses. Ibrahim Abayat ducked through the Door of Humility at seven o'clock, drawing on his ever-present cigarette, waving to Imm Khaled and other family members who had gathered on a rooftop to see him one final time. He still didn't know where he was going, but at this point he didn't care. He was happy to leave the stinking, claustrophobia-inducing Basilica forever. Then the Israelis separated him and the thirty-eight others destined for exile from those remaining behind, and took them to the military headquarters in Gush Etzion for interrogation before driving them to Ben Gurion Airport.

Later that day, as the tanks and armored personnel carriers rolled away in a cloud of dust from Manger Square, Samir Zedan and I joined a throng of priests, nuns, and ordinary worshipers who poured through the Door of Humility to survey their beloved Basilica. Women wept as they wandered through the gloomy hall, gazing upon bedrolls, water bottles, kerosene lamps, and other detritus scattered among the columns. But except for the fire-gutted rooms in the Parish Building and Justinian's Tower, the damage was minimal. Gold and silver crosses, crystal chandeliers, and ancient frescoes gleamed through the murk, as they had for centuries. Despite Israeli claims that the Palestinians had looted and vandalized the church, nothing appeared to have been touched.

As dusk fell on Bethlehem, the priests began to clear the church. Joyful crowds gathered in Nativity and Manger Squares, celebrating the lifting of curfew; for the first time since early April Bethlehemites could move freely through their city without fear of being shot. Ibrahim Abayat and his twelve fellow militants, accompanied by Alistair Crooke, were at that moment aboard a British military flight to Cyprus. Only a few hours earlier Miguel Moratinos had put the last pieces of the deal in place, gaining commitments from seven European nations—Portugal, Belgium, Cyprus, Spain, Greece, Italy, and Ireland—to accept the exiles.

The Basilica was empty now. In the gathering darkness Parthenius left the hall and crossed the courtyard to the Greek Orthodox bell tower. He began to ring the great bells, yanking the heavy rope with all his strength. The tolling echoed across Manger Square and through the alleys of the Old City—a resounding, joyful clamor that quickened and gathered force. The priest pulled and pulled until he felt he could go on no longer, and then, as he faltered, he heard the bells from Saint Catherine's Church in the Franciscan monastery picking up where he left off. Parthenius dropped the rope and caught his breath. After thirty-nine days the Church of the Nativity siege was over.

EPILOGUE

∽⟡∼

WE DEPARTED EARLY FROM BARCELONA, BEATING the rush-hour traffic as we drove from Las Ramblas through the elegant heart of the city. The national highway led west across the dusty plains of northern Spain to Zaragoza, and from there the landscape changed dramatically: red-rock escarpments, centuries-old churches and monasteries perched on cliffs. The road dipped and rose through rolling hills covered with a crazy quilt of yellow, green, and pink agricultural fields. Ancient Spanish towns rolled past. In the hamlet of Bulbuente, graffiti on an abandoned café proclaimed, *"Yanquis, Judios son genocidos!"* Americans and Jews commit genocide.

On an unseasonably cold and windy afternoon in early July 2002, Samir Zedan and I were on our way to a village called Lubia, in the province of Castilla y León, to interview Ibrahim Abayat, now beginning his third month in exile. The thirteen Palestinian militants had remained incommunicado since the end of the Church of the Nativity siege, and I had been curious to find out what had happened to these violent men after they had been stripped of their identities as guerrilla fighters. Zedan, who had established a good relationship with Ibrahim Abayat, had called him in late June and proposed that we visit, and Abayat had readily accepted.

Passing the central Spanish resort town of Soria, we drove for a few miles through a valley hemmed in by pine-forested mountains, then turned right onto a dirt track that wound through a grove of eucalyptus trees. A Palestinian flag flapped from a tree branch inside a fenced compound. Two green-and-white jeeps of the Guardia Civil were parked in front of the gate, and as we approached, a half dozen uniformed policemen and a plainclothes officer spilled from the vehicles. Abayat had told his guards that he was expecting visitors, but the government had banned journalists from the compound in Lubia, not wanting to draw attention to the presence of Palestinian militants. As we'd planned, Zedan told the officers in fluent Spanish that we were family friends of Abayat's from Bethlehem, bringing photographs and news from home. He withdrew from his jacket pocket a handful of snapshots that Imm Khaled had given us in Wadi Shaheen a few days earlier.

"You just want to bring him some pictures?" the plainclothes security man asked, perusing the prints.

"*Sí,*" Zedan replied.

He took our passports and went into a booth to make a call, while the uniformed officers searched the trunk and peered beneath the car with a mirror attached to a long pole. Minutes later the plainclothes cop returned. "You can drive in," he said, opening the gate and pointing to a parking lot near the guard booth.

Then as the Guardia Civil ran metal detectors over our bodies and rifled through our bags, Ibrahim Abayat emerged from the house. It was strange and unsettling to see the former commander of the al-Aqsa Martyrs Brigades in this context. Abayat wore a gray tee shirt, blue jeans, tennis shoes, and a black-and-white checkered kefiyeh tossed around his neck. He embraced Samir Zedan warmly, in Palestinian style—a firm hug and a kiss planted on each cheek. To me he offered a brisk, businesslike handshake and a nod of recognition. Stripped of his assault rifle and plunked down in this isolated compound in Western Europe, he seemed defanged and rather ordinary. If I hadn't known his violent background, I could have mistaken him for a Palestinian exchange student. "I always wanted to travel to Europe," Abayat told us, leading the way to his home away from home, "but I never thought it would be like this."

We walked across a wide lawn dotted with picnic tables and long pine benches, toward a two-story whitewashed stucco villa with a red tile roof and balustraded wooden terraces. Bathed in the shade of towering oak trees, it had a rustic, homey feeling to it. Inside the wood-paneled living room, decorated with mounted deer antlers, stuffed birds, and other hunting trophies, a large-screen television was blaring al-Jazeera, the Arabic satellite network. Abayat's two comrades in exile—Aziz Abayat of Hamas and Ahmed Hamamreh of the al-Aqsa Martyrs Brigades in Doha—sprawled on the couch, watching footage of Israeli tanks sweeping back into Bethlehem. They stood and extended their hands in welcome.

The men had arrived here six weeks earlier, after a drawn-out odyssey from Bethlehem, Abayat said. Landing in Cyprus aboard a British military flight, they spent a week at the seaside Flamingo Hotel in Larnaca while waiting for Miguel Moratinos to finalize the distribution of the thirteen exiles among six other European nations. Arriving in Madrid on May 22, the three were each given two thousand dollars in cash by the Palestinian Authority ambassador to Spain, then packed into a police car and driven one hundred miles northeast to this government-owned hunting lodge—built during the regime of Francisco Franco and used most recently as a weekend retreat for Spain's former prime minister Felipe González. It was a way station, a temporary stopover while Spanish politicians and security forces bickered about how to handle these sensitive strangers in their midst. Their arrival caused commotion at first: Spanish journalists from the nearby town of Soria massed around the compound gates, begging the Guardia Civil to let them interview the exiles. A local citizens' committee held an angry meeting to protest the presence of the "terrorists." But the interest faded, and the three men were left alone in their remote quarters in the forest, their only company a live-in Spanish-Moroccan housekeeper-cook who also served as a translator between the Palestinians and their Spanish guards.

The cook served us Arabic coffee, and we sat around the dinner table discussing how Abayat was adjusting to exile. Not well, it turned out. He was still brooding about the decisions he had made in the church—rejecting a chance to flee with his friend Chris Bandak, persuading his comrades not to make a suicidal escape attempt through the Door of Humility. The Israelis had mocked him after taking him into custody, he said. After Abayat's arrival at Israeli military headquarters in Gush Etzion, a settlement five miles south of Bethlehem, an intelligence officer known as "Captain Sabreh" had paraded him through the offices like a trophy. Sabreh had then taken Abayat alone into a room, locked the door, and told him: "You know I could kill you now if I wanted to."

"I don't give a shit," Abayat said he had replied. "I have always been willing to accept death for my country."

Sabreh had looked at him skeptically. "If that's true, you would have stood firm in front of our tanks. But you ran into the church."

Abayat said he had replied, "I know it hurts you that I'm still alive, but I'm ready to die a martyr."

But it was too late for martyrdom, and Abayat knew it. Lighting up a Marlboro, he fingered a key chain adorned with two laminated photos of his predecessors as head of Bethlehem's al-Aqsa Martyrs Brigades—the late Hussein Abayat and the late Atef Abayat. Both had met bloody ends, both had entered the pantheon of Fatah heroes whose exploits would be celebrated by future generations of Ta'amra. The knowledge of his predecessors' glory, and his own abject surrender, gnawed him to the core. "I feel that perhaps I did not live up to my promise to die as a martyr," he admitted. "I think it would have been a more honorable end."

ABAYAT'S LIFE HAD been drained of its drama. He had thrived on danger and conflict. Now he spent his days sitting in front of al-Jazeera, chain-smoking his stash of Marlboros, and making cell phone calls to his family and fellow exiles using phone cards purchased with his two-thousand-dollar allotment from the Palestinian Authority. He was a prisoner, and he hated it. "We talk about ways of improving the situation," he told me. "One week ago we held a protest. We hung up signs on the street outside asking for our freedom. Somebody from the Interior Ministry came and said, 'We are aware of your troubles. We will try to improve things.'" Since then a volunteer Spanish teacher had visited them every morning, and the exiles had received permission to make three shopping trips each week to Soria, accompanied by plainclothes guards. Two days earlier they had spent five hours horseback riding in the forested mountains that rise just outside Soria. And signs had emerged that their forced isolation was about to end: Spanish authorities had returned their passports, assured them they would soon receive resident permits, and granted visas to the wives of Aziz Abayat and Ahmed Hamamreh. But I had the feeling talking to Abayat that it would take months, perhaps years, for him to accept the parameters of his new life. "The worst part of it is the homesickness," Abayat told us. Turning to Zedan he said, "Samir, you lived abroad, you speak English, you had advantages, but still you suffered. Imagine how it must be for us." He took a drag on his Marlboro. "A week ago I asked to return to Palestine, whether they put me in jail or not," he admitted.

Against my expectations I found myself sympathizing a bit with Ibrahim Abayat. Languishing in this hunting lodge in the middle of nowhere, he seemed lost and forsaken by the high-ranking figures who had empowered him during the intifada. But then I considered Ibrahim Abayat's violent record—the shootings of unarmed Israeli settlers, his acquiescence, if not full-scale participation, in the murder of seventy-two-year-old Avi Boaz, the abuses his Tanzim gang had committed against their own people. Given the code that Ibrahim Abayat had lived by, I thought, he should probably consider himself lucky that he wound up in comfortable exile, rather than a grave.

Zedan and I lingered with the exiles throughout the day,

walking the grounds, watching the latest news from the Middle East on al-Jazeera. Late in the afternoon two officers of the Guardia Civil burst into the house and to my dismay ordered me to leave at once: I had made the mistake of carrying my laptop computer into the house, not wanting to leave it in the trunk of my car, and the Guardia had after consideration decided that I was indeed a journalist. Zedan argued strenuously in Spanish with the men, and after about fifteen minutes they relented. Zedan chuckled as they walked out the door.

"What did you tell them?" I asked.

"I said that you were engaged to be married to Ibrahim Abayat's sister and that you had every right to visit a member of your family."

The Spanish-Moroccan cook prepared dinner for us. Gathered around the dining room table, we shared a generous spread of chicken paella, beef, hummus, and tabouli, with watermelon for dessert, while discussing the politics of Palestine. Abayat was in a convivial mood—the first time I'd seen him so relaxed in all our encounters. He told us that he had always opposed the suicide bombings of civilians and had argued vigorously against the attacks with Ahmed Mughrabi, the leader of Deheishe's suicide cell. But he said he understood why Mughrabi had chosen that path. "Sometimes you are caught in a situation where there is a popular demand," he explained, "and you risk falling out of favor if you don't do it. For me, confronting settlers was always my first priority." I asked him whether he considered Osama bin Laden, who had expressed support for the Palestinian cause, to be an ally. "Maybe in Germany the neo-Nazis also support the Palestinian cause," he replied. "Does that mean we have to be friends with them?" As the night wore on, the former Tanzim commander grew by turns melancholy and defiant. He said that Ariel Sharon had crushed the intifada this time around but added, "The Israelis have to ask themselves, is the question resolved? Or will the next generation be filled with even more hatred?" Abayat told me that Moratinos, the European Union special envoy, had assured him that he would be able to return home when Palestine achieved statehood, but he recognized that the day lay in the distant future. "I will live to the last second of my life waiting to go back to Palestine," he said as we shook hands good-bye. I felt another flicker of sympathy for the former Tanzim commander, but it dissipated quickly. In my eyes Ibrahim Abayat was a sociopath whom the intifada had elevated into a freedom fighter. Whatever one's opinions about the Israeli settlers who occupied Palestinian land, the sniper attacks carried out against them by the Abayat gang along the bypass road had been cowardly murders. Moreover, the Tanzim's reign of terror in Bethlehem had victimized their fellow Palestinians as much as it had Israelis. Arafat and his underlings certainly bore the primary responsibility for transforming volatile, violent characters such as Ibrahim Abayat into evanescent heroes. But, I thought, credit also belongs to Ariel Sharon, whose determination to crush the Palestinian uprising by force, and force alone, had helped create a whole generation of militants and martyrs.

FOR THE TEN other Palestinian exiles scattered across Europe, conditions varied greatly. Abdullah Daoud, the head of the intelligence division in Bethlehem, had irritated his Cypriot hosts with belligerent interviews in which he criticized his living conditions; in November 2002 the government expelled him to the destitute West African nation of Mauritania, the only Arabic-speaking country willing to take him in. The two militants in Greece were studying in universities and moving about the country freely; the two in Italy—including Mohammed Said, the member of Ahmed Mughrabi's suicide cell—had been prevented from talking to the press, hidden in undisclosed locations, and warned that they would be turned over to the Israelis if they abandoned these tight security arrangements. Italian officials compared their situation to that of "mobsters who turned state's evidence and entered witness protection programs."

Jihad Ja'ara and Rami Kamel, the two members of the Abayat militia who had been dispatched to Ireland, were faring better. Zedan and I met them in the lobby of the seedy Royal Dublin Hotel on a brisk afternoon in October 2002, after they had shaken off the Irish intelligence agent who accompanied them around the clock. Kamel, whom I had last seen cradling an M-16 in his one remaining arm in Manger Square, was nearly unrecognizable from our previous encounter. Kamel was clean shaven and smartly dressed; the European Union had provided him with a flesh-colored prosthetic limb so technologically advanced that he could manipulate all of the fingers through neuroelectric impulses transmitted from his brain. I found it ironic that so many innocent Palestinians were suffering under Israeli occupation, yet Kamel, a suspected murderer, was enjoying benefits he'd never have received in the West Bank. Although he had agreed to talk to me for the book project, Kamel was keeping a low profile: a female Australian doctor in Dublin who had examined Kamel shortly after his arrival had asked him, "How did you lose your arm?" The former guerrilla had replied, "In a car accident." The doctor had looked at him askance and said, "You're lying." At that point, Kamel said, the intelligence agent lurking in the background had stepped forward and told her, "Just keep working."

Unlike Kamel, Jihad Ja'ara seemed to revel in his infamy. As we sat in the lobby of the Royal Dublin, surrounded by elderly locals and tourists sipping tea, Ja'ara recounted in lurid detail how he had organized the kidnapping and murder of the elderly American Israeli Avi Boaz nine months earlier, and shot dead seven collaborators the morning that the Israelis invaded Bethlehem. He was a chilling character. At one point, speaking to him in my beginner's Arabic, I said something that set off an intense exchange between him and Zedan. After the interview was over and Ja'ara had gone, Zedan told me that I had unwittingly pronounced the word "Bethlehem" in a Hebrew accent. Zedan had had to swear to him that I wasn't an Israeli to keep him from storming off. It occurred to me that, had I made the same mistake while interviewing Ja'ara on his own turf in Bethlehem, I might not have lived to write about it.

THROUGHOUT THE SPRING and summer of 2002 Israeli tanks and troops swept through Bethlehem's refugee camps to hunt militants who had eluded them during the Church of the Nativity siege. On May 27, five days after a sixteen-year-old boy from Bethlehem blew himself up in a pedestrian mall in Rishon Lezion, killing himself and two Israelis, two dozen soldiers, acting on a tip, surrounded a house at the top of Deheishe camp. When the troops demanded that all inside surrender or die, a tall, bearded guerrilla appeared at the door with his hands in the air.

"Who are you?" the Israeli commander asked.

"Ahmed," the man replied.

"Ahmed who?"

"Ahmed Mughrabi."

The leader of Deheishe's suicide cell was taken into custody, and the Israelis danced jubilantly on the balcony of his hideout, located yards from the Mughrabi family home. Israeli troops arrested Ali Mughrabi, Ahmed's sixteen-year-old brother, the same day in a nearby house. They also picked up Ibrahim Sarahneh, who had driven Ayat al-Akhras and two other teenaged bombers to their deaths. Mughrabi's passive surrender was deeply disillusioning to many in Deheishe camp. "Ahmed Mughrabi was ready to send kids to be suicide bombers, but he refused to engage when surrounded by Israelis," Mohammed Laham, the Fatah godfather in Deheishe, told me. "This raised a lot of questions about him. People said, 'It was easy for you to sacrifice people's children, but you weren't willing to sacrifice yourself.'"

In November 2002, six months after Ahmed's arrest, his wife, Hanadi, gave birth to an eight-pound boy, Mahmoud, named after Ahmed's "martyred" younger brother. The boy had been conceived, Hanadi told me, while the couple was living underground, just before Mughrabi orchestrated the suicide bombing outside a yeshiva in Beit Israel that left ten Israelis dead. "Ahmed always wanted to have a son," she told me one day at Yusuf Mughrabi's home as she swaddled her sleeping child in a yellow blanket. "You can see he is a big boy, just like his father." Barring an unlikely amnesty or prisoner swap with the Hezbollah guerrillas of Lebanon, who periodically kidnapped Israeli soldiers and released them in these sorts of exchanges, young Mahmoud Mughrabi would never know his father outside an Israeli prison cell. Israeli military prosecutors were asking for a sentence of eighteen consecutive life terms, one for each Israeli whom Ahmed Mughrabi was accused of murdering.

Later in the summer of 2002 the Israeli Defense Forces began a new campaign through the West Bank of demolishing the homes of family members of suicide bombers and expelling some to Gaza. The military argued that this would both punish relatives who had abetted the terrorists and act as a deterrent against future attacks. Before dawn one August morning Israeli troops swept through Bethlehem, giving the parents and siblings of two Islamic Jihad bombers half an hour to pile their belongings on the sidewalk before blowing up their houses with dynamite. Afterwards the troops handed out leaflets in Arabic to the families and their neighbors: "The Israeli Defense Forces are implementing these missions to prevent terrorists from acts of savage killing," the leaflet read. "You must know that each one who helps will pay a heavy price. Stop and think. Your destiny and that of your family are in your hands. [signed] The Commander of the IDF in Judea and Samaria." The father of the Doha bomber tore up the pamphlet in front of the soldiers and tossed the pieces in their faces.

That same morning I visited Ayat al-Akhras's family, who assumed that they were next on the Israelis' list. From the end of his alley in Deheishe camp, Mohammed al-Akhras had watched the Israelis destroy the hilltop Doha home of the Islamic Jihad bomber, and afterwards he had swiftly removed all his furniture and stashed it in a neighbor's place. Twice Israeli soldiers had burst into the house and surveyed his rooms, discussing in front of the family exactly how much dynamite they'd need to bring the four-story structure to the ground. "The only thing that's stopped them is their worry that the explosives will destroy the houses built on either side of mine," al-Akhras said as he sat on a frayed piece of carpet in his empty sitting room, smoking a cigarette. Al-Akhras was lucky again: hours after my visit, the Israelis took another look around and left without demolishing the house.

I found it hard not to have sympathy for Mohammed al-Akhras, who had been oblivious to his daughter's deadly entanglement with Ahmed Mughrabi and was guilty only, perhaps, of passing on to her his own hatred of Israeli occupation. I also thought it was doubtful that these house demolitions would dissuade young would-be martyrs. Most were swept up by rage, by a thirst for revenge, and by the sick exaltation of suicide bombers that still infected Palestinian society, and they gave little thought to the fate of their families. At the same time it was difficult to challenge Israel's right to take punitive action. In the two years since the uprising began, ninety-six Palestinian suicide bombers had blown themselves up inside Israel's pre-1967 borders, killing more than three hundred Israelis, and the Palestinian Authority was long past being able to stop the forces it had unleashed.

The problem was that Ariel Sharon's dependence on retribution alone to put down the uprising promised only the perpetuation of the dismal status quo. For the foreseeable future, Israelis and Palestinians were faced with the long-term reoccupation of the West Bank, economic misery on both sides of the Green Line, and a devastating suicide bombing every couple of months to remind Israelis that even full-scale reoccupation could not totally protect them. Sharon had come to office early in the al-Aqsa intifada promising to restore Israel's security. But he had proved to be a man without vision, relying only on escalating military tactics to maintain a tolerable level of terror. As long as Sharon tried to bring the Palestinians to their knees, I thought, while offering them no incentives to end the uprising, the wretched state of affairs was likely to continue.

Many Israelis countered that argument with a reference to recent history: Yasser Arafat had blown a historic opportunity to make peace by rejecting Ehud Barak's offer at Camp David in July 2000, they said. The Israelis had tried negotiation—they had offered the Palestinians a state—and had gotten murder and mayhem in return. The time was past for deal making, they argued; Israel's only possible course of action was to defeat the Palestinians militarily, then enforce a policy of total separation by constructing a physical wall between the two societies. Yet such reasoning struck me as based on shaky evidence. For one thing, it was by no means evident that Barak's offer was especially generous. The offer, if accepted, would have kept the West Bank divided into noncontiguous Bantustans, maintained Israeli control over the would-be Palestinian state's water supplies and its eastern border with Jordan, and guaranteed the perpetuation of many Israeli settlement blocs. The uprising had been as much the result of Israeli arrogance and intransigence in the post-Oslo years as of Arafat's and his people's misplaced belief in violence, I thought, and until the Israelis were willing to accept that, there could be no movement toward peace. Offering the Palestinians a few carrots along with the sticks, I thought—freezing settlements, easing the harsh conditions of closure, even withdrawing unilaterally from the Gaza Strip, where 6,500 Jewish settlers effectively hold hostage more than 1 million Palestinians—would help to break the violent cycle by lifting the atmosphere of despair in which the extremist groups Islamic Jihad and Hamas flourished.

Sadly, nothing in the prime minister's character or history indicated he was prepared to offer such incentives. The man who had orchestrated the bloody 1982 invasion of Lebanon and bore indirect responsibility for the massacres at Sabra and Shatila refugee camps seemed even now, in his old age, to understand only the language of force when it came to dealing with the Palestinians. It seemed to me, as well as many other observers, that Sharon was willing to accept an occasional attack against his people as an excuse to stall on any rollback of the state of occupation. He paid lip service to the creation of a Palestinian state—on 40 percent of West Bank land, an offer that would remain forever unacceptable to Palestinians—but he shared much of the agenda of the Israeli hard right, who believed ardently in the expansion of Israel's hold on the West Bank and Gaza and the abandonment of Oslo. The 210,000 settlers living in 145 Jewish settlements in the Occupied Territories remain the greatest obstacle to a lasting peace between the Israelis and Palestinians, according to the 2001 Mitchell Report, but Sharon said repeatedly that he would never give up a single settlement as long as he remained in power. And indeed he was going in the other direction: according to data compiled by Peace Now from aerial photographs, fifty new settlement sites have sprouted across the West Bank since Sharon defeated Ehud Barak in the February 2001 elections.

Sharon was a masterful politician, and his greatest achievement in his first term in office was persuading both the Israeli electorate and the international community that he was a force of moderation. By repeatedly laying siege to the Palestinian leader in his muqata, humiliating him, emasculating him, yet stopping short of harming him or dispatching him to exile, Sharon deftly set himself against even more hawkish figures who wanted to banish or kill Arafat. And by making the case that the Palestinian uprising was linked to al-Qaeda and Islamic fundamentalist terror, Sharon received a green light from the United States to intensify his harsh measures. The world was well aware of the duplicity of Yasser Arafat, the corruption of his Palestinian Authority, the nihilistic acts of terror that still had the support, according to polls, of the majority of Palestinians. Few people took notice anymore of the suffering inflicted upon the Palestinian population by Sharon's government: the many killings of unarmed civilians committed by overzealous Israeli soldiers; the failures of the Israeli military to prosecute any of those troops;

the miseries inflicted upon hundreds of thousands locked into a
state of endless curfew; and the seeds of hatred that Sharon was
sowing in the youngest generation of Palestinians.

THREE MONTHS after the church siege, I attended a reunion
of participants at the Arab Orthodox Club in Beit Jala. Governor
Madani welcomed Father Parthenius, the archimandrite of the
Armenian Orthodox Church, Anton Salman, Salah Tamari,
Mayor Hannah Nasser, and the entire Palestinian negotiating
committee. At the start of the meal the governor held up bowls of
lentils and macaroni and urged everybody to take some as an ap-
petizer. "I thought this would bring back happy memories," he
told them. The room erupted in laughter. Madani spoke about
Bethlehem's unique diversity, how the siege had brought Muslims and Christians closer together, and how Father Parthenius
had wept when the corpse of the last "martyr" was carried from
the church. "Jesus Christ said, 'Knock on the door and it shall be
opened,'" Madani told them. "And we did the same. We knocked
on the door and it opened for us." Of course that wasn't quite
true: armed Palestinian militants had shot off the locks, but nobody thought it appropriate to mention that unpalatable fact.

It was a moving performance, yet the governor's ecumenical
spirit wasn't all-encompassing. I caught up with him one August
evening in the small office he kept down the hall from his apartment, where he was faxing a plea to Pope John Paul II to pressure
the Israelis to withdraw from Bethlehem. The anti-Semitic over-
tones of the letter were deeply unsettling. "We address your holiness on behalf of the inhabitants of occupied and besieged
Bethlehem, from the vicinity of the grottos containing the skulls
of the children killed by the sword two thousand years ago by the
ancestors of those who are now killing the children of Bethlehem
by hunger and bullets," he had written. "[The children's only
crime] is being witnesses to the message of peace of Jesus Christ,
which is rejected by the grandsons of those who crucified him."

Reading this screed shook my favorable opinion of the governor. He had always struck me as a reasonable man, but now he seemed to be surrendering to the same primitive passions that had swept up so many others. Or perhaps, I thought, remembering the experiences that had driven him into exile from Israel as a young man, he had always felt that way.

A few weeks later Madani left for medical treatment in Amman, Jordan, and while there he submitted his resignation to Yasser Arafat. Madani had grown weary of the continuing political infighting, and he found it impossible to run a functioning government while under Israeli occupation. Madani had been gone a couple of weeks when Arafat rejected his resignation and ordered him back to Bethlehem. Arafat, it appeared, was reluctant to upset the status quo within the Palestinian Authority and create even more instability at a time when he was confined to Ramallah, unpopular among his citizens, and for all intents and purposes powerless.

Arafat was now more an object of ridicule in the West Bank and Gaza than a figure of respect. Palestinians joked that his domain consisted of the second floor of the Ramallah muqata, and everywhere I went in Bethlehem, I heard little but disgust and weariness expressed in regard to the Palestinian leader. "He arrived in Gaza in 1994 promising that he would make Palestine into the next Hong Kong," Sheik Suleiman Abayat, Ibrahim Abayat's older brother, told me in August 2002. "Instead he turned us into Somalia." After the devastation of the spring and summer, a consensus was slowly building in Palestinian society that Arafat—undemocratic, corrupt, wedded to the rhetoric and mechanisms of revolutions—belonged to the past and that his dream of "liberating Palestine with a rifle" needed to be pushed aside if his people were to move forward. General Ala Hosni, Bethlehem's outspoken police chief, told me that Palestinians had an unfortunate tendency to idolize failed revolutionaries, and Arafat had successfully exploited that mind-set. "Gamal Abdel Nasser had a history of defeat, but he died a hero, and millions wept for him," Hosni said. "Anwar Sadat recovered land through negotiations, and yet he died a traitor in the eyes of his people. We are very subjective, we Arabs. For us it's a pity."

And yet reform and new leadership did not appear imminent. Ironically the Israeli reoccupation had worked to Arafat's advantage. Each time Ariel Sharon sent in his tanks to lay siege to the muqata, he whipped up Palestinians' rage and reinvigorated their beleaguered leader. The dismantling of the Palestinian Authority and its replacement by a de facto Israeli military regime had allowed Arafat to postpone elections indefinitely, delay reforms, and maintain his grip over government bank accounts and the Palestinian cabinet. For both Sharon and Arafat, two aging leaders mired in the past, the rolling back of Oslo had its benefits.

OMAR HABIB, the seventeen-year-old student whom Madani had dissuaded from leaving the Church of the Nativity in mid-April, remained, like so many boys his age in the West Bank and Gaza, torn between his education and the lure of militancy. In late July, after a five-month battle in Israeli courts, his family succeeded in forcing the Israeli Defense Forces to turn over the body of Habib's twenty-three-year-old brother Ihab, who had been buried in an "enemies' cemetery" in Be'er Sheva. Habib's mother along with an older brother made the long journey to the Negev Desert and brought Ihab's corpse back in a private ambulance. Habib and several family members wrapped the wooden coffin in a Hamas flag and, in violation of curfew, buried it in a hasty ceremony in the martyrs' graveyard in Irtas, keeping their eyes out for Israeli tanks. Habib had resumed his studies at the Terra Sancta School, but his experiences inside the church, the violent death of one brother, and the retreat underground of several surviving siblings had hardened his anti-Israeli feelings. Habib had no father to keep him on the straight and narrow path, and his mother was deeply worried about his future.

*   *   *

IN THE SPRING of 2002 Samir Zedan moved into the new apartment in Beit Jala—Chez Intifada—that he had constructed with the profits of his flourishing new career as a freelance journalist and translator. Zedan was working steadily, despite the fact that the right-wing ideologues in charge of the Israeli government press office, who viewed all Palestinian journalists as security risks, denied him press credentials. It was also becoming harder for Palestinians to leave their hometowns, but Zedan had, with typical resourcefulness, acquired a travel permit for the whole West Bank, as well as documents allowing him to cross the Green Line into Israel and even fly from Ben Gurion Airport. Though he had a privileged life compared with that of most Palestinians, occupation still weighed on his family. On April 28, in the midst of the Church of the Nativity siege, Zedan's wife, Denisa, gave birth to their daughter, Mary Lourdes, following a harrowing journey by ambulance to the Holy Family Hospital in Bethlehem. Zedan and his wife found the hospital ringed by Israeli tanks, and a cannon swiveled menacingly toward them as they rushed to the front gate; the Israeli troops fortunately had let them pass. Zedan's new apartment in the Maya Building overlooked a thoroughfare used by Israeli armored vehicles, and his five-year-old son, Nikolas Andreus, often watched, petrified, from the balcony as the convoys rolled by. "He used to say that he wanted to become a journalist like his father," Zedan told me one afternoon in the summer of 2002. "Now he says he wants to become a martyr."

The life of Zedan's friend Khader Abu Abbara had gone through more ups and downs than the Brazilian stock market since the Church of the Nativity siege. When the Israeli Defense Forces rolled into Bethlehem on April 2, the local leader of the Popular Front for the Liberation of Palestine had dropped out of sight. On the afternoon of April 21, however, the Israeli Defense Forces traced his cellular phone signal to a friend's house in Beit Sahour, surrounded the place, and captured Abu Abbara without a struggle. The Israelis imprisoned Abu Abbara in the Russian

Compound in Jerusalem in a tiny cell next door to the Tanzim leader Marwan Barghouti. Three months into his captivity, he was given a series of lie detector tests, exonerated of culpability in the Wadi Qilt killings, and released from jail. "The Shin Bet man said, *'Mabrook'* [Arabic for congratulations]," Abu Abbara told me. "Then he said, 'Be warned, Khader. If you come back, this time you will be locked up forever.'"

Abu Abbara made a 180-degree turn after his release from prison on July 17, 2002. He resigned from the Popular Front for the Liberation of Palestine, called for an immediate end to the uprising, and announced his candidacy for mayor of Beit Jala. But the campaign went nowhere. Disgusted by the corruption and lawlessness of the Palestinian Authority, resigned to the long-term reoccupation of the West Bank by the Israelis, Abu Abbara investigated emigrating with his family to Australia. He was awaiting a visitor's visa from the Australian Embassy in Tel Aviv when, shortly after the New Year, Abu Abbara's life took another bizarre turn: his twenty-six-year-old nephew shot him in the shoulder with a nine-millimeter pistol during a dispute over property. He soon recovered, but the injury only hardened his resolve to emigrate.

THE ISRAELI Defense Forces withdrew from the city in late August under the terms of the "Bethlehem First" plan, conceived by the then Defense Minister Binyamin Ben Eliezer, to restore control of the West Bank step by step to the Palestinian Authority. This time, however, few people rejoiced: almost everybody assumed that the Israeli withdrawal would be only a temporary respite. Even with the Israelis physically gone from the city, their lethal operations continued. One night in mid-October 2002 Zedan and I were sitting in a restaurant on Manger Street when somebody reported an explosion in front of Beit Jala's al-Hussein Hospital. We rushed over there to discover that a low-level member of the al-Aqsa Martyrs Brigades named Mohammed Abayat had ducked inside a phone booth after dropping his ailing mother off in the emergency room—and been blown to pieces by a booby trap planted in the receiver. (The Israelis, it turned out, killed him by mistake; the intended target had been his brother.) When we arrived, the Palestinian police were still hosing the blood off the sidewalk; the blast had reduced the phone booth to a pile of twisted metal. I spotted Chris Bandak, a close friend of the murdered man, sobbing in front of the hospital. Governor Madani, convening an emergency security meeting, ordered his commanders to prevent the Tanzim from shooting at Gilo in revenge.

But the balance of power had shifted in Bethlehem, and no shooting erupted at Gilo that night. Crippled by killings, arrests, and deportations, the Fatah militias no longer held the city in their grip. A top associate of Kamel Hmeid had openly challenged Hmeid's leadership of Fatah in Bethlehem, calling the intifada a "dead end" in the Arabic newspaper *al-Quds*. When Chris Bandak and a half dozen Tanzim cronies surrounded the author of the *al-Quds* article at Mohammed Abayat's funeral and beat him up, the police chief threw them in jail for several weeks. The days of chaos in Bethlehem were over.

Still, in the current political atmosphere, it would take only a single act of terror to make life miserable again for tens of thousands of Palestinians. In late November 2002 an Islamic Jihad suicide bomber from al-Khader blew himself up in a bus on Mexico Street in southern Jerusalem at rush hour, killing eleven Israelis, and the Israeli Defense Forces reoccupied Bethlehem. The Israeli government claimed the town had become a safe haven for Hamas, Islamic Jihad, and al-Aqsa Martyrs Brigades militants from other parts of the West Bank; bomb labs were returning to Deheishe, the Israelis claimed, and the gunmen were building back their forces. The evidence for that claim was shaky, but round-the-clock curfews and daily sweeps through the refugee camps became the norm again. Chris Bandak returned to hiding; the Israelis would arrest him in a house near the Church of the Nativity on February 5, 2003 and charge him with the murders of two Jewish settlers and complicity in Ahmed Mughrabi's suicide bombings. He faced the prospect of spending his life in prison. In December 2002, an Israeli demolition squad drove up to the house of Ibrahim Abayat in Wadi Shaheen and, as his elderly mother watched, blew a hole in the roof above the exiled militant's bedroom. The explosion cracked the walls and weakened the steel roof supports. Ibrahim's older brothers surveyed the damage and said the structure might be uninhabitable. After forty years Imm Khaled would have to leave the home in which she had raised her four sons and a daughter. The Abayat family called it revenge, plain and simple, serving no greater purpose than to satisfy Israeli public opinion, and the whims of a military commander.

Ibrahim Abayat learned about the demolition of his family home while settling into his new apartment in the Spanish city of Zaragoza, to which he had moved after four months in the hunting lodge in Lubia. His period of house arrest and tight security was behind him, and the former al-Aqsa Martyrs Brigades commander was learning Spanish and searching for a job in his new land. In Jerusalem, meanwhile, the man who had pursued Abayat and his gunmen to Manger Square, Captain Mike Aviad, had recently received word that he was about to be called up for reserve duty again. In February 2003, nearly one year after the Church of the Nativity siege, Aviad and the soldiers of the Jerusalem Brigade were going back to Bethlehem.

ACKNOWLEDGMENTS

ʚ៶ɞ

I'M GRATEFUL TO A NUMBER OF PEOPLE FOR helping me bring this yearlong project to fruition. Elizabeth Rubin of *The New Republic* and *The New York Times Magazine*, Adrian Jaulmes of *Le Figaro*, and *The New Yorker*'s Gilles Peress joined me on forays in Bethlehem and elsewhere in the West Bank during April and May 2002. They were inspirational traveling companions who lifted my spirits and kept me laughing during otherwise grim times. Arnon Regular of *Ha'aretz*, a fount of knowledge and insights about Bethlehem, helped map out the complex political and social landscape for me at the beginning of my reporting and allowed me to bounce ideas off him during the writing process. James Bennet of *The New York Times* shared some vital information with me about suicide bomber Ayat al-Akhras's fatal mission, and Michael Matza of *The Philadelphia Inquirer* offered suggestions, insights, and companionship. Andrew Purvis, *Time*'s Central Europe bureau chief, was a continual long-distance voice of encouragement. Joanna Chen generously devoted her time to research and to reading the manuscript in progress while she kept the *Newsweek* bureau and my own quotidian life in Israel running smoothly. She is a marvelous editor, forthcoming with criticism and gifted with an uncanny sense of how to reshape a narrative. Dan Ephron, my colleague at *Newsweek* in Jerusalem, filled in admirably for me during my writing leave.

I'm deeply indebted to Samir Zedan, without whom I could never have written this book. We spent literally hundreds of hours together over the past year and a half, ducking bullets in Bethlehem, tooling around the Judean Wilderness, meeting exiled militants in Ireland and Spain. Samir's intimate knowledge of the region and his humor, resourcefulness, and enthusiasm for the project were invaluable; working with him was a delight. The whole Zedan clan—especially Samir's wife, Denisa; son, Nikolas Andreus; and parents, Anton and Linda Zedan—welcomed me to their homes in Beit Jala, fed me countless fine meals, and made me feel like part of the family. Nuha Musleh, my Arabic teacher and occasional translator in Bethlehem, helped me develop a level of comfort with this difficult language and assisted me with several key interviews.

This book would also not have been possible without the support of my editors at *Newsweek*, including Mark Whitaker, Jon Meacham, Fareed Zakaria, Jeff Bartholet, and Marcus Mabry. I thank them for giving me the opportunity to cover the Middle East during this dramatic period, for showcasing my work during the al-Aqsa intifada, and for allowing me to devote the time to this extracurricular project. Flip Brophy, my agent, suggested making my book a "biography of a place" and remained an unstinting believer; Martha Levin, my editor at Free Press, embraced the idea and allowed me to badger her regularly with questions, doubts, second thoughts, and general free-floating anxiety. Maris Kreizman of Free Press shepherded the manuscript through its various stages and ably assisted with research and design. Free Press's Edith Lewis also did a heroic job of preparing the manuscript for publication.

Finally I want to express my love and gratitude to my wife, Nadja Gemmel, and my son, Max. Despite the overwhelming responsibility of caring for a one-year-old, Nadja devoted many hours to reading the work in progress and offered a fresh and insightful eye. For the patience they displayed while I toiled away obsessively in my backyard bungalow, for the balance they brought to my life, and for their love, I will be forever thankful. I consider myself truly blessed.

INDEX

ABOUT THE AUTHOR

JOSHUA HAMMER is an internationally renowned journalist who has worked at *Newsweek* since 1988. Previous to his assignment in Jerusalem, he was the magazine's bureau chief in Nairobi, Buenos Aires, Los Angeles, and Berlin. His first book, *Chosen by God: A Brother's Journey,* was a finalist for the 2000 *Los Angeles Times* Book Award. He currently lives in Jerusalem with his wife and son.